THE WORLD
OF FANTASY FILMS

Also by RICHARD MEYERS:

TV Superstars
The Illustrated Soap Opera Companion
Movies on Movies
Doom Star
Doom Star II
Cry of the Beast

THE WORLD
OF FANTASY
FILMS

Richard Meyers

SOUTH BRUNSWICK AND NEW YORK: A. S. BARNES AND COMPANY
LONDON: THOMAS YOSELOFF LTD

A. S. Barnes and Co., Inc.
Cranbury, New Jersey 08512

Thomas Yoseloff Ltd
Magdalen House
136-148 Tooley Street
London SE1 2TT, England

Library of Congress Cataloging in Publication Data

Meyers, Richard.
The world of fantasy films.

Bibliography: p.
Includes index.
1. Fantastic films—History and criticism. I. Title.
PN1995.9.F36M4   791.43′0909′15   78-69640
ISBN 0-498-02213-7

Printed in the United States of America

CONTENTS

ACKNOWLEDGMENTS

The response and cooperation has been humbling. My thanks cannot exceed your talents: Dick Smith; Ray Harryhausen; Rick Baker; Ilya Salkind; Pierre Spengler; Richard Donner; Stuart Freeborn; Doug Trumbull; Dave Prowse; Brian De Palma; Richard Williams; Chuck Jones; Bob Clampett; Al Brodax; Ralph Bakshi; Donald Duckwall; Bob Lusk; Tom Jones (Walt Disney Productions); David Armstrong (Specialty Films); Robert Mandel (ITC Entertainment); John Goldstone; Anne Henshaw (Python—Monty—Films); Christopher Padilla (Voyage Productions); John Dark (Amicus); Manley Productions; P. Reid (BBC Enterprices); Phil Edwards; Mick Garris; Steve Rubin; Gary Gerani; Nan Bernstein.

Many TV photos were kindly supplied by Howard Frank, Personality Photos, P. O. Box 50, Brooklyn, N.Y. 11230. Supermarionation and *Space: 1999* shots were courtesy of the Gerry Anderson Collection of David Hirsch.

Special Thanks

Tremendous assistance was generously donated by Allen White. Great patience and cooperation were offered by the publishers and editors of *Starlog* magazine: Kerry O'Quinn, Norman Jacobs, Howard Zimmerman, Ed Naha, David Hutchison, Howard Cruse, Ted Enik, Laura O'Brien, James Odell, Robin Snelson, and Rita Eisenstein. Last-minute help came in the form of Phyllis Reison. And, naturally, Melissa.

R.M.

INTRODUCTION

This is not a follow-up to Jeff Rovin's 1977 Barnes volume, *The Fabulous Fantasy Films*; rather, it is a continuation and elaboration. Jeff's book took the reader on a mellow, memory-filled trip across the history of the fantasy film. This volume covers slightly more rocky ground—the fantasy-related movies of the last four years—and takes a closer look at the contributions of television and animation.

And how does the battered genre hold up? How does one compare the splendor of *Stairway to Heaven* to the graphic gore of *The Omen* or the magical *The Wizard of Oz* to the nasty *Squirm?* The answers are, naturally: very well, thank you; and you don't. Thanks to the genre waffling of such major works as *Close Encounters of the Third Kind* (which director Steven Spielberg has publicly proclaimed as fantasy) and *Superman* (which director Richard Donner has purposely eliminated all relevance from), the fantasy film field is all the more rich and ever-growing.

As far as the less-than-classic efforts go, it is fitting to remember that many present-day greats were financial failures and were critically devastated when they first appeared. The *Carrie* of today could very well become the *Dracula* of tomorrow. So join me on the roller coaster of recent film fare. See: Movies of unbearable violence! See: Huge animals eating whole cities! See: Things to come on the other side of 2001! See: A little tube that took over the world! See: The growth of the American animation industry built by a cat, a mouse, and a bunny!

Welcome to the world of fantasy films.

1 THE OCCULT

ACCORDING to Webster's Dictionary, the occult is "matters involving the action or influence of supernatural agencies." The supernatural is defined as "of or relating to an order of existence beyond the visible universe; of or relating to God or a god, demigod, spirit, or devil." And in the recent outpouring of films, devil seems to be the key word. In recent history and in ever-increasing numbers, the public's collective fantasies have turned from optimistic dreams to persistent nightmares, filled with gruesome, unnatural death. It appears that these pessimistic visions are uncomfortably popular, for box office receipts of films that embody them are continually high, and production of such films has not flagged since the premiere of *Rosemary's Baby* in 1968. Indeed, movies in this category outnumber the more enjoyable fantasy films in upcoming chapters by more than two to one.

Primarily, there are two reasons for this. One, the genre is easy. More often than not, these cinematic exercises are inexpensive "quickies," written or directed by the producer to make some fast money. Since he is dealing with the unknown, all semblance of logic and logical plot development can be jettisoned in the name of shock, thrills, and gore. Unfortunately, character development and visual structure often fall by the wayside as well in order to cram in as many otherworldly goings-on as possible.

Nowhere was this aspect more obviously and crudely delivered than in *The Sentinel* (1976), a Michael Winner film from Jeffrey Konvitz's novel. Initially, the production seemed to deserve some avid prerelease interest, since the book had become a paperback best-seller

thanks to a large-scale publicity campaign launched by Ballantine Books. Also, it came hot on the heels of Winner's successful *Death Wish* (1974), released just prior to his dreadful *Won Ton Ton, The Dog That Saved Hollywood* (1976), which should have been regarded as a warning of the travesty that was coming.

Also in *The Sentinel's* initial favor was a cast of experienced actors and a technical crew which included the makeup wizardry of Dick Smith, veteran of *The Godfather* (1972), *Taxi Driver* (1976), and *The Exorcist* (1973). The story, simply put, involves a young model (Cornelia Sharpe) who begins to suffer horrible headaches and nightmares after moving into a New York brownstone.

Her fellow residents include two lesbians on the first floor, one (Beverly D'Angelo) who enjoys abusing herself in front of the model and the other (Sylvia Miles) who enjoys fondling the abuser; a strange little old man (Burgess Meredith) whose roommates include a cat and a canary, and an ancient, blind priest (John Carradine) who does nothing but sit by the window all day.

Her neighbors and her migraines aren't her only problems, however. The model, Alison Parker, also has a boyfriend (Chris Sarandon) who is suspected, by an intrepid police detective (Eli Wallach), of killing his first wife, and a dead father who has the nasty habit of walking around the apartment on the next floor all night. At least that is what the frightened Alison discovers when she investigates the noises—her dead father, carousing with two zombie girls.

Although not exactly used to such a sight, she has seen him thus before. As a child she came upon her living dad

15

enjoying himself with two prostitutes, and then tried to commit suicide. This time, however, she hysterically knifes him in the arm, the chest, the nose, and the right eye.

When the boyfriend, who has hired a private detective to watch Alison, discovers no body, no zombies, and no detective, he figures something is definitely wrong. Upon investigation he further discovers that the real estate agent (Ava Gardner) who sold his girl the apartment has disappeared, the other residents don't legally exist, and the Catholic Church has arranged Allison's new lease to get her in a position to take over the job of the blind priest as the sentinel—the world's guardian against evil. The brownstone is actually the gate over hell.

The film's finale explains that Alison's neighbors are actually Satan's minions, trying to drive Alison to suicide before she can take up her post; shows the boy friend as the murderer of his first wife, which gives them the excuse to bash his head in with a cross and drive a sacrificial knife into his neck; and hustles out a parade of actual circus sideshow freaks, playing a horde of lost souls. Good wins out in the end, but not quality. While the book maintained suspense by keeping the characters' innocence in question, the film was wrong-headed from frame one, becoming an exercise in sadism rather than a tale of heaven defeating hell.

Dick Smith, responsible for the more gory creations in the production, admitted doing the movie like a "Jekyll and Hyde." While the talented artist was against the obvious blood-letting, the technician in him was attracted by the problem of achieving that gore.

"That and the money, frankly, is what I did it for," he confessed. "The bad taste of the director I thought was appalling."

Many others agreed, because *The Sentinel*, even released at the peak Christmas season, did not light audience's fires. Many critics thought the failure of this extension on the occult theme indicated the decline and disappearance of this sort of film, but they were sadly mistaken.

The second, and far more unfortunate, reason for the Devil's persistent cinematic survival is that these films give audience an easy way out for real troubles that can only be solved through mankind's own interaction and peaceful coexistence. Recently, in movie theaters all over the world, Satan has been blamed for assassinations, pollution, mass murder, and the overall lack of morality in our "permissive society."

If these movies allow audiences to sigh a collective "the Devil made me do it," they become not only ugly examples of producers' tastes, but actual detriments to the human progress. A primary example of that is *The Omen*, the surprise hit of the summer of 1976, which blames our current political climate on Satan.

This little film was remarkable on several counts. First, screen-writer David Seltzer packaged this as a literary double-whammy, selling the movie with the book, thereby pushing the sales of one with the other. If the book sold well, then the film would prosper, and vice versa. Second, the mercenary movie, perched firmly on the coattails of *Rosemary's Baby's* and *The Exorcist's* successes, was given a professional gloss thanks to the contributions of director Richard Donner, director of photography Gil Taylor, editor Stuart Baird, special effects man John Richardson, and makeup champ Stuart Freeborn. It was a grade "A" film built around a grade "Z" theme.

Robert Thorn (Gregory Peck) has a wonderful job in politics; a wonderful wife, Katherine (Lee Remick); and a wonderful brand-new son, Damien (Harvey Stevens). Only problem is that the son his wife actually bore died mysteriously, immediately after birth, and to spare her feelings, Thorn accepted a replacement baby that a mysterious priest offered him, no questions asked. With a maneuver like that, many moviegoers felt Thorn deserved what he got. And he got it in spades.

It started with little Damien's fifth birthday, when his young nanny happily went to the top story of their London home, pleasantly cried out, "Watch me!" and hung herself. Then, with a hearty "you ain't seen nothin' yet," the movie is off. It seems that the little angel is actually the Antichrist, predicted by the Bible to appear and turn man against his brother.

The screen parents are offered tiny hints of this, like the child going crazy when he sees a cross and zoo animals going crazy when they see the child, but the two adults continue blissfully on even though the new nanny (Billie Whitelaw) could outdo Boris Karloff in an evil-look contest, and Damien's new pet dog would rather rip your leg off than chase cats. However, the Thorns begin to suspect that something is amiss when people around them start dropping like flies.

A priest (Patrick Troughton) who tries to warn them is impaled through the chest by an eight-foot iron rod that is ripped off his church tower by a bolt of lightning, and a reporter (David Warner) who accompanies Thorn to Rome to uncover the truth is beset by hellhounds and then decapitated by a sheet of glass. Momma and Poppa Thorn don't fare much better. Mom is dumped fifteen feet from a balcony onto a teakwood floor, then thrown out a hospital window to fall several stories into the back of a

Katherine (Lee Remick) gets her first hint that son Damien (Anthony Stevens) isn't the angel he appears to be when zoo animals try to eat through the car to get to him during *The Omen* (© 20th Century Fox).

Ambassador Thorn (Gregory Peck), meanwhile, has a pooch problem in Rome. Hellhounds have attacked him in the cemetery where his real child is buried (© 20th Century Fox).

parked ambulance. Pop, after discovering the skeleton of his real child (who had his skull crushed upon birth) and his murdered wife, has a point of a cemetery fence pushed through his upper arm and then is shot by a policeman before he is able to destroy Damien.

The film's finish sees the Antichrist, smiling happily at his "'parents' " funeral, adopted by, no less than, the President of the United States. The audience, after sitting through this two-hour pagan ritual, rarely smiled, however. The overall reaction was one of numb shock. For, while extensive care was taken in the visual style of the film, it is essentially no more than one well-executed murder after another. The priest is done in only after an exciting "sudden storm" scene, with the wind whipping through the trees and thunder and lightning crashing about. Peck's demise wasn't filmed until a new camera was developed to capture the flight of a bullet fired from a policeman's pistol in slow motion. Remick's and Warner's deaths were also filmed in slow motion and from four angles as well.

Stuart Freeborn, the number-one British makeup wizard, remembered the "beheading" especially. "I worked very close with the special effects boys," he recalled. "We spent some time on working out exactly how that sheet of glass would go, where it would hit, at exactly what velocity—we went into quite a bit of detail. How much blood would come out at that point, the spinning of the head, was all sort of worked out."

Detail was the key word here since the pain, the human suffering, the empathy, all could be eliminated and replaced with a wealth of detail interjected into each death, like an overdone autopsy. After a while, spirit loses its meaning and only flesh is left. Each of the main creative contributors involved in *The Omen* could not be categorized as cruel people. Gregory Peck is one of the most able, intelligent, and gentle actors in the business. Freeborn is the most affable, good-natured, and enjoyable Englishman imaginable, and director Donner is a likable, talented American with a great love of filmmaking and fantasy.

So who was to blame for such a morally hollow enterprise? Who, when the last buck was passed, was responsible for a film which did not allow one vestige of on-screen human dignity to remain? The answer must be everyone and no one. *The Omen* went on to make over 60 million dollars in the Unites States and over 100 million world-wide. Music composer Jerry Goldsmith won an Oscar for his score over the likes of veteran composers Bernard Herrman and John Barry. Peck got a boost to his flagging career, and Richard Donner and Stuart Freeborn were to team once again for the largest movie undertaking in history, *Superman*.

Freeborn, who also headed the makeup on *2001: A Space Odyssey* (1968), had some final words to say on the graphic horror of *The Omen*. "You think, quite frankly, this is not what I like to do, but this is what is called for, so who am I to say you mustn't do these sort of things? In the script, it called for much more than we did, and some of the things we did do were, let's say, rather too successful. They were so horrifying they had to be cut down."

Damien's ongoing screen life was not cut down, however. Such monetary rewards called for a sequel, and 20th Century Fox was up to the task, hiring producer Harvey Bernhard to write up the last two sections of a trilogy based on the first film. However, as with other projects of this type, that is, one capitalizing on an initial success, all did not go smoothly.

The final shooting script of *Damien: Omen II* (1978) was penned by Stanley Mann, Al Ramrus, and John Shaner. Then it was further modified by its initial director Michael Hodges, who was later replaced by Don Taylor. Hodges had a reputation as an avant-garde talent from his work on *Get Carter* (1971), *Pulp* (1972), and *The Terminal Man* (1973). Taylor was pegged as his successor, after some "creative conflicts," because of his dependable work on *Escape from the Planet of the Apes* (1971) and *The Island of Dr. Moreau* (1977).

The signed cast included William Holden, Lee Grant, and Robert Foxworth who were to act out the continuation of the Antichrist's campaign of total annihilation. Although some critics gave the sequel better reviews than its predecessor, it failed in the money department, disappointing the studio and putting an *Omen III* in doubt.

Warner Brothers, who, strangely enough, had the initial option on *The Omen* but let it expire, was responsible for *The Exorcist II: The Heretic*, an attempt to capitalize on success of the original, the granddaddy of all modern possession films. And they certainly had their hearts in the right place.

Richard Lederer, the vice president of Warner's advertising and publicity department, was teamed with director John Boorman as coproducer of the new work, and they encircled themselves with some of the finest technical and artistic talent they could. The director of photography was William A. Fraker, late of *Rosemary's Baby* and *Bullitt* (1968). The music was composed of Ennio Morricone, responsible for *The Good the Bad and the Ugly* (1966), *The Bird With the Crystal Plumage* (1969), and *The Burglars* (1971), among others. Dick Smith, again, was makeup chief for the original tale and this sequel. Albert Whitlock, the undisputed king of the matte painters, who has displayed his fine work in

DAMIEN OMEN II

The first time was only a warning.

COLOR BY DeLUXE° PANAVISION®

Copyright © 1978 Twentieth Century-Fox

R

Omen II

The happy family as they were before Devil-spawned disaster hits Lee Grant (left) and William Holden (right) as the parents of *Damien: The Omen II* (© 20th Century Fox).

The little devil returns for *Damien: The Omen II* (© 20th Century Fox).

19

Max Von Sydow is subtly aged through the makeup magic of Dick Smith for *The Heretic: Exorcist II* (© Warner Brothers).

Earthquake (1975), *Bound for Glory* (1976), and *High Anxiety* (1978), lent his talents. And an excellent cast was signed. To the holdovers from the original—Linda Blair, Max von Sydow, and Kitty Wynn—they added Richard Burton, Louise Fletcher, Ned Beatty, and James Earl Jones.

The Heretic begins four years after *The Exorcist* ends. Father Merrin (von Sydow) and Father Karras (Jason Miller) had given up their lives exorcising the demon from little Regan (Blair), but she is still affected by that experience, haunted by dreams and seemingly able to understand other people on a mental plane. Meanwhile, the church sends Father Lamont (Burton) to verify Merrin's exorcism, which they have begun to doubt in the intervening years.

The child and priest meet at the office of a Dr. Tuskin (Fletcher), a psychiatrist who is putting Regan through a unique form of "dream synchronization" aided by a "brain-wave" machine—a handy item no one in real life had ever seen before. It seems a little bit of the Devil is still left over in the young lady—a demon which Father Lamont tracks down across several continents. The trail ends in Africa where Kukumo (Jones), a scientist who Merrin exorcised years ago, details the secret of the demon harassing Regan. Lamont races back to Washington in time to join the girl in an attempt to rid her of the supernatural affliction once and for all.

A horde of locusts attacks her town house. Regan's babysitter, Sharon (Wynn), bursts into flame, Regan turns into a lecherous nymphet, and the entire town house is ripped to shreds. The shrink arrives and confesses she understands now—which is more than the audience can claim—and the priest and the girl, unharmed by the devastation, literally walk into the sunrise.

The movie was a total disaster, artistically and monetarily. Even with the experienced crew, the William Goodhart script was so ludicrous that the premiere audience was openly laughing in all the wrong places. What would have been subtle flaws under normal circumstances became jagged tears in the light of the ridiculous screenplay. Richard Burton went unaccepted as a priest. Linda Blair had developed in the intervening years, but only in the weight department. Her voluptuous "baby fat" was the subject of widespread ridicule. Fletcher, fresh from an Oscar for her portrayal of Nurse Ratchett in *One Flew Over the Cuckoo's Nest* (1976), nearly killed her career with a part that was originally written for a man but shuttled to her when no "appropriate" male actor could be found.

The film's only success was visual. Boorman, the director of *Point Blank* (1967) and *Deliverance* (1972), is nothing if not a stunningly stylistic artist. *The Heretic* mirrored this ability but aggravated his shortcomings in the plot department, a sad situation that also marred his previous genre effort, *Zardoz* (1974).

Naturally, Whitlock's contributions were breathtaking, but Dick Smith was disappointed by his inability to convince the producers to let his imagination run free. This situation finally culminated with the movie having three climax changes. Boorman came down with an intestinal disease which put him in the hospital before the final sequence was filmed. Laid up, he had plenty of time to work on the shortcomings of the finale as originally written. Both Smith and the director worked out scenes they considered better, but Warner Brothers rejected Smith's ideas, which included a multifaceted visage of the actual Regan demon. The powers that be settled for Linda Blair playing the vamp. Smith went to a local screening and admitted that he "laughed with everyone else."

Even after extensive publicity to the contrary, *The Heretic* was bombing in every theater engagement, a situation owners found more horrible than the film, since they had to put up a lot of money and guarantees to insure the studio's investment. In other words, they had to assure Warner Brothers that *The Heretic* would run a certain number of weeks and pay exorbitant prices for the right to show it.

When no one showed up to see it, the theater managers got angry and let the studio know it. Warners, desperate for some face-saving tactic, pulled every print and edited out most of the truly detrimental moments within two

20

Linda Blair and Richard Burton dance cheek to cheek in a hot bed of locusts during the climax of *The Heretic* (© Warner Brothers).

weeks of the premiere. Then, instead of stupidity, the public got overall boredom. Finally, John Boorman was recalled from Ireland to re-recut the master print into a new semblance of intelligence.

However, by that time it would have cost Warners too much to re-recall all the prints, so the third incarnation of *The Exorcist II* was only seen by the rest of the world, where the opening date was months in the future.

After such a catastrophe it would seem hard to believe that any fly-by-night producer would want to capitalize on the demon breed, but many still felt there was a market, and even *The Heretic*'s poor returns would be a fortune to these schlock artists. So the studios continued to roll out more and more tales of devil worship, repossessing everything in sight.

The Peppercorn-Wormser Distribution Company blanketed the States with *The House Of Exorcism* in the summer of 1976, publicizing it as nothing more than an entertaining reworking of *The Exorcist* theme given fuller box office impact by the presence of Telly Savalas, Elke Sommer, and Robert Alda. They were right—that was all it was. Still, it was refreshing in the light of cruder endeavors and benefited enormously from a tongue-in-cheek Savalas performance.

The plot revolves around Lisa (Sommer), who comes under the influence of the satanic Savalas during a vacation in Spain. She divides her time hysterically tearing up a hospital ward, throwing up, and levitating, and visiting Savalas's villa, where extremely odd rites occasionally take place. Enter good guy Father Michael (Alda), who succeeds in exorcising a demon named Elena from the girl and in destroying Savalas, who is discovered to be a devil in human form.

This is a long way from zip code commercials and "Kojak," but director Mickey Lion—who many think is actually the famous Italian genre director Mario Bava—managed to invest the proceedings with some vitality and allowed Telly to suck a lollipop all the way through.

Simultaneously released was an American feature

21

detailing the possession of an innocent, thrusting the selfsame innocent into a new and deadly world. Called *J.D.'s Revenge* (1976), it replaced the green vomit with orange purple Technicolor blood and the white victims and Swedish priests with black gangsters and cabbies. American International distributed this extravaganza, written by Jaison Starkes and produced and directed by Arthur Marks.

Glynn Turman, an up-and-coming young actor who starred in *Cooley High* (1975)—upon which TV's "What's Happening" is based—starred as a law student who is possessed by the spirit of J.D. Walker, a gangster murdered in a slaughterhouse by a vengeful Lou Gossett, who thought J.D. the killer of his girl way back in 1942.

The REINCARNATION OF J. D. WALKER
...who came back from the dead to possess a man's soul, make love to his woman, and get the Vengeance he craved!

J.D's REVENGE

An AMERICAN INTERNATIONAL PICTURE [R] RESTRICTED

STARRING
GLYNN TURMAN · LOU GOSSETT · JOAN PRINGL
Written by JAISON STARKES · Produced and Directed by ARTHUR MARKS · Production Services by CoCaCo SERVICE COMP/ · Music by ROBERT PRINCE · COLOR by MOVIELA

J. D.'s Revenge.

Now, because of hypnotism performed in a night club, Turman turns from a nice New Orleans guy into a violent, obscenity-spouting, rod-packing hoodlum who is out for a little blood.

He gets some by cutting up a pimp but is frustrated in his vendetta against Gossett by the fact that the murderer is now an evangelist with a daughter who looks exactly like the war-time girl friend. The unaffected part of Turman takes a liking to the girl which allows the filmmakers to throw in some partial nudity in the "R" rated occurrences.

Finally, the dead spirit forces a showdown with his old enemy only to discover that it was Gossett's brother, Fred Pinkard, who actually killed the girl because she was really his wife and was going to expose their relationship to Lou. And that makes Gossett's daughter really Pinkard's daughter. By now the plot was so hopelessly confused that it made little difference that Pinkard's accidental death allows J. D. to leave Glynn's body and return to the great beyond avenged.

Lou Gossett left the production to star in "Roots" and *The Deep* (1977) but the theme of gangster possession and other-worldly revenge did not leave. It resurfaced in late 1977 thanks to Dimension Pictures, distributors of many a horror-exploitation film, in the form of *Ruby*. Piper Laurie played the title role, seemingly a step up from her supporting lead in *Carrie*. But while many of her fans hoped it would be her return to acting grace, since her departure from the screen after her Best Actress nomination for *The Hustler* (1961) it failed to generate extensive interest in or out of the horror genre, even with the participation of actor Stuart Whitman and director Curtis Harrington.

The *New York Times* went as far as to say, "Even within its own modest league, this movie is a dull concoction." The ingredients break down thus: Ruby is an ex–gun moll for a notorious gangster named Nicky (Sal Vecchio), who had been unceremoniously shot in the neck, cheek, and forehead, and then dumped into a swamp. Since then, Ruby has run the drive-in theater and lived in the nightclub Nicky left her for her autistic daughter, Leslie (Janit Baldwin).

It is now the mid-fifties and the open-air theater is doing booming business thanks to the horror/monster film cycle—all through this picture glimpses of *The Attack of the Fifty Foot Woman* (1958) are seen. Nicky chooses that moment to both rise from the dead and possess the autistic daughter in order to wreak revenge on the members of his treacherous mob who work in or around the drive-in. Soon, bullet holes appear on Leslie's face, she starts speaking with Nicky's voice and

She's a holy Terror!

JENNIFER
...makes "CARRIE" look like an angel!

A STEVE KRANTZ Production
"JENNIFER"

Starring
LISA PELIKAN · BERT CONVY · NINA FOCH
AMY JOHNSTON and JOHN GAVIN as Senator Tremayne

Co-Starring JEFF COREY · LOUISE HOVEN
RAY UNDERWOOD and WESLEY EURE As Pit

Director of Photography   Story by
IRV GOODNOFF · STEVE KRANTZ

Screenplay by   Produced by
KAY COUSINS JOHNSON · STEVE KRANTZ

Directed by BRICE MACK   Color by CFI · Prints by MOVIELAB

An American International Release   **PG** PARENTAL GUIDANCE SUGGESTED
SOME MATERIAL MAY NOT BE SUITABLE FOR CHILDREN

Just one of the *Carrie* rip-offs that appeared shortly after the initial horror film's success. Another film that tried to copy *Carrie*'s ingredients for success was *Nurse Sherri* (1978).

Ruby's employees start winding up hung, impaled, and crushed.

Dr. Keller (Roger Davis), a prison doctor who also happens to be a parapsychologist, is called in to explain what is going on. Finally, Ruby goes to her ex-lover's grave site to join him in death, and the last we see of her

is in an underwater skeletal embrace. The film's steady, nation-wide appearances allowed critics to cluck over the salad days of various participants while affording the young Baldwin better reviews than her experienced fellows.

Laurie's "comeback" was better served by her role as the psychotically religious mother of *Carrie* (1976), though her pre-finale fate remains the same. November offered the horror genre a much-needed Thanksgiving in the form of this well-received United Artists release, directed by the much-interviewed, much-critiqued, always-intriguing Brian De Palma.

Sissy Spacek played the title role of a repressed, ridiculed teenager whose discovery of supernatural powers leads to tragedy only because of the ignorance and cruelty of others. The film opens with a volleyball game at a high school where Carrie White's well-meaning confusion and awkwardness is established. Then the primary conflict is detailed, as well as the film's motif of discomfort and frustration, in the credit sequence where De Palma's cameras lovingly drift through a steamy girls' locker room where well-developed California girls frolic in various stages of nudity.

A boyhood wet dream turns into a nightmare when Carrie menstruates for the first time in her life, naked, in a shower stall and reacts hysterically, to the delight of her cliquish classmates. They taunt her unmercifully as she cringes in a corner until the sympathetic gym teacher breaks it up. Thus does De Palma's exercise in audience expectation begin. The talent and understanding of character development and interaction that he only hints at in the over-bloody *Sisters* (1973) and rock satire *Phantom of the Paradise* (1975) are well orchestrated here as he skillfully creates scenes of psychological and physical pain then thrusts his audience's noses in it, essentially making patrons semi-reluctant voyeurs in someone else's great personal tragedy.

The only real monster in the movie is Margaret, Carrie's mother, whose religious fervor is crazy in temperament and homicidal in application. She sees her daughter's period as the first sign of ultimate damnation and drags her into a disintegrating dust closet where a macabre Christ figure is hung, its eyes glowing from an outlet installed in its head. From there on, the film adds layer upon layer of tension, each locking into the larger catastrophe like pieces of a Shakespearean jigsaw puzzle.

The gym teacher, Miss Collins (Betty Buckley), convinces Carrie that she could be quite attractive, while punishing the rest of the class for their torment, a move that makes the nice Sue Snell (Amy Irving) regretful and the nasty Chris Hargenson (Nancy Allen) revengeful.

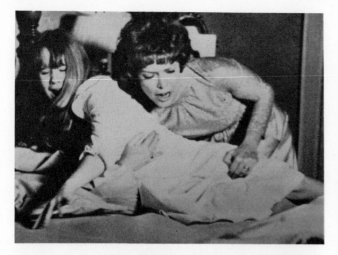
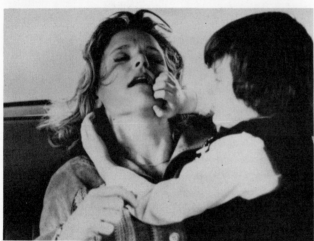

Montage of parent/child supernatural relationships: From upper left then clockwise, Linda Blair and Ellen Burstyn from *The Exorcist*, Anthony Hopkins and Susan Swift from *Audrey Rose*, Piper Laurie and Sissy Spacek from *Carrie*, and Anthony Stevens and Lee Remick from *The Omen* (© United Artists).

Meanwhile, Carrie is discovering her latent telekinetic ability, the power to move things by thought.

The opposing forces, rather than shock at regular intervals like most horror films, build to a violent climax at the senior prom. Sue, as atonement, convinces her boy friend, Tommy Ross (William Katt), to ask Carrie to the dance while Chris convinces her boy friend Billy Nolan (John Travolta) to aid her in a monstrous retaliation. Mother Margaret, in the meantime, has discovered her daughter's prom plans and mental ability, naturally assuming them to be the final sign of demonic possession. She is kept in check by Carrie's power only until the youngster leaves for the dance; then she plans a retribution.

The prom is the movie's centerpiece. It is there that

Carrie turns from a wallflower into a radiant princess. It is also there that De Palma pulls every ballroom cliche out, from the circular camera moves, spinning around the angelic couple as they dance, to the mirrored ball casting points of light around the gymnasium. Carrie and Tommy are picked as prom king and queen and are paraded onto a raised platform to receive their crowns and bouquets. At this point it seems as if all Carrie's dreams have come true.

But this too turns out to be of someone else's manipulation. At the very last moment, Chris releases a bucket balanced above the stage, and a waterfall of pig's blood falls atop Carrie. The cruel couple, Chris and Billy, run out the door as the bucket itself falls and knocks Tommy unconscious. Suddenly, the picture is bathed in red and a split screen appears. The camera settles on Carrie's face as a third transformation takes place. Before one's eyes Spacek turns into a blood-coated banshee, her arms stiff at her sides, her fingers claws, her eyes enlarging until they are two blue beacons in her head. The full destructive force of her telekinetic power is unleashed.

Lights burn, the fire hose goes crazy, the electrical system bursts into flame, decorations become hurtling weapons, people are thrown left and right and teachers are electrocuted. Miss Collins is crushed against a wall. Carrie stands transfixed on the stage. Only when the gym is almost completely consumed by fire does she move slowly to the doors, which swing open before her and close soundly behind her, sealing in the last survivors. Chris and Billy wait in a car, hoping to run her down, but again Carrie's power holds sway, throwing the hurtling auto away into a flaming heap. Finally, she stumbles home like a zombie—where her mother waits.

Carrie washes the blood off herself and changes back into her plain clothes, going to Margaret for comfort and absolution. They sink to the floor together and in the middle of a soothingly told but chilling story of her warped life she drives a kitchen knife into Carrie's back.

The poor girl hurtles backwards down the stairs and manages to crawl into the kitchen, the camera keeping pace on the floor beside her. Her mother smilingly trails her, the knife raised high for the death thrust. Just before she can drive the blade home, Carrie's power starts shooting implements across the room. Knives pin Margaret upright in a doorway. Can openers and spatulas slice into her white-garbed torso. Finally, she stands dead, with a look of peace on her face. Her stance and wounds *match exactly* those depicted by the plastic crucifix in the dust closet.

Carrie's life begins to flow out of her body along with her power. Its might begins to bring the house down upon their heads. In pain and emotional torment, the dying Carrie pulls her mother into the prayer closet and under the glowing eyes of the artificial Christ. They meet their ultimate end together.

But the movie is not over. Up until now, there had not been one honest scare in the entire film. Whatever horror there was came from the audience's empathy for the tragic events De Palma set up. We all knew what was going to happen in advance—the script and the director laid it all out for us. But one of De Palma's recurrent themes is that death and the supernatural are not ends in themselves. Just because the threat is gone does not mean that the horror is over.

The final scene of *Carrie* begins with a telephone call to the mother of the only prom survivor, Sue Snell. While she discusses the situation with a friend, we see Sue, in angelic white, slowly walking down a street with a bouquet of flowers. She comes to a rock-filled lot where Carrie's house once stood. In the center of the vacant patch of rubble is a for sale sign with the legend scrawled across it, "Carrie White Burns in Hell!" It is there that Sue sinks to her knees and places the flowers. At that moment a bloody hand reaches out of the ground and grabs Sue's forearm.

The next moment, most of the audience is scraping themselves off the theater's ceiling. The surprise is so well timed that even if one knows the scare is coming, the fright still manages to get through. *Carrie* really ends with Sue's mother assuring the distraught girl that she has just woken from a momentary dream. But the point is made that tragedy is not a closed circle. The innocent survivor will be affected by the deaths until her own demise.

Carrie's effect on the rest of the world was almost immediate. Sissy Spacek was catapulted to stardom, garnering a *Newsweek* cover, an Oscar nomination for Best Actress, and roles in *Welcome to L.A.* (1977) and *Three Women* (1977). John Travolta went on to complete *Saturday Night Fever* (1977) and *Grease* (1978), cementing his stardom, and William Katt was signed for *First Love* (1977) and *Big Wednesday* (1978).

Brian De Palma retained the services of Amy Irving for his next film, basically an extension of the ground covered in *Carrie*. He was now a "bankable" director; the success of his modest horror film and Hitchcock homage *Obsession* (1976) guaranteed that his future projects would get ample financial backing. Indeed, *The Fury* (1978), from the novel by John Farris, got the red-carpet treatment at 20th Century Fox, especially since the production chores were being handled by Frank Yablans, the packager of *The Silver Streak* (1976) and *The Other Side of Midnight* (1977), and the man generally described as the "hit maker." Besides De Palma and an all-star cast, he had a lot of plot to work with.

Here, instead of one pitiful waif, we get two powerful young people who are all too aware of their telekinetic abilities. Robin's (Anthony Stevens) father, Peter (Kirk Douglas), is an experienced agent for a super-secret spy organization run by Childress (John Cassavetes). Gillian's (Amy Irving) family is one of the most wealthy and powerful in the country. But both children have the same mental powers, which are so strong that they can hemorrhage people nearby.

Childress wants the mind control under his control. Toward that end he sends Peter on a mission, kidnaps Robin, and informs each that the other is dead. Then he sets a death-trap for Peter, but Peter escapes, blowing off Childress's arm in the process. He goes underground to stay alive, a move Gillian mirrors when Childress becomes aware of her presence through a sympathetic

Kirk Douglas has the mugging of the elderly problem well in hand during *The Fury* (© 20th Century Fox).

mind link with Robin. The corrupt Dr. Roth (Charles Durning) locates the girl and spirits her away to the spy organization's mansion-like Psi Facility, where Robin's steadily declining mental condition is kept in check by the sexy Gwyn (Fiona Lewis).

Meanwhile, Peter has been retaliating through Hester (Carrie Snodgress), a lovesick employee of Childress's, who assists the ex-agent in a daring plan to rescue his son. They, in turn, are tripped up by faulty timing and a misplaced bullet. Though Hester winds up a bloody mess, Peter has Gillian as new conspirator. She leads him to the Psi H.Q., but they're too late on several counts. The constant diet of mental power, booze, drugs, and sex has destroyed Robin's moral fiber to the point where he is a vile shadow of his previous fun-loving self.

When he gets tired of Gwyn, he kills her by levitating, spinning, and making her bleed from every orifice. Then, once Peter locates the psychotic boy, they fight and fall

Amy Irving has the blood shortage problem well in hand during *The Fury* (© 20th Century Fox).

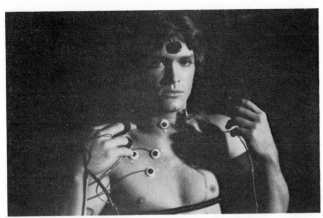

Andrew Stevens has no problem in hand. His problems start with his psychically powerful brain in *The Fury* (© 20th Century Fox).

The author sits with director Brian De Palma discussing the complexities of De Palma's latest fantasy effort *The Fury*. (Photo courtesy of David Hutchison).

out the window to the edge of the roof. Peter manages to hold onto both his son and the ledge, but when he is further attacked and sees what Robin has become, he drops the lad to his death. Screaming once in rage and grief, he follows in a suicidal leap. Childress merely suggests someone "get them out of my sight," then tries to convince Gillian that he is really a good guy the morning after.

In final retribution, Gillian turns her concentrated power on the evil government official, and, in what must be the most gruesomely effective finish in decades, literally blows him all over the room. Thus is another fine family film created. This virtuoso bit of fantasy with Shakespearean overtones made $6 million in less than two weeks, then nearly spiralled into obscurity. Too many critics and viewers found De Palma's "razzle-dazzle" direction too intrusive and the plot too muddled. The movie, thankfully, boasted great ensemble acting

and all-too-credible makeup effects by Rick Baker and Dick Smith. Sadly, because of conflicting responsibilities, Smith took his credit off the horrifying entertainment.

The innocent subject at the whim of powers within or beyond their control, the supernatural tot, could practically be a separate catagory in itself. Above the already mentioned titles, the last three years have also seen the unfolding of the frightening tales concerning poor little *Audrey Rose* (1977) and the boy with *The Shining* (1978-9).

The Shining was a hardcover best-seller in 1977, a paperback best-seller in 1978, and Warner Brothers hopes, the movie blockbuster of 1979. Steven King, the author of the original novel *Carrie* and the vampiric *Salem's Lot*, was also responsible for this eerie vision of a six-year-old with ESP fighting the combined powers of long-dead spirits and a hellish demon in a snowbound, upstate New York hotel. He also wrote the original screenplay, but then the project was taken over by Stanley Kubrick to become the follow-up to his relatively unsuccessful *Barry Lyndon* (1975). Kubrick, one of the finest filmmakers in the world, is nothing if not original and is justly famous for his complete control of a project. So while King's screenplay is rife with psychological torture, a vicious demon named Redrum, living hedges in the shapes of wild animals, hornets that will not die, abundant violence, and a climax that incorporates a woman in a bathtub who has been dead for thirty years, no one is quite sure how the screen version will finally turn out.

All that is known presently is that Jack Nicholson and Shelley Duval have been signed, and the world's greatest makeup men, Freeborn and Smith, who many insiders bet will be tapped to create *The Shining*'s many bloody wonders, have yet to be contacted.

Audrey Rose has been contacted, though. Contacted by the spirit of a girl who was born the moment she died. Ivy Templeton (Susan Swift) was born to Bill (John Beck) and Janice (Marsha Mason) the moment after Elliot Hoover's (Anthony Hopkins) wife and child were killed in a car crash. Through years of long searching, Elliott tracked down his daughter's soul in Ivy's body. His claims of reincarnation are given weight by the girl's strange behavior, especially on her birthdays.

Janice begins to believe, but Bill does not and the case goes to trial. There, in front of a jury, the climax of a tragedy is played out when Ivy is placed under hypnosis and regresses back to her time as Audrey Rose. The spell cannot be broken, however, and Ivy remains locked in another girl's past. Before her three parents' horrified

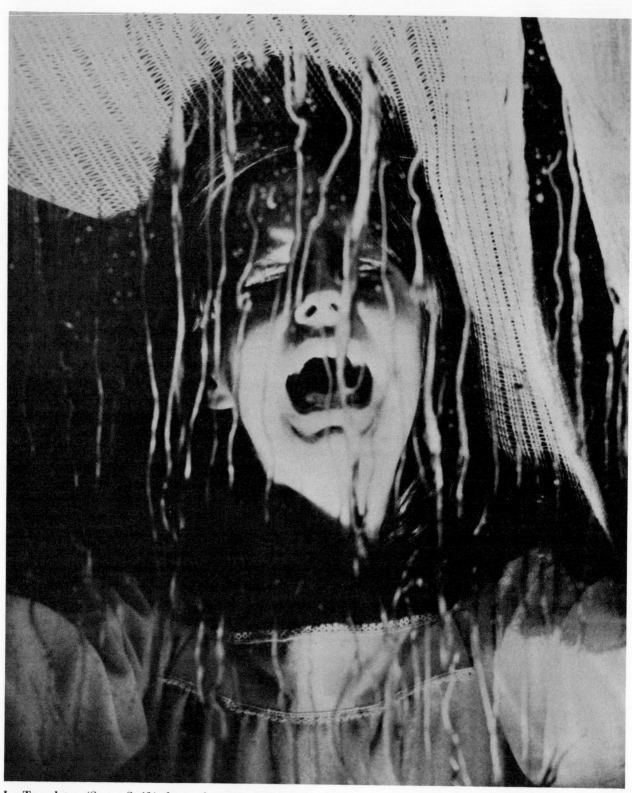

Ivy Templeton (Susan Swift) shares the pain of the spirit
of *Audrey Rose* (© United Artists).

eyes, she relives her death, trapped in the flaming wreck of a car, although actually in a doctor's office.

At the time of its release, *Audrey Rose* had been a best-seller as a novel written by Frank DeFelitta. Although it did not swell the ranks of the "believers," it did deliver to its readers enough chills to plop it firmly on the booksellers' order forms and the film producers' option sheets. DeFelitta was after more than quick money, however. His own son had shown signs of what was called "incarnation leak" by expert Barbara Ryan and had become an accomplished jazz pianist at the age of six without previous musical aptitude or a single lesson. DeFelitta had done extensive research before attempting the novel and became a firm believer in the hereafter.

Thereafter, he became the producer, with Joe Wizan, of the film version, hoping to translate his work undiluted to the screen without succumbing to the voyeuristic thrill seeking of other supernatural vehicles. In that, he succeeded admirably by acquiring Robert Wise as the director. Whatever success this maligned film enjoyed is due, in no small way, to the taste and craftmanship of this experienced showman. From the very first, editing *Citizen Kane* (1941) and *The Magnificent Ambersons* (1942), Wise's work displayed quality.

Then, from his first feature—*The Curse of the Cat People* (1944), taken over from Gunther Von Fritsch—on, the supernatural has subtly permeated his filmography, giving the genre several classics, *The Body Snatcher* (1945), *The Day The Earth Stood Still* (1951), *The Haunting* (1963), and *The Andromeda Strain* (1970) all bear Wise's directorial stamp.

The same strikingly intelligent handling shone through *Audrey Rose*'s shortcomings as a movie. The shortcoming was credibility, for while the book page can be emotionally acceptable given the proper framework, a visual cinematic scene needs more than the author's assurances that such a thing can exist. People need a reason to believe reincarnation exists, and *Audrey Rose* fails to deliver.

This fact is compounded by a flagrant contradiction in the story. DeFelitta's main pro-reincarnation characters powerfully promote the concept, but no one seems to note that they are giving affirmative testimony at a case where a girl is being slowly tortured to death by an insufficient spirit transfer. Wise does not capitalize on her suffering, thankfully.

His visualizations are constantly stunning and unpretentious, his motifs being glass and water. The water pounding on the windshield in the film's opening shot causes the car carrying the female Hoovers to crash.

Little Audrey Rose pounds on the car windows as the rain fails to quell the flames raging about the auto. Ivy Templeton stumbles from room to room in her New York apartment, pounding the windows, crying from unknown heat, the streaks of rain on the panes becoming her tears. And, finally, the release as she pounds on the two-way mirror in the doctor's office, dying her second death, and her first father breaks through to her. Even beyond the thin plot line and unsubstantiated premise, the power of these moments is extremely effective and makes one wish that Wise could always work with a script worthy of his abilities.

No sooner had these top-quality films been released than the smaller production companies saw an opportunity to bankroll with the paranormal punches. January 1977 saw the release of the Robert Dadashian produced, Robert Voskanian directed, Ralph Lucas written, and Boxoffice International released *The Child*, an *Omen*ized

The Child.

29

Night of the Living Dead with a dose of *Carrie* thrown in.

While its popular Antichrist predecessor used semi-classy publicity campaigns, incorporating a child with a wolf's shadow or a cross with the legend "You Have Been Warned," *The Child* pulls no punches. Its poster depicts a glowing-eyed girl behind a cemetery fence and a teddy bear in the foreground with its head ripped off. In case that wasn't a big enough hint the film's tag line was, "Let's play hide and go kill . . . !"

Essentially, it is the "R" rated tale of little Rosalie Norden (Rosalie Cole), whose mother was killed by the family gardener at the request of the Norden father (Frank Janson). The little girl retaliates by communicating and controlling the ghouls and ghosts who inhabit the cemetery near her house. Into this wholesome atmosphere comes young and attractive Alicianne Del Mar (Laurel Barnett), who has been hired as a housekeeper and governess. Out of all the major characters, she gets

to survive after a neighbor and her dog are killed and eaten, a scarecrow comes to life and attacks her, the gardener is shot, old man Norden is half-consumed, and Len, Rosalie's big brother, is destroyed while protecting Alicianne from the climactic attack of the ghouls.

Finally, alone in a pumphouse with an ax for protection, she goes for the first thing that moves. It is Rosalie, and, since she now has an ax in her head, the zombie-like flesh eaters drift back into the surrounding woods. Alicianne drifts into the sunrise, "hopelessly insane," according to one review, and "bewildered," according to the production notes, as we wander over to a far more faithful and successful derivation of the *Omen* concept.

Holocaust 2000 was its original title, but early in 1978 the title was changed to *The Chosen* and picked up by American International Pictures for a March release. This move incurred the wrath of other producers who had options on the Chaim Potok novel of the same name, but

The seven-headed hydra—a nuclear power plant—destined to bring on a holocaust in the year 2000 under the control of the Antichrist. From *The Chosen* (© A.I.P.).

The Redeemer.

the American distributors felt the latter title more acceptable to audiences who had been recently inundated by occult films bearing the word "The" followed by Exorcist, Heretic, Omen, Fury, Shining, Sentinel, and Redeemer.

The Redeemer is a picture concerning a lad from a lake taking over a priest in order to indiscriminately massacre six sinners at a deserted school, but back to *The Chosen*. No matter about the title, it still stands as an entertaining, interesting film with decent production values and a capable cast overcoming the awkward aspects of having three different nationalities playing members of the same family.

Edmondo Amati produced and Alberto De Martino directed the Sergio Donati, Michael Robson, and De Martino script. Kirk Douglas finished his leading role here in Italy during July just before starting *The Fury*, but he plays an essentially more interesting role of the head of a technological company commissioned to build a massive thermonuclear power plant in a third world country.

So far shaping up as a disaster film, the occult influences show when the plant's building site is discovered to be cursed with the ancient rune IESUS. According to Sara Golen (Agostina Belli), a local Government attaché, the word protects the area from a mythical beast prophesied in ancient times to rise from the sea under the guidance of the Antichrist to destroy mankind in a rain of fire. Robert Caine (Douglas) just smiles at the superstition, but the audience knows better.

Against the wishes of his wife, Eva (Virginia McKenna), and Prime Minister Harbin (Spiros Focas), the industrialist orders the land leveled, thus putting his world and his family on the road to ruin. A knife-wielding assassin charges him at a party, only to have the death blow deflected by his son, Angel (Simon Ward), into Eva's chest. It is she who dies and with her all emotional opposition to the nuclear plant. Shortly thereafter, Harbin and the political opposition die. Then all Caine's scientists and experts approach him with disturbing signs of supernatural sabotage. Professor Griffith's (Anthony Quayle) computer goes haywire, spitting out an anagram of IESUS before destroying itself and the professor.

With the help of Father Charrier (Romolo Valli) Caine becomes convinced that his own plant is the seven-headed beast of the old prophecy and that the unborn child he had helped create during an affair with Sara must be the Antichrist. The girl manages to escape in time for Robert to realize that it is the helpful Angel who is the real demon, the one who has been doing everything in his power to see that the plant is built so he can "purify" the world by setting off a chain of nuclear holocausts in time for his thirty-third birthday—in the year 2000.

Robert's reaction manages to get him shut into a madhouse where a Dr. Kerouac (Adolpho Celi) has planned a horrible death for him. Charrier arranges his escape and reunion with Sara at the cost of his own life. He dies hoping that the girl that Sara has borne embodies good the way Angel embodies evil and that the three can somehow prevent the terrible fate facing the Earth in just twenty-one years.

On that inconclusive note, the Italian/British co-production ends, brought to you by the team who had introduced the concept of an Antichrist to Italy more than five years before with a film called, naturally, *The Antichrist*, but with weaker results. Stateside, equally weak results were displayed by *Suspiria*, an International Classics release of August 1977, helmed by another Italian, director Dario Argento.

For years this Romanized, watered-down Hitchcock has been putting out tales of murderous mayhem unparalleled for consistent nastiness. From *The Bird With The Crystal Plumage* (1970) to *Four Flies on Grey Velvet* (1971) to *Deep Red* (1976) to his codirected (with Ned Romero) sequel to *The Night of the Living Dead*, *Dawn of the Dead* (1978), Argento has featured consistent death, the bloodiness outdone only occasionally by his bold directorial style.

Suspiria (1978) is his first occult excuse for gore, but the change of pace does not dampen his taste. The opening credits, for example, are spelled in pulsing letters made from vein-covered organs that beat like hearts. Following this is a pulse-pounding scene in which a pretty girl is attacked by supernatural forces in a dormitory room of a dance school. As she looks out her window, disembodied eyes open suddenly and stare back. Her scream of fear is drowned by an arm reaching through another window to push her head against and through the glass.

Once this shocking bit of business is finished, the plot drips out. Susy Banyon (Jessica Harper) enrolls in the Frieburg Tanz Akademie, a German ballet college where horrible things are happening, like the previously described episode. From there on, more blood is let, thanks to razor blades, shards of glass, loops of wire, and other common household implements. Susy is attacked by bats, witches, and, during the finale, by the school itself when the walls begin to tear themselves to pieces around her.

It seems that the faculty, led by Madame Blank (Joan Bennett), is really a coven of witches who enjoy doing in their students for reasons that are never fully revealed. Unfortunately, very little is fully revealed in this movie outside of wounds. It seems to exist as merely an atmospheric experiment in color and sound. The sets, designed by Argento and Giuseppe Fraticelli, were created to set moods. The halls and rooms are jagged, "twilight-zone" expanses that lead nowhere. The overall color is red, naturally, but, at other times faces are lit for emotional purposes like mood rings—blue for fear and green for doubt. The music, scored by Argento and played by the rock group Goblin, is orchestrated with screams, moans, and heavy breathing, a technique Dario used a lot more subtly in his past work.

Susy winds up killing Blank with a spike and escaping the establishment with the same speed and relief of many that left the theater. But audiences' relief was short-lived for the marquees were full of possessed women, tele-kinetically blessed children, Antichrists, and satanic cults. So many, in fact, that it wasn't long before every variety of filmmaker, from pornographers to independents to major studios, had at least one horror film scheduled for late-seventies release.

Even prestigious Walt Disney Productions got into the act with a pair of "Witch Mountain" films, *Escape to Witch Mountain* (1975) and *Return from Witch Mountain* (1978), both directed by John Hough. Here we have two children, Tony (Ike Eisenmann) and Tia (Kim Richards) Malone, who are not only telekinetic but alien as well. They are part of an enclave of earth-dwelling extraterrestrials who reside in the confines of Witch Mountain where they had fled at the end of the first film with the help of Eddie Albert to keep out of the industrial clutches of Ray Milland.

Now, three years later, they are dropped off from their flying saucer in the Pasadena Rose Bowl by Uncle Bene (Denver Pyle) in order to experience a major city. However, a dog wouldn't deserve the reception they get. While they are taxiing into town, a man leaps off a building. Tony senses the danger and, stopping the cab, saves the seeming suicide with his "degravitational" powers. But the victim is actually under the scientifically created mind control of evil Dr. Gannon (Christopher Lee), who, with his mercenary partner, Letha Wedge (Bette Davis), hopes to perfect this psychic power in order to control the world.

They kidnap Tony and "mindcuff" him with a brain-controlling device while Tia attempts to track down his weak mental signal with the help of the teenage Earthquake Gang: Muscles (Brad Savage), Crusher (Poindexter), Rock (Jeffrey Jacquet), and Dazzler (Christian Juttner). They interrupt Madame Wedge during a murderer as well when detective Paul Burke devises a method to "burn out" Hutton's power as well as his brain. The generally pleasant notices, ranging from "pretentious 'B' picture" to "the very best junk movie it could possibly be," are basically because of Raymond Danton's crisp direction.

Avco-Embassy returned to the occult genre more than two years later with the wildly inventive, highly researched, boldly ambitious and sadly flawed *The Manitou* (1978). William Girdler, the creator of such forgettable work as *Abby* (1975) and *Grizzly* (1976), picked up Graham Masterdon's novel at an airport late in the bicentennial year. Reading the English writer's work on the plane, he knew immediately that he wanted it to be the followup to his previous box office successes.

Using his street-wise savvy, he knew he could produce the incredibly complicated story for about three million dollars, but he went to his production organization of Weist and Associates to convince the rest of the world.

Kim Richards (left) and Ike Eisenmann give Christopher Lee (far right) a telekinetic lift during the climax of *Return from Witch Mountain* (© Walt Disney Productions).

gold heist in a museum, but she manages to spirit Tony away again. Tia follows them back to their hideout, only to discover Gannon plans to hold the world for ransom from inside the walls of a nuclear processing plant.

The Earthquake Gang and Tia race to the rescue, but the psychically-controlled Tony is sent to stave them off. Things literally start flying until Tia manages to exhaust her weakened brother. Soon Letha and Gannon are in the authorities' custody, and the two aliens have learned an important lesson—never trust a human over fourteen years of age. They are picked up by Uncle Bene's flying saucer and it is the last we see of them until the next sequel.

Another example of the psychically mistreated is the Avco-Embassy Production, *Psychic Killer* (1976), originally titled *The Kirlian Force*. Jim Hutton, perennial youth and TV's Ellery Queen, plays a two-bit crook who acquires the power of astral projection from a likewise imprisioned voodoo enthusiast. From then on, he does in everyone who had the least little thing to do with putting him in jail, giving the film its violence and spice as people get bumped off left and right. Among the victims are such old hands as Neville Brand, Nehemiah Persoff, and Whit Bissell. The deaths take their toll on the

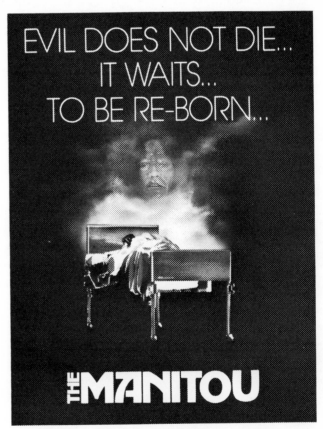

The Manitou.

Mel Gordy, the executive producer of the project to be produced, directed, and written (with Jon Cedar and Tom Pope) by Girdler himself, created a four-inch-thick, 1,100-page "feasibility study" to be sent to investors. The package included audience reaction charts, a film-term glossary, conceptual illustrations by Nikita Knatz, and distribution patterns. It wasn't long before Girdler had his three million and a cast that included Tony Curtis, Michael Ansara, Susan Strasberg, Stella Stevens, Burgess Meredith, and Paul Mantee.

The plot, if anything, is more outlandish than almost anything previously attempted. Karen Tandy (Strasberg) develops a tumor on the back of her neck. Night by night it grows until initially puzzled doctors discover the tissue and bone beneath the skin moving. All of a sudden, the real world of a big-city hospital is turned upside down. Enter Harry Erskine (Curtis), who has discovered that it is the Indian sorcerer Misquamacus returning to life after 400 years to take his revenge on the white man.

Caught between the rock and the hard place, the doctors agree to hire John Singing Rock (Ansara), a modern medicine man, to fight the manitou, or spirit, of the monster. The hospital is sealed off and Misquamacus, all the more powerful from his centuries-long

The horribly mutated visage of Misquamacus, care of makeup man Tom Burman, the 400-year-old *The Manitou* (© Avco-Embassy).

wait, is actually born before our eyes, pulling out of the cocoon on Karen's back. First his hand appears; then his shoulder; then his horribly deformed head, warped by x-rays used earlier; then his truncated legs, also changed by the rays. His rage is all the more horrible for his pain. He buries the floor in arctic conditions and hurls Karen's room into another dimension. Interior earthquakes are formed and firebolts fly. It is only through the intervention of a computer, called Unitrack, and its own manitou that the entire world is saved.

Girdler was enormously successful in translating the terrible tall tale to the screen for the first forty-five minutes of its running time. The last half, although enjoyable, was marred by poor dialogue and sluggish pacing, a situation made all the more surprising by the snap and quality of the movie's beginning. Still, the effects and ingenuity involved were extensive. Misquamacus himself was the result of two midgets hauling pounds of makeup covering every inch of them; one midget for stationary shots, the other for walking across the floor.

Other effects included a "black-screened Lizard of the Trees," a badly designed suit for a stunt man but a well-realized ghostly apparition, a laser beam gone mad, and the single most impressive feat—a demon head rising from the solid surface of a wooden table. The special effects were handled by Dale Tate, Frank Van Der Veer, Gene Grigg, and Tim Smyth; the ample music score was well written by Lalo Schifrin; and a special appearance was made by Ann Sothern.

The true tragedy of the production is that William Girdler did not live to see its premiere. He died at the age of thirty in a helicopter crash while scouting locations for a new movie on January 24, 1978.

His last film comes at the end of a long line of low-budget movies and is representative of producers' attempts to squeeze out every last exciting derivation possible on the possession theme. Girdler's film was certainly more successful than the next four movies put together. *Demon Witch Child* (1976), a Spanish film, told about a little girl who is taken over by a devil worshipper who killed herself. The gimmick here is that the preteen acquires an ancient face whenever she leads a rite or does in a victim.

After that, the Germans sent over their answer, *Beyond the Darkness* (1976), wherein an extremely attractive blonde turns from a shy teen into a foul-minded love machine, upon spiritual takeover. Seemingly the only attraction of this exorcism-less production was to see the shapely Dagmar Hedrich in the nude and a couple of gruesome murders. Immediately thereafter, two young

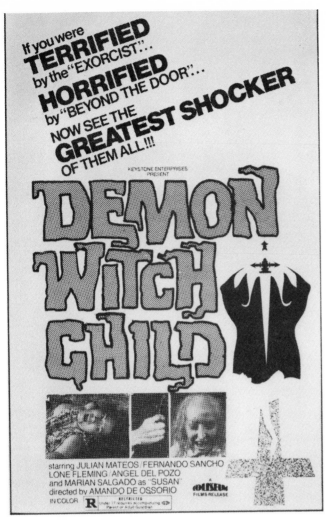

Demon Witch Child.

Americans managed to get their effort, *The Demon Lover* (1976), released to the theaters. It is a little more than an hour of karate, demon-inspired deaths, and genre in-jokes. Sandwiched in the story of "hell having no fury like an occultist scorned," that is, Laval Blessing conjuring up a horned demon to kill his followers when they leave the fold, is Gunnar Hanse, who played "Leatherface" in *The Texas Chainsaw Massacre* (1973), Val Mayerik, the primary illustrator of the syndicated "Howard the Duck," and character names based on the comic and film fields.

Made at about the same time as the *Demon Witch Child* was a minor effort about a professor of the supernatural who gets beat up by some hoods—a la *Clockwork Orange*—and watches them kill his family—a la *Death Wish*—then takes his revenge from his hospital bed with the help of a demon. This Evan Lee–directed story was hardly worth an audience's second thought, but, in the hands of the Group One Production Company, it went the

box office distance thanks to a tacked-on prologue by Christopher Lee and a title that stole a little thunder from the cultist *Texas Chainsaw Massacre*. Thus, *The Hollywood Meatcleaver Massacre* was given a new cinematic career in 1977.

Also given a chance in 1977 was Larry Cohen's bicentennially produced *God Told Me To*, renamed *Demon* to take advantage of the new horror orientation. Cohen, along with Girdler, Argento, and De Palma, is one of a select group of directors whose horror efforts are marked by the consistent triumph of style over content. Simply said, their visual sense is better than their character or plot developments most of the time. So while their movies almost always have a few memorable moments, the films on a whole are usually unsatisfying.

The memorable moments in *Demon* happen early on. A sniper wipes out people, then gives as his motive, "God told me to." Then a father kills his entire family because "God told him to." Suddenly the city is awash with heavenly-inspired murders. These episodes are frightening in their realism—how many times have newspapers in real life reported the same sort of thing?

Here, however, it is not the Devil or the Lord who takes the rap, but an alien race who have been experimenting with the creation of two effective supermen. The first, Bernard Phillips (Richard Lynch), is a young man with flowing blond hair who has grown up thinking himself the second coming because of his power to get people to do his psychic bidding. Soon his attitude turns to revenge, or "purification," in the time-worn religious terminology, which really means normal people dropping like flies. The second, Peter Nicholas (Tony LoBianco) is far more successful because he doesn't realize his power or background until the end of the film. Up until that time, he thought he was a New York City detective of considerable skill and ability, a part that LoBianco is experienced in, having played the same role in many television shows. But when it comes time to face the resurrected son, he literally brings the house down upon him, calling forth his own alien-spawned strength.

As in Cohen's earlier action work, which included two black-exploitation films, blood runs free and most stops are pulled out near the finale, with alien ships appearing, seeming virgin births, and a final-line "twist." When LoBianco is asked why he killed the young hippie at the end he replies, "God told me to."

The acting is consistently superior to the situations, Cohen wisely assigning the supporting roles to Sandy Dennis, Sam Levine, Sylvia Sidney, and Robert Drivas. It was a New Worlds picture release, produced, written, and directed by Cohen, but the finished film is obviously not what he originally intended since the editing credits list four men—Arthur Mendelberg, William Waters, Christopher Lebenzon, and Mike Corey—when most other films credit one. The bad reviews and mediocre box-office returns disappointed Cohen, who professed pride in his work and even went as far as to dedicate it to the memory of Bernard Herrman, the great film composer, but it didn't stop him. He would achieve a monetary revenge the very next year with another re-edited re-release called *It's Alive*. However, the lack of patrons and the critical scorn did kill one of the most famous horror studios ever established—Hammer Films.

Registered in 1934 under the chairmanship of Will Hammer, the studio began its history with comedies, historicals, and action thrillers based on popular radio programs of the time. It wasn't until 1952 that Hammer Films, re-registered, started producing horror and science-fiction adventures such as *Stolen Face* (1952) and *The Four Sided Triangle* (1953), both dealing with doctors' attempts to recreate a lost loved one.

They really hit their stride two years later with *The Quatermass Experiment* (1955), based on a famous English television character, a specialist in the extraterrestrial realms and forerunner to the present British master of the macabre Doctor Who. It is 1957, however, that most fantasy-film enthusiasts remember when Hammer is mentioned, for that is the year when their "monster cycle" began with *The Curse of Frankenstein*, a gory update, followed by the masterful *Horror of Dracula* (1958) starring Christopher Lee as the vampire.

There followed dozens of horror movies which depended more on shock, blood, and nubile female flesh to attract audiences than a genuine concern for the development of character and terror. Some exceptions that deserve mention include *The Devil Rides Out* (1968), *The Curse of the Werewolf* (1960), *Die Die My Darling* (1965), and *Vampire Circus* (1972). *To the Devil . . A Daughter* (1976) cannot be added to that list, unfortunately. Even though the production boasted a Dennis Wheatley source novel and fine performances by Christopher Lee and Richard Widmark as the antagonists, many could not help being disappointed by the lack of true horror substance. It is generally considered Hammer's last gasp.

Father Michael (Lee) wants to make Catherine (Nastassja Kinski) the living embodiment of the demon Astaroth. John Verney (Widmark), a noted occult expert intends to stop him. Thus the doors are flung open to plot and counterplot, shock and countershock. Finally, the two opponents face off in the church courtyard, verbally abusing each other while the wind howls. Up until that

To the Devil . . . A Daughter.

time, no real audience involvement has been courted, since Catherine is played apathetically, like a blank slate ready to be written on. One does not care about her, so one doesn't care what happens to her. Further, no supernatural ground rules are established, so no reality or followable fantasy is created. Whatever drama that could have been pulled in by the end is destroyed by a time-worn cop-out. Instead of taking a stand, establishing that good can legitimately triumph over evil, Father Michael is defeated by a rock knocking him unconscious.

What was refreshing, however achieved, was the fact that good won at all. With the advent of the witches'-coven/devil-cult film of the seventies, the fashionable thing is to have good lose, mirroring the ever-present corruption within reality. With police payoffs, judicial disorganization, political inequities, and the all-too-possible threat to total human annihilation, filmmakers were inclined to let audiences off easy. Evil was winning in the real world, and the cinema gave Satan as an excuse.

Man is always the Devil's instrument in these numerous coven/cult films, the worst of which, or best, depending on your point of view, probably being *Satan's Cheerleaders* (1976), Alvin L. Fast's jolly picture. This opus, directed and co-written (with Fast) by Greydon Clark, tells of Benedict High School's senior cheerleaders, blonde Patti (Kerry Sherman), brunette Debbie (Alisa Powell), redhead Chris (Hillary Horan), and mousey Sharon (Sherry Marks) going up against a small-town satanic cult headed by the high priest (John Ireland), high priestess (Yvonne DeCarlo) and a monk (Sydney Chaplin).

It all begins when head janitor Billy (Jack Kruschen) vows vengeance for the humiliation he has suffered at the hands of the girls. He takes them, along with their young, attractive faculty advisor Ms. Johnson (Jacqulin Cole), to the coven's headquarters instead of to the Saturday

Satan's Cheerleaders.

football game. There, while the other girls are paralyzed, Satan kills Billy and mates with Patti. When the others are unfrozen, they accept the explanation that he died of a heart attack trying to rape the blonde.

Once they arrive at the police to report the accident the sheriff and his wife turn out to be the priest and priestess who plan to do in the girls as sacrifices, only to suffer bloody deaths at the hands of Patti who has the Devil himself as consort. True to form, she uses her new power to further strengthen the cult. About the only interesting aspect of this drive-in fodder was that John Carradine did a walk-on halfway through as a bum who gives directions to the girls.

It does not take half of *The Devil's Wedding Night*'s (1975) eighty-five minutes to know that this was another quickie horror offering from Dimension Pictures, Inc., which also supplied their audiences with *Black the Ripper* (1977) and *Carhops 1980* (1978). The title in question concerns Karl and his twin brother, Franz (both played by Mark Damon), fighting over the Nibelungen ring, once owned by Count Dracula and said to have supernatural powers of its own.

Franz steals a talisman which should protect him from the ring's aura and journeys to Transylvania, where he gets under the covers with a beautiful countess (Sara Bay) and comes under her power when it is discovered she is both the wearer of the ring and a vampire. Karl races after his brother only to find him entombed in the Countess's castle as one of the living dead. He also discovers the secret of the ring's power. On the night of the first full moon every year, it attracts the local virgins to a black sabbath where they are sacrificed to Satan for purposes that are never made clear. Neither is the fact that no virgin who hypnotically appears seems to be under the age of seventeen nor over the weight of 120 pounds. On this particular celebration night, Franz is to become Dracula's heir and wed the Countess amid an orgy of death.

Clever Karl manages to stake out his brother and replace him at the ceremony. Although he doesn't save the virgins, he does hack off the Countess's ring hand with an ax. She and her followers are then blasted into nothingness by lightning.

The infamous count made a guest appearance in that 1975 effort, so it is only natural that the next film of this type feature his hairy confederate, the werewolf. The Atlas International Presentation let the audience know exactly where they stood. "Prepare yourself for the Horror of *Psycho!*" cried the poster. "The Terror of *Exorcist!*" And then below the photo of a naked woman on an altar, "Damn The Exorcist! The Devil won't let go!"

The Devil's Wedding Night.

The story of *Curse of the Devil* (1975), however, tells of a curse put upon Irenius Daninsky, an Inquisitor under the rule of Wladislao III. Four hundred years after the fact, Daninsky's descendant Waldemar (Paul Nashy) accidentally kills a gypsy during a hunt. The rest of the tribe calls on the Devil to carry out the curse, so Satan possesses Maria (Faye Falcon), who seduces the man then cuts his skin with the teeth of a werewolf, turning Waldemar into a beast on the night of the full moon. From there on it is straight hairy murders, without an exorcism or heavenly retribution in sight.

The wolfman is finally done in by his fiancée, Kinga (Maria Silva), freeing him, and us, of the curse. In the middle of 1976, another mistitled film was released by Independent-International. Called *They're Coming To Get You!*, it seems to be promising monsters, but this Italian feature, filmed in England, delivered a demon cult instead, trying to take over and do in a lovely girl named Edwige Fenech. Toward this end, she is assailed with terrible dreams, gang raped by members of the cult, sent to a sanitarium where the caretakers are murdered, then she's arrested by the disguised cult leader when they kill her boy friend and blame it on her. She meets the same fate as her loved ones by the end of the movie seemingly for the simple reason that demon cults like to kill people.

For a while, the titles appeared regularly, using the occult theme to grind out a steady supply of gore and sexual stimulation, unashamedly using popular successes as their basis. Newspapers advertised uncredited films that appeared with regularity and disappeared with speed.

"WARNING! If the abnormal love of a sex-psycho frightens you . . . STAY AWAY!" *Lynn Hart, the Strange Love Exorcist* (1976) was the title. The blurb beneath read, "Lynn Hart WAS POSSESSED BY A DEMON! This one starts where *THE EXORCIST* leaves off!" It was actually the story, made years previous to its late-seventies release, of a girl who could not kiss without killing.

The same goes for *The Touch of Satan: A Story of Exorcism* (1976). "To Love Her is to be Cursed!"

"A walking corpse lusts for revenge. Hot fire consumes his body . . . Burning passion consumes his soul! *SCREAM OF THE DEMON LOVER*."

"Black Belt Vs. Black Magic! See: A Kung Fu Master Battle An Army of Savage Midgets! See: Deadly Flying Bat Men! See: The Terrifying Lady of Snakes! See: The Unstoppable Men of Stone! More Action! More Horror! More Power Than Ever Before! *Bruka, Queen of Evil* [1975]!"

This film and *Beyond the Door* led the surge of foreign produced *Exorcist*-like horror films that swamped the United States from 1973 on. More recently audiences were treated to the Italian import *The Tempter* (1978).

And along the same lines: "The Baddest Dudes That Ever Walked The Face of the Earth Fight a Battle to the Death with Satin's [sic] Sinister Sister! *Devil Woman* [1976]: The Ultimate Evil. She has a Sexy Body and Soft Silken Skin and . . . the Kiss of Death!"

Finally, things began to improve with a small offering from Crown International Pictures. *The Land of the Minotaur* (1977) was a Greek/English coproduction with a refreshing casting change, making Peter Cushing the villain and Donald Pleasence the hero, positions that are usually reversed. Also refreshing, if a bit old-fashioned, was its optimistic, upbeat ending. The rest of the cast were unknowns, on this side of the ocean, as were producer Fixos Constantine and director Costa Carayiannis. Originally designated *The Devil's People* for United States release, the present title was returned when the movie was religated to one-half of a double bill.

Baron Corofax (Cushing) makes a habit of sacrificing young tourists to keep the spirit of the Minotaur, beneath

This 1977 title joins the ranks of obscure, nearly untraceable films within the fantasy film genre.

his castle, happy and his pagan village running well. He makes a mistake in kidnapping Tom, Ian, and Beth (Bob Behling, Nikos Velekis, Vanna Revilli), for Tom's fiancée, Laurie (Luan Peters), goes to Father Roche (Pleasence) and New York private eye Milo (Costa Skouras) for assistance.

Black-hooded people soon appear and Laurie disappears, leading Roche to believe that he is dealing with an ancient, faceless power that can control people. The only solution—exorcism! Moonlight falls and the forces of good and evil battle. In a subterranean room filled with statues of the horned demon, the victims, placed on recliner-shaped alters, are prepared for the sacrifice. On the verge of death himself, Roche completes his own ritual, and the entire castle collapses, the power on which it was based totally destroyed.

Quite possibly the two best films of this kind met a similarly sad fate. *The Tenant* (1976) was ignored critically and commercially, and *The Wicker Man* (1977) was never fully released. *The Tenant* was Roman Polanski's first major film after *Chinatown* (1974) and followed in the steps of his *Repulsion* (1965) and *Rosemary's Baby* by examining reality from an insane, paranoid, possessed point of view. It is almost a combination of the most pitiable aspects of a Woody Allen character and the darkest side of Russian writing. Indeed, Polanski himself plays a character named Trelkovsky, who moves into an apartment vacated by the suicide of the previous female tenant.

From the beginning, he is cowed by life and is, essentially, terrified by everything. The concierge of his

Land of the Minotaur.

Roman Polanski chokes himself up during *The Tenant* (© Paramount).

new dwelling (Shelley Winters) belittles him, Mr. Zy (Melvyn Douglas) makes Polish jokes about him, and no one else considers him of the least importance. However, he takes their apathy and builds it into a major conspiracy, thinking that the rest of the building's occupants are trying to drive him to the same end as his room's previous tenant.

This 125-minute film, for which Polanski collected a large, talented crew of French and Swedish technicians along with French and American actors, is so unremittently depressing, it is little wonder that it was not a success. However, the power of the story, as well as the beauty of the visuals make it a fascinating, if painful, film to watch.

It is also in these visuals that the fantasy aspects reign. During a variety of dream sequences, Polanski's head replaces a volleyball, his room grows in size, a neighbor suddenly sports golden pupils and a forked tongue, and

all the residents gather below his window to provoke him. Nothing can save Trelkovsky, not an unconsummated relationship with a "liberated" woman (Isabelle Adjani) or reality. His room becomes a prison, his mind the executioner. Soon, he is seeing other tenants attack him, but it is his own hands around his throat. Then he starts trying on the clothes of the dead girl and painting his lips and fingernails. Finally, he jumps from his window and only then achieves freedom, but after he survives the first fall, he crawls up the stairs to jump again, declaring, "I am Trelkovsky." He succeeds in killing himself the second time, bloodied and in woman's clothing.

The Wicker Man was shorter, more accessible, and made by some of the finer British talents, but it has been deemed no less important. Originally made in 1973, it has passed through a bureaucratic nightmare that rivals the plot of many other horror films. Going through four or more distribution centers from EMI to Warner Brothers

41

to New World to Abraxas and beyond, it found none that were interested or capable of promoting it.

It was cut from 102 minutes to eighty-seven, though many felt it was too short even at the former length, with the original version being almost lost in the process. In the space of four years, *The Wicker Man* became a symbol of embarrassment to many in the rocky British film industry. Still, the word from the horror-genre critics is that the film is the finest of its type in years. Made entirely in Scotland by producer Robin Snell and director Robin Hardy, it is still unavailable for viewing in theaters, at fan conventions, or on television.

Anthony Shaffer, author and screenwriter of *Sleuth* (1972), *Frenzy* (1972), and *Murder on the Orient Express* (1974), wrote this film concerning Sergeant Howie (Edward Woodward), who is called to the remote island of Summerisle to investigate the reported disappearance of Rowan Morrison (Geraldine Cowper). There he is met with oddity after oddity, concerning both the supposed disappearance and the nature of the residents.

On the first day, he comes upon naked lovers in a cemetery. The second day, the innkeeper's daughter (Britt Ekland) frolics naked next door, singing a dirty tune and enticing Howie with melodic suggestions. When he visits a school, he discovers that the lessons are about pagan rituals, using the powers of the earth and the elements as gods. Only when he meets Lord Summerisle (Christopher Lee) does the film cement its theme of a pagan island assaulting the sensibilities and, ultimately, taking the life of this "civilized" Catholic.

The disappearance has been arranged only to get Howie to the island so he can be given to the god of the coming harvest. The film ends with a lengthy May Day procession, incorporating traditional songs and poetry into a highly stylized, sensual demise for the mainland policeman. He meets his end in the Wicker Man, a gigantic, standing figure made of wood, with different compartments for animals, the largest being for Howie. He dies screaming that if the crops do not grow the coming year the people will be coming for Lord Summerisle.

The cliches of previous fantasy films are pointless to dwell on with such a unique movie as *The Wicker Man*. Almost universally touted by those involved and those who have seen it—Lee called Lord Summerisle, ". . . the best part I've ever had."—it is still doubtful that the movie will ever be released to the national audience. It was last reported that Abraxas and National General Pictures planned the official American premiere for October 28, 1977 in New Orleans. Since that time nothing more has been heard.

While the producers struggled to get their film seen, other occult adventures of considerably less quality and intelligence were making money hand over foot. *Race With the Devil* (1975), an American International release, teamed Peter Fonda with Warren Oates as two campers who are pursued by a satanic cult after they witness a black mass with their wives.

This framework was merely an excuse to mount all sorts of outlandish motor-vehicle stunts, using motorcycles, cars, vans, trucks, and campers. One by one, the intrepid foursome wipe out the coven members in fiery crashes until they settle, supposedly safe, in the last reel. Suddenly, a ring of fire appears around their camp site, and the hooded living dead move in for the kill.

The movie satisfied the thrill-seeking car fans, of which there must be many, since the box office returns for this pessimistic vision were hefty. It also led the way for two almost simultaneously released tales of "radials beyond the grave:" *Crash!* (1977) and *The Car* (1977).

The Car was the more prestigious effort, coming from Universal Studios, home of *Jaws* (1975) and *Earthquake*, (1975) but the overall critical reaction to the two was the same. Demolition Derby, with people as the targets. Dennis Shryack and Michael Butler wrote the screenplay, a chore they repeated for *The Gauntlet* (1977), a Clint Eastwood picture which also dwelled on rapid transport. But, while the Eastwood film had a plot firmly entrenching it in reality, *The Car*'s storyline is stationed somewhere beyond "The Twilight Zone."

Santa Ynez, for no particular reason, is being terrorized by a huge black car which is driverless, never runs out of gas, and is made of seemingly indestructible

Another victim is about to be chalked up by all 5000 pounds of *The Car* (© Universal).

material. It never bends, chips, breaks, or loses its shine. It also has a tendency to kill those who are undeserving of death, like beautiful young women, innocent hitchhikers, battered wives, children, and intrepid lawmen.

Sheriff Everett (John Marley), Deputy Wade (James Brolin), and Assistant Deputy Luke (Ronny Cox) are hot on the black car's trail until it does in the sheriff. Then Luke mentally disintegrates, becoming a drunk and forgetting to cancel a school parade, where the car wipes out more innocents. When the survivors hole up in a cemetery, the motorized killer won't enter. It does, according to the production notes, "race its engine in fury," however. Lauren (Kathleen Lloyd), Wade's fiancée, taunts the vehicle while a friend radios for help.

Following is a long chase where the car pushes one police vehicle over a cliff then crushes some others while on two wheels. The final straw comes when it kills Lauren by driving right through her picture window, "plows across the room and crashes out the far wall," again according to the press releases. And without being damaged in the least. Bullets can't hurt it, other autos can't stop it, it won't be baited, so the grief-ridden Wade decides cleverly to blow it up with explosives.

He fills some vans with dynamite and leads, on motorcycle, the car to the dead end of a canyon, where more dynamite is planted. Wade and the reformed Luke lead the car in, the detonator is hit, and the whole area goes up, the deputies safe on the cliff above. The film leaves an open end, however, or, as the press release says, ". . . it's all over. But . . . is it?"

If the audience and critics have anything to say about it, the answer is definitely yes. The film was universally panned and seemingly left even avid car freaks in the dark as to the plot's purpose. No supernatural rationale was introduced, no occult terminology, no cause and effect, and very little suspense, since it was established that nothing could damage the auto and that it had a tendency to avoid running over essentially evil people.

Producer-director Elliot Silverstein, whose previous credits include *Cat Ballou* (1965) and *A Man Called Horse* (1970), spent more than a year in planning *The Car* with designer George Barris and stunt director Everett Creach. The vehicle itself was 240 inches long, ninety-two inches wide, 5500 pounds, and made from eighteen gauge steel on a Lincoln Mark III chassis with a 455 cubic-inch engine. It took twelve men eight weeks to build the monster, with double air shock absorbers, double bumpers, and extra roof bracing to protect the stuntmen. Furthermore, the windows were of laminated amber on the outside but smoked on the inside so no one could see in, but the driver could see out.

Many critics wished the movie screen had been laminated amber as well, but that didn't stop Group One from releasing Charles Band's *Crash!*, where a car is not only a killer, but possessed as well. Jose Ferrer starred as a crippled occultist whose young wife (Sue Lyon) is confined to their home. He watches old home movies while she manages to step out and discover a relic with supernatural powers at a "swap-and-shop drive-in."

Since his handicap was caused by a car accident and she is blamed, the antique's power manifests itself into the family car after having possessed an old wheelchair to crush Ferrer's vicious dog. Auto accident follows auto accident until Jose traps Sue in a sauna and turns the heat all the way up. But the power holds sway, and it is Ferrer who dies while handsome doctor John Ericson saves the sweaty Lyon. John Carradine returned from giving directions to *Satan's Cheerleaders* to appear momentarily in this.

Possession of another kind appeared in 1976, not so much of soul or auto, but of character. One film was essentially an homage to all aspects of the horror film, while another took the shape of a murky dream. One was as entrenched in the cliches and audience expectations, as the other was an audacious experiment. One was the work of an established horror enthusiast, while the other was critically acclaimed as a premiere American filmmaker who had only used a fantasy theme once before. The films in question are Dan Curtis' *Burnt Offerings* (1976) and Robert Altman's *Three Women* (1977).

Robert Morasco, whose previous effort, *Child's Play* (1972), which was also a Tony award-winning stage work, wrote the book on which the movie *Burnt Offerings* is based. Both the novel and the film were moderate successes, since both interjected style for substance. The screen work seemed especially to exemplify the credo "if you've seen one, you've seen them all." Many knew what to expect from the rolling of the credits, and hardly a surprise was to be found as the plot unfolded.

That is not to say the film didn't have its share of shocks. Dan Curtis, who has spent his career mounting horror productions on television—Dark Shadows, Dracula, Trilogy of Terror, Curse of the Black Widow—was well versed in the time-worn devices of the genre and employed them professionally. However, the screenplay he wrote with William F. Nolan, author of *Logan's World*, is hollow at the core.

Marion (Karen Black) and Ben (Oliver Reed) are looking to get away from the city for the summer with their son David (Lee Montgomery) and Ben's Aunt

Oliver Reed discovers it isn't nice to fool Mother Nature in this scene from *Burnt Offerings* (© United Artists).

Elizabeth (Bette Davis). They find a huge mansion run by Roz (Eileen Heckart) and her wheelchair-bound brother (Burgess Meredith) which is available for an incredibly low price. Against Ben's better judgement, they become the tenants, a decision that turns doubtful when dead plants start blooming at the sight of blood.

Suddenly, Ben's nightmares about his mother's death return, Marion starts to become aloof, and Elizabeth, normally vital, starts to grow weak and bedridden. It all seems to revolve around the landlord's invalid mother, who never leaves her attic flat. Her waiting room is decorated with antiques, including a table top of portraits ranging from Victorian times to the present. Marian takes an intense interest in the house and the old woman to the detriment of her loved ones, and Ben's condition continue to deteriorate until he attacks his son and "shares" one of his nightmares with his Aunt, bringing on her heart failure.

Finally, one night, Ben sees the house ripping off its rotted wallboards to expose fresh wood beneath, and he puts two and two together. The house is alive and lives off the strength of others within. It slowly saps them every moment but gets stronger, in spurts, upon wounds and death. The family's escape attempts are foiled by Marion's obsession with the house and nature's cooperation with the real-estate's power. Trees fall to block their car's path and plants try to choke Ben.

The film ends as modern audiences would expect. Just when it seems escape is assured, Marion takes on the persona of the "invalid mother," who existed only in evil spirit, and hurls Ben out the attic window. This particular shot seems to be Curtis's trademark since he uses it in almost every production. But, since this is a "GP"-rated movie, he gets to frame the aftermath—Ben's ruined face dripping at David through the shattered car windshield. The terrified boy runs out only to have a chimney collapse on him. The final shot has Roz and her brother gloating over the portraits, to which Marion's,

44

Ben's, Elizabeth's, and David's have been added.

Paintings are also the central symbol in *Three Women*, but these are sinuous, sensual, macabre works painted by Bohdi Wind in reality but attributed to Willie Hart (Janice Rule) in the film. They line the bottoms of swimming pools in Desert Springs, California where the two central characters, Pinky Rose (Sissy Spacek), a blank-faced child of Texas; and Millie Lammoreaux (Shelley Duval), a flighty girl who is more affectation than character, work at an old-age clinic, giving hydrotherapy to elderly patients.

Pinky idolizes the character Millie has made up for herself, using mail order catalogs and popular women's magazines, piecing together her version of the perfect lady. Pinky is so plain as to be transparent, and Millie is so shallow that no one pays attention to her. They become roommates, and the first half of the film unwinds like a heat mirage until Pinky tries to commit suicide by leaping off the Purple Sage Apartments into the swimming pool.

Upon awakening from a coma she starts to assume Millie's persona to the point where she's wearing Millie's clothes and writing in Millie's diary. Meanwhile, Millie starts to lose her own identity like a glass being emptied from a hole in the bottom. Then the movie whirls into greater nightmare images as Willie's baby, sired by a fading cowboy-film star, is stillborn, heralding the rebirth of the trio until a man is murdered and the three women control the entire community. The telling of the "plot," as it were, cannot completely describe the mystic, magical quality of Altman's film, which he wrote from a dream he had. Many articles have been written, and many reviewers have tried to translate the movie in readable terms, but all have failed to incite audiences. *Three Women* was a box office disappointment, the same as all his other films, except for *M*A*S*H* (1970).

Reviews, like Roger Greenspun's *"Three Women* belongs with the magical transformations," and Bruce Williamson's "Compared with Altman's sophisticated witchery, such high-grossing conventional shockers as

The new, improved Sissy Spacek takes aim after a personality possession during *3 Women* (© 20th Century Fox).

45

The Omen and *Carrie* look like Halloween pranks," didn't prepare people for the humor, the dream sequences, and the mystery of Altman's first fantasy vision since *Brewster McCloud* (1970). Though *Three Women* was filled with female flesh and occasional blood, it didn't even make as much money as the inexpensive pornography films glutting the market.

These sex-filled opuses are appearing everywhere and have turned from back-alley business to front-page news with the advent of high-budget, high-quality fare like *Emmanuelle* (1975). The occult storyline is a natural for these filmmakers since the sexual aspects of possession and other supernatural phonomena were grossly represented in the controversial crucifix scene of *The Exorcist*. Since then, producers have been urging other actresses to "let go" under the Devil's influence.

Appearing immediately after *The Exorcist*'s success, but probably made earlier, was *The Joys of Jezebel*, (19?) the poignant story of a ninth-century Phoenician princess who is plotting her revenge on Joshua in hell, while Satan looks across his domain for a virgin to despoil. This allowed the filmmakers—who rarely record their real names for posterity—to portray Goliath being thrown into a pit of nymphs; Eve ranting against Lucifer for her Garden-of-Eden woes until Solomon, credited as the original dirty old man, soothes her; and a cast portraying the likes of Rachel, Ruth, Lust, Sol, Sarah, Isaac, and other biblical greats.

Slightly more serious in concept, but only slightly, was *Lucifer's Women* (1975), a story of a stripper being enticed into a satanic cult in 1954. Also released after *The Exorcist*, it has a young scholar (Larry Hankin) being forced by his sadistic publisher, Sir Stephen (Noorman Pierce), to convince the sexy Trilby (Jane Brunel-Cohen) to give her life up to the dark realm. Much skin is exposed before the student falls in love with the long-haired lass, then much blood is spilled when they decide to fight their way out of their predicament.

Constellation Films was responsible for releasing that, while Boxoffice International took the credit for two more porno-plagiarisms of 1976. *Dream No Evil* was the superior of the two, if only because it was longer and dealt in blood rather than flesh. A little girl, demented by her treatment in an orphanage grows up, finds her dead father capable of eliminating all her problems. The man only has to rise from the grave and mutilate anyone who shows the least interest in the girl. Many brutal murders are depicted before it is discovered that the psychotic girl is doing the killing, using her dead father's memory.

The second of these two winners was humorous in its

Lucifer's Women.

obviousness. It has had a three-year release record since its appearance as *The Virgins and the Vampires* in 1973, changing first to *Crazed Vampire* in 1975 and finally becoming the subtly proclaimed *Caged Virgins* in 1976. This French import was directed by France's leading creator of "naked terror" films, Jean Rollin, and was filled with blood and nudity.

This particular effort concerned two unsympathetic young girls who kill a policeman while running away from school on New Year's Eve. They come under the control of a vampire cult in an old castle and are hypnotized into luring victims for the blood-thirsty band. Love saves the more attractive of the two, who hides her first, handsome victim while the vampires hurl her failing friend into a tomb where she is buried alive. The remaining two humans fight off the others until the head bloodsucker seals off his domain for the rest of eternity.

This was the last of Rollin's four garish films, which started with *The Vampire's Rape* in 1967, made for a friend who wanted thirty minutes of sex in an hour-long American film, using only an inexperienced cast and crew. *The Nude Vampire* (1970) came next, utilizing a

$70,000 budget, which was $65,000 more than they had for the first. Finally came *The Vampires Thrill* (1973). Rollin was last reported making a new picture, called *The She Devils*.

Stiller waters returned with three straight, out-and-out pornography films appearing at the end of 1976 and at the beginning of the new year. September held a surprise box-office hit with Bill Osco's musical *Alice in Wonderland X* (1976). It was a colorful and humorous version of the Lewis Carroll classic, but adapted to fit a sexier plotline. Small-town librarian Alice (Kristine DeBell) uses the Carroll novel as her transport to a magical land where song and sex abound. Soon she is femininely aware and mature, able to return to her own world prepared and experienced.

The December offering was Jonas Middleton's *Through the Looking Glass*. Although not a sequel to the "X" rated *Alice*, it did concern another innocent in a fantasy land. Catherine Burgess's narcissism leads her to a full-length mirror in her attic which reflects a fantasy world wherein a blue-skinned demon (Jaime Gillis) frolics. Playboy's consensus was that it was "beautifully photographed, sharply edited and spooked up with a richly atmospheric score by Arlon Ober."

January 1977 delivered *The Devil Inside Her*, an "X-" rated play on the recent low-budget *The Devil Within Her* (1976), starring Joan Collins, Eileen Atkins, Ralph Bates, and Donald Pleasence in yet another *Rosemary's Baby/Exorcist* derivation. *Inside* has the Devil impersonating every member of a repressed New England family of 1826, affording them the chance to blow off some steam. Rod Dumont is Satan and Terri Hall is the object of almost everyone's affections.

Less than a year later, an "X-" rated *Cinderella* appeared, cut from the *Alice X* mold but failing to copy even its predecessor's weak humor. The Prince (Brett Smiley) is looking for his true love, and Cindy's (Chryl Smith) black fairy god person obliges by making her the queen of the ball.

The Cinderella fairy tale was far better served by *The Slipper and the Rose* (1976), a marvelously imaginative musical directed by Bryan Forbes and produced by David Frost. Richard Chamberlain was the strikingly handsome prince, and Mary Ann Mobly made a tuneful Cinderella among the opulent pomp and circumstance of the multi-million-dollar production. Unfortunately, this tasteful film was poorly distributed in the United States, appearing and disappearing out of New York's Radio City Music Hall, about the only place it played on the east coast.

Other films of the pornographic type appeared, like *The Erotic Adventures of Pinocchio*, originally released in 1975 and redistributed recently. It has been reported that Bill Osco was planning a *Wizard of Oz X*.

Fairy tales aside, after such an extensive collection of occult titles mostly concerned with the sensational, it is a pleasure to return to the inspired. After all the Satan-concerned themes, it is difficult to remember that the supernatural also concerns itself with the other end of the spectrum. The Heavenly Father made his triumphant return to the motion picture screen, hilariously, first in 1975, and then with an award-winning performance in 1977.

The former production pictured the Lord as a bearded miracle worker who grew impatient with all the human fuss that had grown up around him to the point that when his subjects averted their eyes or bowed, he testily advised them to "knock it off!" The same movie also pictured such diverse fantasy elements as King Arthur

two young girls... trapped with no escape!

Forced to submit to the Horrors of the Pit!

Color

THEIR INNOCENCE VIOLATED BEYOND DESCRIPTION— IN AN ENDLESS NIGHTMARE OF TERROR

HARRY NOVAK presents

CAGED VIRGINS

R

starring MARIE CASTEL · MIREILLE D'ARGENT · PHILIPPE GASTE · DOMINIQUE   directed by JEAN ROLLIN   executive producer SAM SELSKY

Caged Virgins.

Prince Charming (Richard Chamberlain) gets the girl (Mary Ann Mobley) at the finale of *The Slipper and the Rose* (© Universal).

and the Knights of the Round Table, the Three-Headed Knight, the Black Knight, the Nine-Foot Tall Knight Who Says "Ni!", Roger the Shrubberer, the Sorcerer Tim, the Killer Rabbit, and the Legendary Black Beast of Arrrghhh. It is, of course, *Monty Python and the Holy Grail*.

The English satirical group, made up of Terry Jones, Eric Idle, Michael Palin, Graham Chapman, Terry Gilliam, and John Cleese, have wormed their way into the American heart through reruns of their anarchic half-hour comedy show, "Monty Python's Flying Circus," on the Public Broadcasting System. That success

Neal Innes (left) and Eric Idle (center) get three heads for the price of one in the form of the dreaded three-headed knight (Terry Jones, Graham Chapman, and Michael Palin). From *Monty Python and the Holy Grail*, not surprisingly (Courtesy of Python (Monty) Films).

prompted the importing of their first film, *And Now For Something Completely Different*, in 1971. It is an anthology of some of their best routines, including "The Upper Class Twit of the Year Contest" and "How to Protect Yourself From Fresh Fruit."

The initial effort suffered from a lack of publicity, but their second movie came at a time when their following in the United States was at a peak. *Monty Python and the Holy Grail* takes place in A.D. 932, but the tone is set by the film's credits, which start with subtitles in mock Swedish, then degenerate into a subtitled monologue about a moose bite the subtitler's sister sustained while carving her initials in a moose's hide with a toothbrush.

A hasty apology is offered and the credits continue, interrupted only by outlandish duties concerning mooses, including "Moose Costumes by Siggi Churchill" and "Moose's Noses Wiped by Bjorn-Irkestomslater Walker." Another hasty apology is offered and the credits recontinue, attributing each of the creative efforts to a different breed of llama, including "Executive Production by Ralph the Wonder Llama" and "Direction by Forty Specially Trained Ecuadorian Mountain Llamas."

John Cleese as the Sorcerer Tim in *Monty Python and the Holy Grail* (Courtesy of Python (Monty) Films).

The real directors were Terry Gilliam, who also handled the animation which binded the different episodes together, and Terry Jones, who guided this demented tale of King Arthur (Chapman) scouring the countryside for knights to join his Round Table. Only after he discovers Sir Bedevere (Jones), Sir Lancelot the Brave (Cleese), Sir Galahad the Pure (Palin), and Sir Robin the Not-Quite-So-Pure-As-Sir-Lancelot (Idle) and they decide Camelot is a silly place, does God appear and give them a purpose: the Quest for the Holy Grail.

From there on they meet the previously mentioned characters, as well as many others (a French Castle Guard-protector of Guy de Loimbard (Cleese), the Trojan Rabbit, the beautiful young blondes "all between sixteen and nineteen and a-half" at the Castle Anthrax, the old man from scene twenty-four, the Holy Hand Grenade of Antioch, and the Bridge of Death where the bridgekeeper may ask them the Questions Three: "What is your name? What is your quest? What is your favorite color?"), before growing close to their objective—the Holy Grail. Unfortunately, they never gain it since a knight had killed a "very famous historian"—according to the subtitle—and the police enter the last scene, knocking the cameraman down without so much as a "The End."

The film simply runs out and the theater lights come on. Hopefully, the same finale will not appear in the group's new film, set for production in the summer of 1978. Since the six members write separately and then get together to make some coherent sense out of their comedy scenes, the plot line is unavailable at this writing. Their organization, Python (Monty) Films, Ltd., has suggested, however, that it could deal with biblical times, so God may make another guest shot with them. Until the time of release, their many fans only have their books, record albums, fan clubs, T-shirts, and PBS re-re-repeats to keep them happy.

Millions upon millions were made happy by the Lord's return in late 1977. Avery Corman, Larry Gelbart, and Carl Reiner conspired to bring His message back to movie theaters in *Oh, God*, the award-winning tale of a supermarket manager pegged to make like Moses by a whimsical, patient eternal Father. George Burns played God to John Denver's Jerry Landers, a confused, put-upon modern man, trying to deliver the Lord's message of peace, cooperation, and understanding to the masses while keeping his family solvent and his career afloat.

Terri Garr plays his sympathetic, but confused, wife, while David Ogden Stiers, William Daniels, George Furth, Barry Sullivan, Donald Pleasence, and Jeff Corey are just some of the people thrown in his way, being

49

Would you believe . . . Moses? John Denver in *Oh, God* (© Warner Brothers).

The crew prepares to film the Bridge of Death crossing in *Monty Python and the Holy Grail*. According to the clapper board they are ten days ahead of schedule (Courtesy Python (Monty) Films).

The face of our Lord, circa 1977. George Burns in *Oh, God* (© Warner Brothers).

bosses, reporters, doctors, and professional religious men who question Jerry's sanity. Finally, the right reverand Willie Williams (Paul Sorvino), the very picture of a white-garbed, money-grubbing media preacher, takes Landers to court on a defamation-of-character charge when the Lord gives Jerry a personal message to deliver to the phony evangelist.

This causes God to appear as a character witness, and he proves his existence to judge Bernard Hughes with a card trick. This is God's style, according to the Gelbart script, based on the Corman book, directed by Reiner. Sometimes he appears as a park custodian picking up litter, sometimes as a black woman buying cornflakes, and sometimes as a cabby who can make it rain inside of a car. Thankfully, the Lord goes on to make all the cards and then himself disappear, proving to at least the court that miracles can happen.

This funny, poignant, and meaningful movie delighted the public, who escaped the dreadful mayhem of other occult pictures to make this one of the biggest-grossing films of the year. Reiner's low-key control only served to juxtapose this comedy with the more strident contributions of Marty Feldman's *The Last Remake of Beau Geste* (1977), Gene Wilder's *The World's Greatest Lover* (1977), and Mel Brooks's *High Anxiety* (1978), all three not coming close to *Oh, God*'s financial return.

Although the future of the supernatural film seems assured, all such films planned in the coming months don't reflect the stylish delight of the Burns/Denver team. *The Dark* (1978), starring William Devane, Cathy Lee Crosby, and Keenan Wynn, is shaping up to be another horror tale written by Stanford Whitmore and directed by John Bud Cardos.

Harlan Ellison has finished the screenplay of William Friedkin's *The Whimper of Whipped Dogs*, based on Ellison's story about a god of city violence. *Cry of Cthulu*, a screenplay based on the tales of H. P. Lovecraft, is lying on its producer's shelf, waiting for financial backing.

Amidst all this mire is a light, however. Warren Beatty has chosen to follow up his successful *Shampoo* (1975) with *Heaven Can Wait* (1978), a delightful comedy based on a script by Elaine May about a pro football player who, through a celestial mistake, is taken to Heaven before his time, but is permitted to return to life for a while in the body of an elderly millionaire who has also recently died. The proven acting talents of Beatty, Julie Christie, James Mason, Charles Grodin, Dyan Cannon, Buck Henry, Vincent Gardenia, and Jack Warden are employed. In addition to starring in the film, Beatty both produced and co-directed it (with Henry).

But until more movies like Beatty's are made, one will just have to be satisfied with the likes of *The Tempter* (1978), an Italian import made by the *Chosen* team; *The Evil* (1978), a New World picture which has garnered reviews comparing it to *The Haunting* and *Legend of Hell House*; and *The Legacy* (1979), an English import starring Katherine Ross. It's a cinch that the little devils in the film world will make sure that all Hell breaks loose for many years to come.

2   BEASTS

WHETHER THEIR LAIR be as vast as the ocean, as barbaric as a South Sea isle, as dank as a swamp, as crowded as a hive, as terrifying as a crypt, or as tiny as an ant hole, the beasts of imagination know no rules but their own. In reality, all earth's creatures follow the laws of nature, but in the realm of fantasy they know no bounds. How else can they attack us with malice aforethought, or live on after death, or transform on nights of the full moon? How else can modern man find mythical lands, investigate legends, or have our own science manifest and turn against us? Every year in the motion picture houses, eternal laws change and the impossible takes shape before us. From as small as a worm to as big as a dinosaur, the beasts are alive and well and eating us up.

The summer of 1975 saw one of God's nastiest creatures achieve stardom through the dedicated patronage of millions. The shark, a fish that seemingly exists only to swim, sleep, and eat, started to base its mealtimes around the beach habits of Long Island residents, tearing them apart whenever they appeared in the water, sometimes swallowing them whole in its massive *Jaws*.

This problem-plagued, much-patronized thriller went on to make more than $200 million and a bankable commodity of its director, Steven Spielberg. Starting as an exceptionally gory novel by Peter Benchley, the rights were bought by Universal and assigned as the second project of the young director who had one other feature to his credit—*The Sugarland Express* (1974)—and some television experience. The studio saw it as a small action picture with a budget to match, since they were saving their real special effects money for the likes of *Airport '75*

and *Earthquake*. Thus, when Spielberg brought semi-retired Bob Matty into the workshop to direct the building of the shark, only a half-hearted effort went into its construction.

This was just the beginning of the production's problems. The Benchley script did not have the cinematic flair Spielberg was looking for—a problem that plagued Benchley's *The Deep* (1977) as well. So with friend Carl Gottlieb safely tucked away in the back room of the inn where they were staying, the two would adapt, edit, rewrite, and alter each day's material.

Then, with a cast composed of a reluctant Richard Dreyfuss ("Who wants to do a fish story?", he was quoted as saying), second-choice Robert Shaw (Sterling Hayden had been the first considered for the role of Quint, but tax problems eliminated him), and Roy Scheider, the crew hit the sea. The sea hit back. It was discovered that Bruce the shark, the name coined for the huge monster machine, would not work properly at best, and would not work at all at worst. Further problems developed when the rear of the boat they were filming ripped off. An exact duplicate had to be built.

Finally, after more than twice the original budget, and most of Universal executives' patience, had been spent, the principal photography was finished. Shaw went back to Ireland, Scheider to New York, and Dreyfuss to the press, bad-mouthing the unfinished film to anyone who asked him about it. Meanwhile, Spielberg pieced together his work with crack editor Verna Fields, using his previous genre experiences to play with the audience's expectations, introducing steady shocks to the narrative *when* they were expected, but not *where*.

The poster ad art for *Jaws* (© Universal).

Later, he was to jettison all pretenses to subtlety when a sneak preview audience failed to react for more familiar horror fare, such as the dead fisherman's head floating in the bottom of the boat. Originally that particular scene was filmed in the daylight but the response was so apathetic that Spielberg admitted he "pulled the oldest trick in the book!" in his words.

Many monster enthusiasts also pointed out similarities between the shark's underwater attacks and those in the *Creature from the Black Lagoon* (1954), but most criticism paled in the light of the overwhelming financial success and the abundance of nuance Spielberg delivered under cover of the fishy plot. To be blunt, *Jaws* has less than three minutes of on-screen violence, while the rest of the movie is framed around character development and an alternately bracing, then frightening, sea adventure.

Several scenes remain vital in the viewer's memory. Sheriff Brody's (Scheider) spectacular reaction to the audience's first clear view of the shark, when it rises from behind him on Quint's boat. He springs up, then slowly moves back, saying, "We've got to get a bigger boat." Matt Hooper's (Dreyfuss) fascinating autopsies: viewing the first-victim's remains then snarling at the medical examiner, "This wasn't any boat accident," and pulling a whole fish, tin cans, and lisense plates from the stomach of a captured shark. Finally, Quint's stunning retelling of the WWII Wayne tragedy, where more than 1,000 sailors died by shark after the ship that delivered the Hiroshima-bound atom bomb sank.

The film's first half mounts from a chilling murder of a young girl—shot from above the waterline so the audience can't see what is hurling her about, to a suspenseful wharf-side attempt by two men to capture the

Cindy Grover is one of the lucky ones. Just before the shark in *Jaws 2* passed her by, it made two of her friends lunch and dinner (© Universal).

Bruce the mechanical shark makes breakfast out of a boat, the boat's driver, and the water skier who use to be attached to the boat. From *Jaws 2* **(© Universal).**

beast only to be nearly killed themselves, to a mortifying mistake in judgment by Brody, who must pay back his conscience by overcoming his fear of the ocean and killing this unnaturally murderous shark.

Bruce gained an equally murderous sister during the summer of 1977 when *Jaws II* went into production. To prove it had lost none of its cursed bite, technical problems instantly arose. Originally, the project was assigned to the husband-and-wife team of director John Hancock and writer Dorothy Tristan. In a *New York Times* interview, the pair seemed to look at the coming work with disdain but promised to scare everyone off the beaches for a second year. The initial plot line called for yet another massive maneater to prowl the beaches of Amity, Long Island, at one point tearing a shapely water skier up before her horrified boy friend's eyes and at another leaping out of the water to knock down a helicopter.

Soon after, however, Hancock and Tristan left the project because of reported "creative difficulties," and

Jeannot Szwarc, an experienced television director, whose principal feature credit was William Castle's *Bug* (1975), was brought in. Following him came Howard Sackler who adapted the initial screenplay, then Carl Gottlieb, the credited co-writer of the original, who further altered the soggy saga.

Time had not cured the mechanical ills either. Reports filtered out that the shark was just as reluctant to work as before, pushing the project over cost and schedule, trying the patience of returning stars Scheider, Lorraine Grey as his wife, and Murray Hamilton as Amity's weak-willed mayor. The filming continued on Martha's Vineyard and Navarre Beach, Florida, preparing for a summer-1978 release. The word, just before premiere, is that the salaries made all the trouble worthwhile, for the actors and the returning producers, Richard Zanuck and David Brown, thought it was spectacular. Unfortunately, most reviewers disagreed.

Part of the *Jaws* phenomenon was the appearance of an "X"-rated jaunt, called *Gums* (1977). Terri Hall starred as a mermaid who was interested in attacking attractive swimmers but certainly not for consumption. Robert J. Kaplan peopled this pornographic satire with more than its share of crazy characters, including a Nazi sea captain unlikely to win any Quint look-alike contest. But what could have been an honestly funny send-up became an unattractive effort thanks to hard-core action and the lack of a cohesive style.

But for a true professional nightmare, nothing can come close to the disastrous return of the world's greatest fantasy beast. In December 1975, a full-page ad appeared in the *New York Times*. It read, "There still is only one *King Kong*." And beneath a jarring picture of a giant ape straddling the twin towers of the World Trade Center, holding a scantily clad blonde in one hand and a jet plane in the other it continued, "One year from today Paramount Pictures and Dino De Laurentiis will bring to you the most-exciting original motion-picture event of all time."

So began one of the most infamous and ugly episodes of deception, irresponsibility, disrespect, and outright lying the film world has ever experienced. What made the crime even worse was that the cinematic community chose to either play along, ignore, or, finally, *award* this poor example of special-effects filmmaking.

The initial reaction to the newspaper ad was overwhelming. More than 60,000 letters poured in, requesting color copies and information. De Laurentiis's idea, which he said he got from seeing a poster of the original *Kong* on his daughter's wall, was verified by public response. Instead of putting his money down to create an exciting update, however, the Italian entrepreneur decided he would spend the big bucks to push his film around the world and into 900 United States theaters in the space of one year.

In order to achieve this miracle, production had to be rushed and padded with high-gloss, low-cost shortcuts. It also meant making sure that Universal's proposed *The Legend of King Kong* would never see completion. Dino succeeded in blocking the Bo Goldman-written, Joseph Sargent-directed production with a court case that forbade Universal from starting work less than nine months after the Paramount premiere. As time went on, the smaller film, conceived as a nostalgia piece, withered beneath Paramount's *Kong* publicity blitz.

Then the deception began in earnest. The "little white lies" become evident upon reading the production notes, pretentiously retitled The Handbook of Production Information. "The enormous complexity of his undertaking," read the production notes, "became evident to De Laurentiis when, last summer, he began assembling craftsmen." Part of this enormous complexity was handled by the producer's son, Fedrico, who, in his position of executive producer, put an ad in the Hollywood trade papers saying that only Negro body builders need audition for the role of Kong. According to an inside source, they figured it was the closest they could come to a giant ape.

And one of the craftsmen happened to be a young makeup artist named Rick Baker. He had been designing and building ape suits for years and held a special place in his heart for the original 1933 version of *Kong*. He discovered, however, that his new bosses not only disliked the original, but made sure it was taken out of circulation as not to create competition for their pale plagiarism.

It turned out they had reason to worry. Even with all of Hollywood's technological advancements, the new film did not compare favorably with the wonder and beauty of the initial work. Some of the blame has to fall on Lorenzo Semple Jr.'s script, a patchwork quilt of campy comments, borrowed situations, and weak characterizations. When the fifty-foot ape first kidnaps the girl, he had her respond with lines like, "Put me down, you male chauvinist ape, you!" and "What's your sign?" But the major fault lies with the producers' mercenary concept and their attempts to shortchange the audience while telling them how great they were.

"Movies being a form of magic," the production notes continue, "a mystery still shrouds Kong. When the audience . . . sees him storming through a South Pacific Island jungle they'll have to decide if Kong is real or a cleverly crafted illusion." It's not cleverly crafted. Rick Baker tells his horror story of attempting to interject some kind of quality into the creation of the movie's leading character.

"They said, 'How much is it going to cost?' and I said, 'this much,' and they said, 'If it costs half that you can do it.' We had less than one month to do it in, so I needed assistance. 'Fine,' they said, 'You can have *one* assistant.' "

One month and one assistant to do what? According to the production notes, "The Kong that looms on the screen will be an ingenious forty-foot mechanical monster weighing six-and-one-half tons, able to cover fifteen feet in a single stride, electronically controlled by a complex hydraulic valve system. . . ."

De Laurentiis himself echoed this information to millions of people when on NBC's "Tomorrow" with Tom Snyder, professing that this giant artificial Kong was used in 98% of the film. A wonderful advancement in technical achievement? No, an out-and-out lie. A

510

Rick Baker *is King Kong* (© Paramount).

creature of that general description was used in less than three minutes of the final two-hour film. And even then it was a struggle to get the Carlo Rimbaldi–designed monstrosity to work. The funniest example of the filmmaking ineptitude concerned this model, which was designed in the United States, using inches and feet, but built in Italy, which uses the metric system. The report goes that, when the parts were shipped to the States, none of them fit and Kong had *two right hands*.

In reality, the majority of Kong was built and played by Rick Baker and his stand-in, William Shepard. After having been, in effect, demoted to Rimbaldi's flunky, Rick was given less than two weeks to create the final suit and a day to sculpt the head.

"The major fault of the film is that Dino imposed a deadline on it," Baker admitted. Actual production wasn't much better. "It was murder," he further confessed. "I wanted to walk like a gorilla, occasionally rising when it was dramatically correct, but they didn't let me."

Beyond the ape suit, the other technical aspects were given the same "lavish" attention: ". . . most importantly the special effects," the press releases declared, "employing every new technique along with the best of the old ones, to make every frame of *King Kong* realistic and entertaining and assuring it to be a classic textbook on cinematography."

The final film was neither classic nor realistic. Entertainment is in the mind of each individual but serves as no excuse for the shoddy model and matte work that appeared throughout. Outlines where the matte was placed onto a full scale background could be seen regularly. A giant arm matted to the ape-suit's body was a darker shade than the rest of the body. Models of New York apartments that the fake ape could romp through were obviously devoid of people or furnishings.

The lack of detail extended even to simple things. When Kong leaps from the World Trade Tower to another building—he *never* straddles them—the girl is in his

This second full-size model of *King Kong* works better than the first, since all it has to do is lie there (© Paramount).

hand. When he lands, the girl is on his back. Most obviously, the forty-foot robot and the six-foot suit do not even remotely resemble each other!

DeLaurentiis must have known he had an inferior work on his hands, only given a thin sheen of quality through the efforts of director John Guillerman, but he continued the cheap deception, using ignoble techniques to keep the patrons ignorant. Besides the big lie mentioned previously, he commissioned artwork that depicted Kong doing things that were never filmed to be sent along with the usual eight-by-tens. He continued to publicize the feature as the most original movie of all time—while his only deviations from the 1933 version are detrimental—and, somehow, got a cover story in *Time* magazine praising the work *that had yet to be completed*.

The final travesty was soon to be consummated. When April 1977 rolled around and *Kong* had gone through two publicity campaign changes—to a ludicrous "love-story" concept and "Kong-as-superhero" idea—someone decided that flagging box-office returns would be boosted by an Oscar.

Although *Kong* did not appear even in the special-effects nominations, in a maneuver generally described as the "25-million-dollar understanding," *King Kong* was awarded an Academy Award for Special Effects by the Academy of Motion Picture Arts and Sciences Board of Governors, who overruled the special effects people in order to do it! Then, to compound the offense, Rick Baker was ignored and did not receive a statue. Indeed, he's listed on the credits thus: "The Producer wishes to acknowledge that *Kong* has been designed and engineered by Carlo Rimbaldi, constructed by Carlo Rimbaldi and Glen Robinson with special contributions by Rick Baker."

The story goes that when the special-effects nominating committee failed to cite Kong and were circumvented by the board, they retaliated by also giving a special award to *Logan's Run* (1976), another poor attempt at quality special effects. Jim Danforth, the noted model animator, resigned from the academy because of this, angrily refusing to be part of any group that would allow this to happen.

Thankfully, the film's returns were lower than expected, so a sequel, *King Kong in Africa*, was scrapped. DeLaurentiis's productions were not however, nor was his familiar film fare. Hot on *Kong's* heels was another giant creature called *The White Buffalo* (1977), who haunted the dreams of Buffalo Bill Cody (Charles Bronson) and Crazy Horse (Will Sampson) in between stampeding over Indian tribes. Here too, Carlo Rimbaldi was called upon to manufacture a machine—this time a

Charles Bronson (center) and Dino De Laurentiis (right) pose with the Carlo Rimbaldi built star of *The White Buffalo* (© United Artists).

4000-pound, fifteen-foot-long, nine-foot-tall albino bison that could do everything but shine your kitchen sink.

The press releases here boasted about its sixty-four separate muscles, twenty-four automatic animation points, and eighteen manually operated animation points. Its screen performance was less than inspired, however. Even with a talented cast and experienced direction of J. Lee Thompson, the movie was quickly shelved as an embarrassment after the derisive reactions of several test audiences.

DeLaurentiis got his monetary revenge later the same year with an obviously derivative piece of schlock called *Orca* (1977), in which a killer whale takes on fisherman Richard Harris after he kills the mammal's mate. Although violent and ludicrous, the film made a bundle from the drive-in and Saturday-matinee crowd, helped along by Dino's regular publicity push.

Far more enjoyable than all the previous efforts put together, simply because it is purposely funny, was the imported English satire *Queen Kong* (1976). It is, as one might have guessed, the story of a giant, red-headed female ape who ruled a prehistoric jungle paradise. But

Orca, the killer whale, brings the house down (© Paramount).

that is just the beginning of the variations in this Virgilio DeBlasi-produced, Frank Agrama-directed movie.

Carl Denham becomes Luce Habit, the world's foremost feminist filmmaker. Jack Driscoll becomes Ima Goodbody, a tough ex-agent turned assistant director. And the lovely Ann Darrow becomes the equally lovely Ray Fay, a small-time male British hippie. The tramp steamer *Venture*, which brought the 1933 group to Skull Island, becomes the tramp steamer *Liberated Lady*, on which are boarded crates marked, "guns," "gas," "monster tranquilizers," "canned tomatoes," and "more stuff," preparing for the trip into deepest, darkest Africa.

Upon arrival, the natives are discovered to be lithesome blondes, brunettes, redheads, and raven-haired Orientals. Their high priestess is a bikini-clad amazon who eyes the long-haired Ray for the biweekly sacrifice to their tribal god . . . Kong. It was only a matter of time before the weak-willed London hippie was stuck in a giant cake and placed atop a giant picnic table, with a

huge red-checked tablecloth upon it, to serve as a tasty tidbit for, what turns out to be, a sixty-four-foot high, brown-eyed female gorilla.

It is love at first sight, much to Luce's chagrin—she had Ray pegged for international stardom. Only after Kong bops a pterodactyl and kicks a trynasauropticus between the legs, does the *Liberated Lady's* all-female crew subdue the big apess with gas. At which point, aping one of Denham's impassioned speeches in the original, Luce intones, "We'll take this baby back to London where she'll be the greatest attraction the world has ever seen! She was a queen on this island, but never forget—half the blokes you meet in London are also queens."

Soon, all England is talking about the great new "Queen Kong" show at the Palladium, but moments before the opening night curtain is to rise, Mr. Woolf, the theater's owner, decides that without the proper attire, Kong cannot appear onstage. So when the giantess is

60

revealed, she is wearing a tremendous two-piece bathing suit. The reporters go crazy, crowding the establishment with flashing cameras and derisive laughter. With a triumphant flex, Queen Kong rips out of her bikini and goes on a rampage from the Thames River to Trafalgar Square. She finally finds her lost human love and climbs the new London Post Office Tower, where Ray delivers an emotional speech to the news media, equating Kong's plight with woman's suffrage. English females revolt and unite, allowing the gorilla and her consort to return happily to their country.

As Queen makes her exit, the Koreans make their entrance with ninety-six minutes of 3-D poetic justice. Paul Leder managed to slap together, advertise, and release a terrible film, called *Ape* (1976), two months before DeLaurentiis's premiere of *Kong*, hoping to steal a little of the Italian's box-office thunder. The obviously inexpensive work employs a man in a tacky gorilla suit fighting the likes of rubber sharks and tin ocean liners before attacking miniature cardboard cities. Given the limitations of 3-D projection, the movie's faults were amplified to make the entire experience worse tha laughable.

Another foreign recreation of a classic beast was *Yeti* (1976), which was originally slated to be another DeLaurentiis project but rushed out by Nicolo Pomilia for 100 Italian movie theaters. Stefano Releasing also thought that it could nip at *Kong's* heels, so they did try a half-hearted attempt at world distribution, only to be circumvented by the inadequacy of the Gianfranco Panolini-directed opus about the thawing of the abominable snowman. Mimmo Crau played the monster, who was hosed from an iceberg after milleniums just in time to save the son and niece of a Howard Hughes type from a billionaire's mercenary plans. The concentration is more on family entertainment than thrilling adventure, however. According to a review in *Variety*, the pacing was slow, the script was ludicrous, the production values showed signs of haste, and, in conclusion, "by comparison, *Kong* was unfairly under-rated."

The Himalayan giant has a cousin in the United States who shares the same reputation. Whenever a producer wants to create a pretty movie with a lot of location work and very little suspense, horror, or action, they call on the legendary Bigfoot. Actually, any big, hairy, humanoid monster in a swamp will do. All the film really needs is a crotchety old mountain man, a small boy— Dutch-bobbed blond hair and pet dog optional—and lots of beautiful countryside. Then a suitably murky title such as *Creature from Black Lake* or *The Legend of Boggy Creek* must be thought up, a publicity budget rivaling the

The Legend of Boggy Creek.

production cost must be raised, and then any old filmmaker can have a money-making property on his hands.

Witness the appearances of *Creature from Black Lake* (1975), *The Legend of Boggy Creek* (1973), *Return to Boggy Creek* (1976), and *Sasquatch* (1977), which came in fairly rapid succession. Each were mildly interesting for a variety of reasons. *Creature* was probably the best of the lot because of the professional performances of Jack Elam and Dub Taylor in the film, written and produced by Jim McCullogh. The *Boggy Creek* duo had atmosphere and a certain murky suspense, while *Sasquatch* took a cue from one of the most unique and powerful production companies in the world—Sunn International.

This company's highly religious director uses a computer to pick concepts, then blasts them into theaters using the "four-walling" publicity technique. That is, inundating patrons with a phenomenal amount of advertising for a short period, meanwhile reserving hundreds of theaters for two weeks only. This concept has worked admirably for the company, through wilderness films, historical dramas, and mysteries.

The organization has done so well that dozens of lookalikes have spawned in their wake, the latest of which is *Sasquatch*. This North American Film Enterprises release of a John Fabien production incorpo-

This eight-foot *Grizzly* is indeed smarter than the average bear—he's just knocked down Andrew Prine's helicopter (© Film Ventures International).

rates Sunn's wildly profitable advertising technique with a mutual lack of cinematic substance. After some establishing shots of a little Indian boy and a frontier trapper, accidentally wandering into Bigfoot's territory, the central story of a bunch of scientists tracking down the modern monster begins and boredom takes over.

The gorgeous scenery and beautiful photography hardly make up for the dull story, awful acting, and unimpressive creature. The team of exploring researchers never catch up with the crafty Sasquatch, making the entire affair hardly worth the trouble for the audience. A far more exciting tale could be found in *Grizzly* (1976), although the leading characters' fates were far more horrible. This wilderness adventure took its cue from *Jaws*, being an almost frame-by-frame copy of it, using a bear instead of a shark, while also losing the humor, the intelligence, and suspense of the fish story.

At that time, it seemed as if William Girdler, who produced and directed the bear story, was going to make his career from ripping off major productions, since this

was his follow-up to *Abby* (1974), which was essentially a black *Exorcist*. As usual, he managed to sign decent acting and production personnel, getting Christopher George, Andrew Prine, and Richard Jaekel to face the paws.

George was back, trodding the same ground less than four months after *Grizzly's* premiere, only this time he brought his real-life wife, Lynda Day, with him. *The Day of the Animals* (1976) had the distinction of being a rip-off's rip-off, trying to capitalize on the good business the bear story had done while also touching on a "nature's revenge" theme which dates back to the popularity of the giant-insect movies of the fifties. Here, however, frontier animals attack humans in return for their threatened extinction. Along the way, everything from a cougar to an eagle (*very* symbolic) to a rattlesnake get into the act, allowing the makeup boys to really ladle up the fake blood.

The return to the idea of tiny creatures growing huge and threatening mankind began a consistent comeback the year before with *The Giant Spider Invasion* (1975), another show under the auspices of Group One Distribution Company. This was a far more enjoyable outing since Bill Rebane, who directed and coproduced it with Richard Huff, did not take the whole affair too seriously. Indeed, they couldn't with a concept like a giant spider riding a black hole to earth. The scientific inconsistencies are too numerous to accept, but with the hard jaw and stiff upper lip of Steve Brodie as the lead, Leslie Parrish as the feminine interest and Alan Hale as the comedy relief, *The Giant Spider Invasion* is a painless entertainment, without enough blood and guts to even get a restrictive rating.

Its surprising success brought a glut of animal-centered films during the next two years. American International brought in a duo of horror vehicles under the creative control of Bert I. Gordon. First came H. G. Wells's *Food of the Gods* (1976), though the Gordon-updated screenplay, based on one chapter of the 1906 novel, bore little resemblance to the classic work. It was fitting that Gordon ushered in the reappearance of the giant-creature theme, since he practically kept it alive during the fifties with *The Cyclops* (1957), *The Amazing Colossal Man* (1957), and *Attack of the Puppet People* (1958).

This prolific man kept his hand in with *The Magic Sword* (1962) and *Picture Mommy Dead* (1966), but his seventies adaptation of the nineteenth-century science-fiction book was his first return to "respectable" filmmaking. He directed actors of consequence, like Marjoe Gortner, Pamela Franklin, Ralph Meeker, and Ida Lupino, through a story of none. Giant flies, caterpillars, and mice attack a quiet farming community after a new growth substance, "boom-food," is introduced into the planting process.

The flies were models, the other bugs were a combination of machinery and mattes, while the rats were both regular-size mice on miniature sets and giant sculptures capable of slight animation. The actors also appeared to be sculptures capable of slight animation, thanks to the thankless script and reduction of Wells's work into just another hack disaster film.

The concept still held its fascination for movie-goers, however, and six months later Gordon's second Wells massacre took place. Production began on *The Empire of the Ants* (1976), starring Joan Collins, Robert Lansing, John David Carson, and Pamela Shoop, with Gordon again writing and producing. This time giant radiation-mutated ants attack the developers and visitors of a new everglade resort, piling shock after shock in the misty rain forests, the cloying swamps, and glass-enclosed

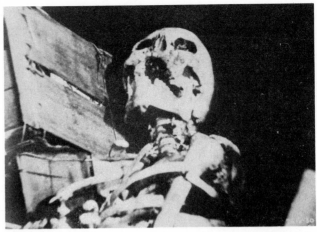

This is what happens when you sleep in a box filled with flesh-eating worms—one of the victims during *Squirm* (© **A.I.P.**).

hotel. The ants themselves were huge, milky-eyed, hairy models whenever they attacked the various characters, but were real insects when showed separately, using a process coined "Matex III" by Gordon. Although it was an interesting matte process, the producer was quoted as describing it as "creating a depth dimension imparting a realism to special effects never before attained." If his dialogue was as awkward as that, it is little wonder that the reviews of *Ants* were unanimously negative.

Far more interesting and better received were two independent productions of 1977. First was Jeff Lieberman's *Squirm*, a new high in nastiness as the picture portrays the attack of *millions* of bloodworms—the kind that move only at night—after a storm topples an electrical tower, pouring thousands of volts into the dirt and mud. The little town of Fly Creek, Georgia, was quiet until people started opening their closets to have a wall of worms fall on them.

In the course of the movie, people are buried by the wiggling strings, and at one point, the worms burrow in between the layers of a man's skin. What set this stomach-churning epic apart from the rest was its practical but inexpensive production values; makeup, designed by Rick Baker; and acting talent culled from the New York soap operas. The subject matter was too gruesome to garner a cult following, but it did well enough to guarantee Lieberman backing for his next movie about a mind-expanding, murder-inducing drug called *Blue Sunshine* (1977).

Secondly was *Kingdom of the Spiders*, released during the fall. Its success was based on a decent budget, dependable actors, and adherence to an ecology theme. That is, humankind will have to pay a terrible price for its

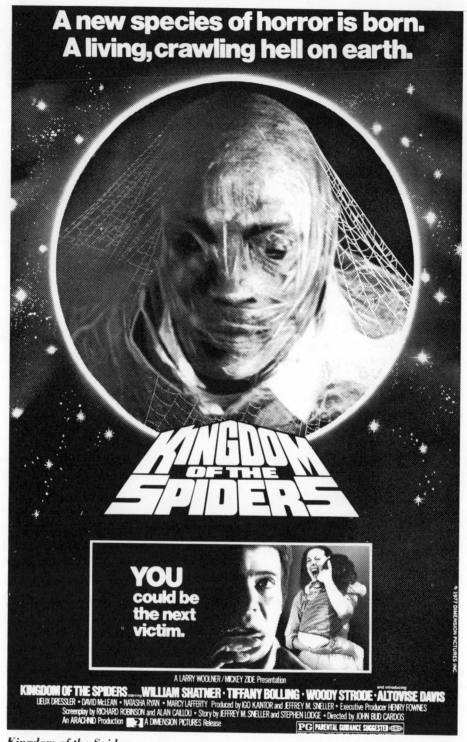

Kingdom of the Spiders.

continued ignorance of nature. The aptly named Arachnid Productions hired Jim Brockett, a veteran animal trainer, to find and "audition" nearly 5,000 live, unaltered tarantulas. For the film's purposes, the six-legged beasts were strengthened, since in reality their venom is weaker than a bee's; and made social, for the plot's sake, since large groups of spiders become cannibalistic.

Producers Henry Fowne, Igo Kantor, and Geoffry M. Sneller, along with director Bud Cardos, worked up a simple plot concerning the mass migration of desert spiders to Rio Verde, Arizona when their food supply is destroyed by pesticides. Suddenly, unnaturally angry insects start killing livestock, then people, for food. William Shatner starred as Rack Hansen, a U. S. Department of Agriculture-veterinarian who teams up with a university entomologist, Diane Ashley (Tiffany Bolling), to combat the deadly invasion.

Spider mounds are found to contain millions of the creatures, but their effective destruction is hampered by the political concerns of the mayor and sheriff, who don't want to ruin the upcoming county fair. They are simply unable to comprehend the threat until the spiders march into town. Then, wholesale horror ensues as bodies are buried under wriggling, fanged insects, then enmeshed in webby cocoons for later ingestion.

The heroes barricade themselves in the town lodge only to have the spiders move in through a cellar window. The finale finds the area destroyed, not, by the spiders, but as the filmmakers stress, by man's inconsiderate abuse of his environment. Shatner, fresh from television success, wasn't at all pretentious about his entrance into the film world. "I can't complain," he said. "I knew what I was getting into. I wanted to do this film because it's a darn good script. Movies have put fear in audiences with sharks, bees, dogs—even worms—but this one could top them all. Those fuzzy, eight-eyed, eight-legged critters are going to send audiences screaming from their seats."

Thanks to everyone's professional work, the crowds didn't run from the theaters, and *Kingdom of the Spiders* made a handsome profit and a commendable addition to the ranks of Dimension Pictures, the distribution com-

In but a few seconds William Shatner will become part of
The Kingdom of the Spiders (© **Dimension Pictures**).

pany that was also responsible for *Ruby* and other films mentioned in this volume. Larry Woolner, the head of the organization, is proud to deal with the less-influential producers.

"The films are better," he said in an article. "Things have never been better." And with the return of the big-budgeted productions, combined with the financial paranoia of the major studios, he also raises an important point concerning the future of theaters. "Too many exhibitors are willing to make deals with the majors—coming up with sizable guarantees and long initial runs. These exhibitors are going to see that the independent is their only salvation."

Not, however, if Irwin Allen can help it. For the past twenty years this active producer/writer/director has been making an art form of the "B" movie. Throughout his history of film production, including: *The Sea Around Us* (1950), *The Animal World* (1956), *The Story of Mankind* (1957), *The Big Circus* (1959), *The Lost World*

(1961), *Voyage to the Bottom of the Sea* (1962), *Five Weeks in A Balloon* (1963), *The Poseidon Adventure* (1972), and *The Towering Inferno* (1974), he has been refining his concept as to what makes a major work of entertainment.

By 1978, he had discovered that by combining a large, well-known cast with a natural disaster of inordinate proportions, you can achieve box-office paydirt. In his new movie, *The Swarm* (1978), the cast includes Michael Caine as a government entomologist, Katherine Ross as a doctor at an attacked military base, Richard Widmark and Bradford Dillman as military men, Henry Fonda, Richard Chamberlain, and Alexandro Rey as, respectively, immunologist, entomologist, and general practitioner. Also in the cast are Lee Grant as a television reporter, Slim Pickens as a water superintendent, Patty Duke Astin as a waitress, Olivia DeHaviland as a school principal, Ben Johnson and Fred MacMurray as her paramours, and all are supporting players to the twenty

Millions of killer bees give these stunt men a run down feeling during *The Swarm* (© Warner Brothers).

million bees kept in the 400 studio hives acquired from scouts in Oregon, Washington, Arizona, Nevada, New Mexico, Texas, and California.

The disaster pictured is the predicted arrival of South American killer bees into this country by the late 1980s. Based on the reality of these mutated cousins of the honey bee, the story begins twenty years ago exactly as it happened. Queen bees were brought from Africa to Brazil for an experiment to cross-breed greater productivity into smaller, weaker insects. Somehow, the test bees escaped, mated with the South American strain, and produced bees that attack and kill. These documented murderers were last reported moving in America's direction at a rate of 200 miles per year.

The Swarm begins when they arrive. The Sterling Silliphant script, based on a novel by Arthur Herzog, was completed and given a twelve-million-dollar budget, circumstances similar to the productions of *Poseidon* and *Inferno*, but with one major difference. Previously, Allen has given the directorial reins to established big-budget directors like Ronald Neame and John Guillerman. But this time he has promoted himself from directing just the action scenes, as in *Inferno*, to helming the entire movie, which includes a full-scale paralyzation of Houston. The big question still remains as to how the successful showman controlled the thousands of stinging insects during shooting. Allowing the stars and their stuntmen to open themselves to unpredictable danger was unthinkable, and simply smearing honey over everthing was ridiculous, so Allen collected a crew of insect handlers and bee experts.

His tests included visual and aural stimulation experiments using light and sound techniques after extensive studies of their actions, reactions, and abnormalities were taken. Master of publicity, Allen happily declared his special-effects achievements after the film's premiere July 14, 1978. Unfortunately the critic's declared the movie's artistic emptiness at the same time.

A killer bee of another kind appeared and was dispatched as early as the time of Scheherazade and tales of *A Thousand and One Nights*. It appeared thanks to a hasty experiment by the wizard Melanthius and was killed thanks to the well-thrown blade of a legendary sea adventurer. Although not exactly recorded history, this episode was given life and vitality on the motion picture screen by the model animation dean, Ray Harryhausen.

Sinbad and the Eye of the Tiger (1977) began its rocky production schedule during June of 1975 in Almeria, Spain. Even then, rumors were in circulation concerning the content of this third of Sinbad pictures, following the successes of *The Seventh Voyage of Sinbad* (1958) and

The Golden Voyage of Sinbad (1973). There had been two previous Sinbads, Kerwin Matthews and John Phillip Law; two planned marriages, to a princess (Kathryn Grant) and a freed slave (Caroline Munro); two previous directors, Nathan Juran and Gordon Hessler; and two previous screenwriters, Kevin Kolb and Brian Clemens; but the producer (Charles Schneer) and Harryhausen figured in all three. Therefore, the formula remained the same, but this time augmented by director Sam Wanamaker and screenwriter Beverly Cross.

Essentially, Sinbad is set to marry another princess, but a terrible curse, which the sailor must rectify, befalls her family. In his quest for a solution, he and his crew meet up with a mighty sorcerer and a variety of impressive beasts. In a last-moment confrontation of monster and man, Sinbad succeeds in his quest, and the way is open for him to "live happily ever after."

Although many of Harryhausen's fans were anxiously awaiting this third flight of Arabian-based fancy, many others derided the production, originally titled *Sinbad at the World's End*, by deeming it *Sinbad at Wit's End*, because of the creators' lack of new inspiration. But, true to his talent, Harryhausen created a wealth of finely delineated denizens of the fantasy world for the work

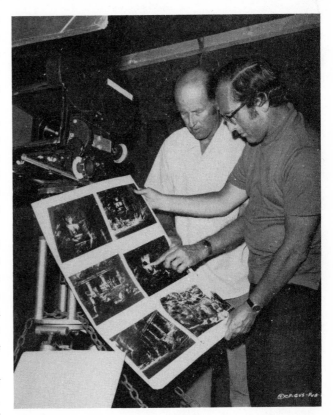

Ray Harryhausen makes a point to producer Charles Schneer on the set of *The Golden Voyage of Sinbad* (© Columbia).

The zomboid ghouls attack through the wonder of Dynarama at the beginning of *Sinbad and the Eye of the Tiger* (© Columbia).

which finally saw premiere almost two years after the cameras started rolling.

Loosely based on the "Fifth Voyage of Sinbad" from "The Story of Sinbad the Sailor" in *A Thousand and One Nights*, the new Sinbad (Patrick Wayne) arrives at Charok to ask permission to wed Princess Farah (Jane Seymour), only to discover that her evil stepmother, Zenobia (Margaret Whiting), has turned her stepbrother, Kassim (Damien Thomas), into a baboon so that Rafi (Kurt Christian), Zenobia's son, will become the new caliph.

In order to eliminate the sailor and his crew, the sorceress makes three weapon-wielding demons appear from a fire. This is a masterful scene, dazzlingly embodying the style and expertise that have made Harryhausen a giant in the cinema world.

The interaction of the live actors and animated models is so well choreographed, so realistic, and so exciting, that no single episode in the rest of the movie can overshadow it.

Surviving the fight, Sinbad takes Farah and sails to the realm of Melanthius, Hermit of Casgar (Patrick Troughton), who alone possesses the knowledge to remove Kassim's curse. He and his daughter, Dione (Taryn Power), guide the group beyond the North Wind, to the World's End, in order to incorporate the ageless wisdom of the Arimaspi into the solution. Meanwhile Zenobia has brought a minotaur—half man, half bull—to life to power her pursuing ship.

Her trip is easier since Sinbad must face the aforementioned bee, a giant walrus, and make friends with a *troglodyte*, a huge prehistoric man with a horn in his forehead, before arriving at Arimaspi's pyramid shrine. But Zenobia's tampering has let hot air in, altering the interior temperature to the point that huge stalactites start shooting to the ground and the entire place begins to fall apart.

Rafi attacks the baboon, who has grown increasingly wild during the voyage so he reacts violently, his strength throwing both of them down a flight of stairs. The evil stepbrother dies on his own knife, and, in desperate grief, Zenobia transfers herself into the ice-encased form of the shrine's guaradian—a saber-toothed tiger. The eye of the tiger opens. Crashing out of her frozen prison, she attacks the Trog, who puts up a valiant battle, but dies beneath her long teeth and sharp claws.

It is up to Sinbad to kill the beast with a well-aimed spear. Zenobia's spirit dies along with the tiger. The curse

is lifted, Kassim finds love in Dione's eyes, and everyone returns to rejoice as the new caliph is crowned.

Sadly, the story suffered in translation to the screen. As exciting and mystical as the plot line sounds, the film's pacing dragged, a variety of effects were curiously ineffective, and the actors labored under bombastic dialogue. "Confrontations with evil can be dangerous," the Wizard declares at one point. The only thing keeping the three-million-dollar movie afloat was its wealth of stunningly executed three-dimensional animation, or, as it is presently known, Dynarama.

Harryhausen is at once amused and perplexed by his fans who insist on reading hidden secrets or extensively categorizing his creatures and effects, so he therefore ignored the ignoble grumbles in fandom circles that the *Tiger's* ghouls resembled the fighting skeletons of *The*

Patrick Wayne, Patrick Troughton, Taryn Power, and Jane Seymour confer over some ancient lore during _Sinbad and the Eye of the Tiger_ (© Columbia).

The ITS ALIVE Baby is back...
Only now there are three of them.

"IT LIVES AGAIN"

A LARCO PRODUCTION • "IT LIVES AGAIN"
STARRING: FREDERIC FORREST • KATHLEEN LLOYD • JOHN P. RYAN as Frank Davis
JOHN MARLEY • ANDREW DUGGAN • EDDIE CONSTANTINE • JAMES DIXON
MUSIC BY BERNARD HERRMANN • WRITTEN, PRODUCED AND DIRECTED BY LARRY COHEN
A LARRY COHEN FILM • TECHNICOLOR • READ THE BALLANTINE BOOK
Released by Warner Bros. (W) a Warner Communications Company
R RESTRICTED ⊖ © 1978 WARNER BROS. INC.

It Lives Again.

Seventh Voyage and Jason and the Argonauts (1963), and that the Trog had a horn like *The Seventh Voyage's* Cyclops. The characters are entirely different, Ray insists, otherwise looking and acting completely unlike their predecessors.

Many non-believers saw for themselves when *Jason and the Argonauts* was re-released during 1978, employing such other fantasy-classic sequences as the fight with a seven-headed hydra and the attack of the winged harpies. Also returning in 1978 is one of the smallest beasts ever to tear, rip, chew, and wet across the screen. This time, however, the "It" of *It's Alive* (1975) is bringing two of his friends.

Larry Cohen's *It Lives Again* (1978) introduces three mutated babies for the price of one. The original killer, born clawed and fanged because of an ill-produced pregnancy pill, escaped from the hospital and carried on a crawling reign of terror, dispatching pedestrians, milkmen, and cops until its father—who had lost his job, sent his other son away, and watched his wife nearly lose her sanity—understands that he helped create the monster who was, in reality, as confused and frightened as his victims.

Initially hunting it down in a sewer, he takes it in his arms and tries to protect it from the blood-thirsty police and corrupt pill manufacturer. Finally, the father is forced to hurl the blubbering killer at the pill maker, who dies beneath the savage baby in a rain of police bullets.

As the creature's parents are taken away in a squad car, the word comes in: another such child has been born in Seattle. The nightmare isn't over yet.

John Ryan, the original *It's Alive* father, returns to assuage his guilt by helping the families of the next three terrible toddlers while Larry Cohen again does the writing, producing, and directing honors. All this may come as a surprise to those who saw the gory newspaper ads for the original film back in 1975. This first publicity campaign, spearheaded by Warner Brothers, alienated most potential customers from seeing the intriguing, and, by and large, tasteful picture.

Then, more than a year later, the movie was re-released with a subtler campaign, employing a wicker baby carriage with a blood-stained claw hanging out as a motif. The tagline held just the right amount of suggested horror: "There's only one thing wrong with the Davis' baby . . . *It's Alive*." The film made a million dollars in the first week of its rebirth, slowly disappearing from nationwide screens after attaining close to a ten-million-dollar return.

Part of its eventual success was due to Cohen's own concept of horror. He purposely kept the appearance of the child dim throughout the film to heighten the audience's imagination. As the suspense builds, a shot of the baby's fiercely toothed mouth would be glimpsed, or its over-large, bloodshot eyes would flash on the screen. "What scares me," Cohen expressed in an article, "is what I never see." It would be remiss, however, not to mention that the never seen doesn't have to be made either, saving much in production costs, a fact that frustrates returning "baby maker" Rick Baker.

After essentially building a doll for *It's Alive*, Baker found himself installing teeth on his wife to do the

The mark of the beast baby! A birthday party spoiled by one of the three monster babies from *It Lives Again* (© Warner Communications).

The poster ad art for *Godzilla on Monster Island* is probably better than the rest of the film (© Cinema Shares).

chewing close-ups, and, on his back in a sewer pipe, animating a stationary baby for a climactic scene. In the sequel, Baker had to repeat these cost-saving techniques, but built a full-scale baby suit which could be worn by a small actor in an oversized set.

"It's much the same situation as everything I do for Larry," he explained. "He wants it cheap and he wants it yesterday." The situation did not change throughout the filming. After spending a bit more time, and building the three dummy babies with a bit more detail, Baker visited the set to discover that the dummies had been made to crawl by being pulled across the floor on a string. "We did it other times and it looked fine," Baker remembered Cohen telling him.

Much the same techniques are employed by the infamous Toho Studios in Japan for the ever-growing Godzilla series. The latest three offerings to make it to the drive-ins, matinees, and secondrun theaters is *Godzilla vs. Megalon* (1976), *Godzilla vs. the Cosmic Monster* (1977), and *Godzilla on Monster Island* (1978). Now being handled by Cinema Shares after a lengthy partnership with American International, the new Godzilla, or Gojira as he is known in his homeland, has been

slowly regressing from the broad and furious monster he once was into a pixie-faced buffoon with a heightened sense of jujitso.

In the first adventure of the trio, the oriental studio reached a new low with what is generally regarded as the worst monster movie ever made. This mish-mash, incorporating film clips from more than a half dozen previous Toho exports, has the vaguely prehistoric hero fighting three monsters: Gigan, a winged, tusked, armored outer-space bird; Megalon, which looks like a giant insect made up of artichoke layers; and Jet Jaquar, a smiling, pointy-headed cyborg who has been stolen from his inventor by an alien race. As usual, this other-worldly group, the Seatopians, want the earth for their own and almost totally destroy the Near East to prove it. Naturally, Godzilla defends the world, defeating all opposing forces, with the help of a reformed Jet Jaquar and a small Japanese boy who cheers from the sidelines.

The film and its audience suffered further when it was cut from its eighty-one-minute theatrical version to fit in a forty-five minute NBC slot hosted by John Belushi of "Saturday Night Live" in a Godzilla suit! Thanks to the

Gigan (right) gives Godzilla the eye and Godzilla breathes on Angorus while Ghidrah delivers a triple whammy in *Godzilla on Monster Island* (ⓒ Cinema Shares).

73

movie's incredibly awful dubbing, Belushi couldn't be funnier than the film.

The following year's offering was much the same. Some ape-faced aliens arrive to take over and destroy earth, but first they must deal with Godzilla. So they invent Mecha-Godzilla, a "bionic" double, who can drill with its hands, use its fingers as missiles, sense with its neck, and zap with its eyes and nostrils. It's even outfitted with a jointed metal tail. Also, as usual, the dubbing and English dialogue are atrocious, and the fights ludicrously enjoyable.

The only thing that is not bad about these efforts are the monetary returns. In Japan, Gojira is one of the consistent big attractions, and he always seems to turn a profit in the West, so Cinema Shares continues to bring him over and unleash him. *Godzilla on Monster Island*

The usual chaos ensues, at least in this ludicrous publicity still for *Godzilla vs. the Cosmic Monster* (© Cinema Shares).

features not only the big lovable lug but such old standbys as Ghidrah the three-headed winged dragon.

Close cousins of the oriental beast are his low budget United States counterparts, nearly always produced on a shoestring. Whether they be dinosaurs, bats, zombies, or lagoon creatures, they invade theaters with alarming regularity. In April 1977, the beast was a cross between the Loch Ness Monster and a brontosaurus, and filled the top of a double bill with *The Land of the Minotaur*. *The Crater Lake Monster* was its name and its creature rose only intermittently because of a variety of production problems arising from its low budget.

Several sequences that were originally planned had to be scrapped; the acting talent was pedestrian; and the direction was hurt in the editing phase; all because of cost. The creature itself had a dinosaur's head and a frog-like body with fins and a tail. Little more than a foot long, it was given life through model animation at the hands of David Allen, John Berg, Phil Tippet, and Randy Cook; all of whom have done better work in their time. Allen handled the Pillsbury Doughboy, Swiss Miss and the Volkswagen commercials featuring *King Kong;* Berg and Tippet created the three-dimensional chess-game animation for *Star Wars* (1977). Because of cost and conflicting schedules, the team got the *Crater Lake* work done in 2½ months on double shifts.

The plot tells of a group of people who travel up to a mountain resort after a meteorite has warmed up the waters of Crater Lake. Beneath the waves lies an egg which is hatched from the heat of the meteorite. The monster rises to make mincemeat out of various people and things until a snowplow does him in. Director/producer William Stromberg and screenwriter Richard Cardella wanted to make a family picture featuring Bigfoot at first, but settled for the animated dinosaur when too many Sasquatch films appeared, hoping to make enough to continue in the picture business.

Crown International, the distributor of both *Minotaur* and *Crater Lake*, entered into the production phase to help the latter along. Fueled with the returns from films like *The Van* (1976) and *The Pom Pom Girls* (1975), Mark Tenser, the company's president, had most of *Crater Lake* reshot, and supervised the editing himself. Being the moneyman, he was in the position to handle the creative aspects in any way he saw fit in an attempt to make the final product more attractive to the theater owner.

It is this sort of direct consideration for exhibitors that makes the small distribution companies prosperous, but as Crown's general-sales manager, George Josephs, was quick to point out in an article, "We need the majors for their expenditures and their big pictures, or there is no motion-picture business."

Big money was certainly not a consideration of

Horror of the Zombies.

75

Independent-International's *Horror of the Zombies* (197?) an "R" rated film which puts its money on two time-tested ingredients: female flesh and the guts that lie beneath. Its official synopsis runs thus: "Three young, pretty models are cast adrift at sea on their pleasure boat. They encounter a weird, ancient ship in the night's fog and board it. One by one they are sadistically slaughtered by cannibalistic ghouls who must have human flesh to live." And everybody lived happily ever after.

Other than its title, this gross little film has nothing in common with the 1965 Hammer production *Plague of the Zombies*, a cult favorite directed by John Gilling. *Horror* lists no director but does name stars Maria Perschy, Jack Taylor, Carl Leonard and Barbara Hey, and incorporates makeup left over from *Tombs of the Blind Dead* (1972).

Slightly better, since its intent was openly pornographic, was *The Beast* (1977), a French import by Walerian Borowczyk depicting the slow alteration of a man into a horse because of the mating of his great, great, great, great, great grandmother with a half-man/half beast centuries before. Hard-core complications arise when an aristocratic heiress arrives for a previously arranged marriage.

The zombie, or flesh-eating creature, hasn't had the kindest treatment in movies, as evidenced by *The Ghoul* (1976), Tyburn Studio's England-produced film concerning an "inhuman thing in the old Lawrence House." Peter Cushing starred as the tortured Dr. Lawrence, the same sort of part he had often enacted in his work for the Hammer studio. Not surprisingly, the film was rife with other Hammer alumni, since Tyburn is headed by Kevin Francis, horror movie director Freddie Francis's son.

The screenplay was written by John Elder, who also penned the scripts for *Frankenstein Created Woman* (1966) and *Dracula Has Risen From the Grave* (1968); the music was composed and supervised by the Hammer-experienced team of Harry Robinson and Philip Martell. Naturally, Kevin produced and Freddie directed.

The tale begins in the Roaring Twenties at a roaring party where Billy (Stewart Bevan) challenges Geoffry (Ian McCulloch) to a car race, with their girlfriends, Daphne (Veronica Carlson) and Angela (Alexandra Bastedo)—who's also Billy's sister—as seconds. In the mist of a moor Daphne and Billy wind up out of gas in a ditch. While Billy is out in search of fuel, the girl is waylaid by Tom (John Hurt), the Lawrences' handyman and resident pervert. She's eliminated when the Lawrences' Indian servant, Ayah (Gwen Watford), unleashes the ghoul on her while Billy is dispatched by Tom.

Gwen Watford leaves some bloody refreshment outside the door of *The Ghoul* (Courtesy Tyburn Films).

Meanwhile, Geoffry and Angela have been looking for their competition only to wind up in the same danger. Angela is held captive in Tom's shed while Geoff forces Tom to talk. Racing into the main house, he confronts Lawrence, who admits that his son is a flesh-eater worshiped by his Hindu servant. The only reason he didn't stop the slaughter years before was that he had made a promise to his late wife not to destroy the boy.

The information does Geoffry no good since he is subsequently killed by a quickly thrust blade when the ghoul suddenly appears. He next murders Tom, but, before getting to Angela, he is shot by his own father, who no longer can stand the violence. Both Lawrence and Ayah commit suicide, leaving the hysterical Angela alive to run, screaming, from the house.

From the bloody to the slimy, Don Barton and Capital Productions raised a new sea creature from *The Blood Waters of Dr. Z.* (1975). Shot entirely in Florida by an amateur crew and featuring an amateur cast, it is obvious that much money and time was spent hyping the picture with two-color T-shirts, radio and television commercials, four posters, a preview trailer and an advertising manual. In concept and execution, the exploitative horror film is classic grade "Z" work—from dealing with a mad scientist to not having even one person, let alone a doctor, with a "Z" in his name.

Dr. Leopold (Marshall Graver) has invented a serum he calls ZaAt that changes him into a seven-foot killer catfish (Wade Popwell) complete with gills and fins. He takes the opportunity to revenge himself on a society that would dare call him insane. He starts by polluting the waterways with ZaAt, causing fish to mutate. This, according to the production notes, causes, "hazards on streets, highways, and lawns."

Sheriff Lou (Paul Galloway) calls in Rex, a marine biologist, and a team from the Inter-Nations Phenomena Investigation Team (INPIT) consisting of Walker Stevens (Dave Dickerson) and the beautiful Martha Walsh (Sanna Ringhaver). After numerous deaths, fights, traps, and escapes, the creature kidnaps Martha in order to make her his mate.

The sheriff and Rex arrive at Leopold's lab just before Martha is to be dunked in a vat of ZaAt, but they pay the ultimate price for their interference. Stevens manages to wound the monster, but it escapes in the end, carrying with it a life-long supply of ZaAt. Just as the two team members seem destined for a reunion, Martha follows the creature, trance-like, into the sea.

The film did not receive much national play, a fate that also befell American International's *The Bat People* (1975), the heart-warming film about a person who literally changes into Batman. Lou Shaw wrote and produced while Jerry Jameson directed this tale of Dr. John and Cathy Beck (Stewart Moss and Marianne McAndrew, married in real life as well) vacationing in a small town for a delayed honeymoon. The problem starts when a diseased bat bites John on the forehead, instigating a degenerative disease.

A Dr. Kipling gets involved when his medicinal shot causes nightmares with Beck thinking his hand has turned into a bat's claw. Sergeant Ward (Michael Pataki) gets involved when a series of night murders start. Dr. Beck hysterically runs from the hospital with Ward in hot pursuit. The policeman searches for a few days but loses the man in the hills where he suffered the initial bat bite.

Cathy is desperate to be reunited with her husband, a wish that is fulfilled when John comes to her one night, metamorphosizing into a six-foot human bat before her eyes. She faints at the sight, but, upon awakening, leads Ward to the hill caves where thousands of bats attack the cop while Cathy begins to display the same symptoms that first afflicted John. At the film's end, Ward is devoured by the bats and the couple are reunited on a batly plane.

It was a long way from Yale University Drama School, where Moss attended, and the movie version of *Hello, Dolly* (1969) in which McAndrew costarred. The same could be said for Marilyn Chambers. Her starring roles in some of the better-known pornographic films was a long way from her original public appearance as the mother on Ivory Detergent boxes.

And her starring role in David Cronenberg's *Rabid* (1977) was another quantum leap, since it was the Canadian's follow-up to *They Came From Within* (1975), or *Shivers* as it was known elsewhere. Each is mildly pornographic; each concerns a modern parasite; and each is extremely revolting in concept and execution.

They Came From Within concerns slug-like, crawling creations of a mad scientist which invade a highly exclusive, highly expensive, and highly populated residential tower. The twist is that the little monsters make their host bodies into love machines, affectionate creatures who want desperately to fulfill lusts. The semi-sterile environs of the "Starliner Towers" make an

Blood Waters of Dr. Z.

After the sun has set and the night wind has died comes the hour of The Bat People!

THE BAT PEOPLE

a Lou Shaw Production
"The Bat People" starring Stewart Moss · Marianne McAndrew **PG** PARENTAL GUIDANCE SUGG
co-starring Michael Pataki · Paul Carr · Music by Artie Kane · COLOR by DeLuxe
Written and Produced by Lou Shaw · Directed by Jerry Jameson · an American International release

The Bat People.

interesting juxtaposition to the orgiastic sexuality that is occurring within. The technical aspects are also interesting, if not disgustingly, well done. Many set pieces of powerful nausea follow one another with frightening speed.

Rabid isn't much nicer. Chambers is used as a test for a new skin-grafting method which leads to her developing a living organism in her armpit which sucks blood from others, infesting the victims with a disease that makes them visually repulsive crazies. More-detailed delineation of the plot would be impossible given the boundaries of taste—no small achievement considering the caliber of films that have thus far been considered.

Cronenberg has finished his next film, *The Brood* (1978), of which nothing is presently known, but, based on his previous work, several things can be assumed. It will probably be graphic, rated, at least, "R," and have a downbeat ending. Both *Shivers* and *Rabid* saw the disease winning out at the finale.

Still, it would be pleasant if Cronenberg suddenly followed the example of director Paul Morrissey. After helming two famous Andy Warhol monster films, both unrelentingly violent and pornographic, he teamed with the famous English comedy team of Peter Cook and Dudley Moore to send up Sherlock Holmes and the legendary *Hound of the Baskervilles* (1978). Jeff Rovin described Cook and Moore's first fantasy film, *Bedazzled* (1967), as a movie where "lunacy reigns supreme." The same could be said of their new effort.

Dr. Mortimer (Terry Thomas) approaches the great Victorian detective and asks that protection be given Sir Henry Baskerville (Kenneth Williams) against the curse of the hound, which has killed all the preceding Baskervilles. Holmes (Cook) however, is too busy investigating the massage parlors of London and offers Watson (Moore) as a substitute. The amiable doctor is described in the production notes as ". . . a Victorian Clouseau [the clod portrayed by Peter Sellers in the "Pink Panther" pictures], but not as smart."

He accompanies Sir Henry back to the estate where he must investigate the following characters: Mr. and Mrs. Barrymore (Max Wall and Irene Handl), the maid and butler; Stapleton (Denholm Elliott), who's been feuding for years over the right to let his chihuahua relieve itself on Baskerville land; his sister Beryl, who has the nasty habit of spewing pea soup and turning her head in 360-degree circles, Frankland (Hugh Griffith), whose six-foot amazonian mistress (Dana Gillespie) carries oxen on her shoulders; and the Notting Hill ax murderer, Seldon (Roy Kinnear).

Watson plods on, but, thankfully, is rescued by the arrival of Holmes just before accusing himself of the crimes since, ". . . whenever something sinister happened, I was there." First, Sherlock instructs Watson to construct a bog. Then he puts the suspects in it. Next he finds the hound, which is actually quite a nice pooch and heir to the family fortune. Seldon is accidentally croaked, the servants leave for America to invent Kentucky Fried Chicken, the neighbors are arrested, and everyone else is blown up by a long-dormant volcano beneath Baskerville Hall.

Moore, Cook, and Morrissey wrote the hysterical screenplay and were aiming for the same audience that flocks to Mel Brooks and Monty Python films. Not unnaturally, John Goldstone, the film's producer, is also the Python's producer and executive producer of *Jabberwocky* (1977), a satirical send-up of the Lewis Carroll creation.

Directed and cowritten (with Charles Alverson) by Terry Gilliam, the film starred Michael Palin and featured such other Python alumni as Terry Jones and Neal Innes (the group's songwriter and musical performer). Advertised as "Bigger than the Black Death, faster than the 14th Century, cheaper than the Crusades," and "At last! A film for the squeamish," *Jabberwocky* begins with a medieval poacher's death at the claws of a savage Jabberwock, a bird-like creature so horrible "it can turn your teeth white overnight."

This monster has been terrorizing the kingdom of King Bruno the Questionable (Max Wall) until there are almost no peasants left to pay taxes. The King wisely decides to hold a tournament to find a champion who will kill the vicious beast. When the mud and blood settles, there is left the "almost-as-dreaded-as-the-Jabberwock" Black Knight (Dave Prowse) and his squire Dennis Cooper (Palin), a cooper's apprentice who has been renounced by his father the cooper (Paul Curran) from the family coopering business and is presently trying to make it big in the kingdom in order to secure the pudgy hand of the obese Griselda Fishfinger, whom he loves faithfully for some reason even though the beautiful Princess has mistaken him for her "Prince who has come," whom she has been waiting for all her life.

Through a series of mistakes, Dennis does in the long-necked, globe-eyed, winged terror; is wed to the beautiful Princess; and takes over half the kingdom. But in *Jabberwocky* it is not so much what happens but how it happens. The aura of medieval times is marvelously evoked, filled with dirt and death. Heads roll constantly, poverty is a way of life, and panhandling is an art form with one beggar chopping off his feet for better business. The humor is extremely broad and violent, while the

Beneath the black armor and horned faceplate of the knight on the right is Dave "Darth Vader" Prowse, fighting for the right to kill the dreaded *Jabberwocky* (© Columbia).

entire film, costing less than one million dollars, has the look of a multi-million-dollar effort. Gilliam must have learned a lot about stretching money from his work on *Monty Python and the Holy Grail*, which cost less than $500,000 even in inflation-ridden Great Britain.

The only thing bigger than the eccentric comedy teams in England is the British-produced, American-based "The Muppet Show." Although a more detailed look at this half-hour program will appear in the television chapter, it would be remiss not to mention the upcoming, multi-million-dollar *Muppet Movie* (1979). Although not fully delineated at this writing, it has been announced that dozens of top stars will be approached to guest in the Jack Burns' screenplay, which broadens the basic concept of the show.

Naturally, most of the performers will be furry, hairy, wide-eyed animals, monsters, and things of no definite definition, made and controlled by Jim Henson and Frank Oz. A little of that group's bright, inventive originality could have been used on *The Blue Bird* (1976), heralded as the first great Russian/American movie collaboration, a movie that said much for detente but nothing for audiences. The lovely book about two children looking for the blue bird of happiness was as leaden as a bowl of bad borsht on screen.

Even with the direction of George Cukor, the old master of such works as *The Philadelphia Story* (1940), *Gaslight* (1944), *Born Yesterday* (1951), and *My Fair Lady* (1964), and a cast headed by Elizabeth Taylor, 20th Century Fox pulled it from distribution as fast as possible. Many felt that it looked like a bad cross between *Willy Wonka* and *Potemkin*.

The bespectacled director talked about the film's difficulties in an interview two years after the fact. As nice as the Russians were, he remembered, disorganization plagued both nationalities, especially in terms of the crew. "Time seemed to mean nothing to them," Cukor explained. Add to that laxness, with the unavailability of proper movie equipment and the harried schedules of American stars, and you get what the director recalls as a "long and sometimes painful experience."

Cukor also had once been set to direct *Gone With the Wind* (1939) until difficulties with Clark Gable saw him replaced with Victor Fleming, who had just finished filming *The Wizard of Oz*. This only serves as an introduction to a story as American as garbage strikes and corporate takeovers: the story of one's discovery of oneself. Back in 1939 it meant going from Kansas, to Munchkinland, to the Emerald City, and back again. In 1978 it meant hitting the track from Harlem to Manhattan.

Instead of Judy Garland following the yellow-brick road, it's Diana Ross "ease on down, ease on down" ing the road along with Michael Jackson as the Scarecrow and Nipsy Russell as the Tin Man, in the movie version of the all-singing, all-dancing, all-black *The Wiz* (1978). The original Broadway hit had anything but a yellow-brick road on the way to its success. Initially, it was flopping in test engagements until Geoffrey Holder, the multitalented actor/dancer/artist, took over.

He didn't just go over the script, he redesigned the whole production top to bottom, recostuming, resetting, and rechoreographing until he had whipped up one of the most dazzling musicals ever, which garnered seven Tony Awards. He has gone on to rework *Kismet* into the black musical *Timbuktu* while *The Wiz's* cinematic recreation was handed to Sidney Lumet, a director well versed in New York from his work on *The Pawnbroker* (1965), *The Anderson Tapes* (1971), *Serpico* (1974), *Dog Day Afternoon* (1975), and *Network* (1976).

It's Oz, circa 1979. But some things never change: like Dorothy (Diana Ross), the Scarecrow (Michael Jackson), the Tin Man (Nipsey Russell), the Cowardly Lion (Ted Ross), and the wonderful Wiz, himself (Richard Pryor). From *The Wiz* (© Universal).

Charles Grey, Calvin Lockhart, and Peter Cushing (left to right) discuss the mechanics of chess and werewolves during *The Beast Must Die* (© Cinerama Releasing).

Father/director Freddie Francis and son/producer Kevin Francis discuss the script of *Legend of the Werewolf* (Courtesy Tyburn Films).

After the babies, sharks, apes, buffaloes, bees, whales, dogs, worms, diseases, bats, Bigfeet, zombies, muppets, walruses, minatons, troglodytes, spiders, ants, and mice, it is pleasant to return our attention to the classic shenanigans of two fantasy staples: the werewolf and the vampire. Dating back to 1922 on screen, these two monsters, created by hereditary and communicable diseases, were well represented in the seventies.

The wolfman made a less than triumphant return with *The Boy Who Cried Werewolf* (1973) and the *Werewolf of Washington* (1974), both announced in Jeff Rovin's volume, but Amicus Productions, an English contemporary of Hammer and Tyburn, tried to get back on the right track with *The Beast Must Die* (1975). Adapted from a story by James Blish, Michael Winder wrote and Paul Annett directed the tale about a big black game hunter (Calvin Lockhart) who collects a group of people at his estate, knowing one is a werewolf.

He wants the creature's head for his mantel. Among the suspects are Peter Cushing, Charles Grey, and Anton Diffring. Not much suspense is mustered by *The Most Dangerous Game/Ten Little Indians* aspects of the movie as, one by one, the house guests are dispatched by the mystery lycanthrope. Still, it was a diverting hour and a half with good production values and a nifty monster who looked more like a wolfhound than a hairy man.

Not to be outdone, Tyburn was mounting its own wolfman story at the time of the Amicus's beast release. Holding over practically the same crew from *The Ghoul*, *Legend of the Werewolf* (1975) was made in the autumn months of 1974. John Elder wrote the script, Freddie Francis directed, Kevin Francis produced, and Peter Cushing moved once more into the breach by starring as Paul Cataflanque, a police pathologist. Thankfully, he is joined by such noted English pros as Ron Moody and Hugh Griffith to help embody this nineteenth-century Parisian adventure.

During a pogrom, a group of starving refugees is killed by a wolf pack, save for a newborn baby boy who, astonishingly, is raised by the animals. A traveling showman, Maestro Pamponi (Griffith), captures the boy several years later and makes him the prize attraction of a

touring circus. The boy grows into a handsome, well-mannered young man (David Rintoul) which, unfortunately, diminishes the patronage. But his peaceful life is once again shattered by a wolf pack which surrounds the caravan. Unable to contain his bestiality any longer, he kills one of Pamponi's assistants and runs into the night.

When the sun rises, the young man, named Etoile, is in Paris where a zookeeper (Moody) hires him. For a while he is content tending the animals until he makes the mistake of falling in love with a prostitute, Christine (Lynn Dalby). Then a series of vicious murders occur, all victims wealthy patrons of the brothels, all ripped to shreds. Professor Cataflanque and Inspector Gerard (Stephen Gryff) are called in to try to solve the mystery from a "legendary" point of view.

Just as they are making headway, the police prefect (John Harvey) foolishly orders all the zoo wolves destroyed, a task that befalls Etoile. Pushed to the edge, the full moon rises and even Christine's professed love

David Rintoul really sinks his teeth into his role in *Legend of the Werewolf*—note the obvious contact lenses (© Courtesy Tyburn Films).

A TRUE STORY SO BRUTAL AND HORRIFYING it was kept from the public for over a century!

See Daniella's Reincarnation!

©1977 DIMENSION PICTURES INC

THE LEGEND OF THE...
WOLF WOMAN

A LARRY WOOLNER Presentation starring ANNE BOREL and FRED STAFFORD
Screenplay by HOWARD ROSS Directed by R.D. SILVER Produced by MICKEY ZIDE
A DIMENSION PICTURES RELEASE [R] RESTRICTED

The Legend of the Wolf Woman.

cannot keep him in check. Armed with a dying victim's description and a silver bullet, Cataflanque follows the wolfman into the sewers. There the white-haired, broad-nosed, pointy-eared creature is seen clearly for the first time. And, unlike other screen werewolves, he speaks, asking the pathologist to help him.

Unfortunately, Gerard is not sympathetic. Tracing the semianimal back to Etoile's lodgings, he uses Cataflanque's pistol to destroy the tortured creature. No such relief was available to the next screen lycanthrope. Though no one said otherwise, movie history has always portrayed murder sprees by confused wolfmen. It was up to Dimension Pictures to release *The Legend of the Wolf Woman* (1976) to the wide eyes of American audiences.

It told the supposedly true story of Daniella Nesneri, an Italian woman who was institutionalized in 1968 after killing her sister's husband and others, thinking herself the embodiment of a wolfman that had died over 100 years earlier. Anne Borel starred in this "R" rated adaptation filled with violence and sex. It starts and ends on the night of the full moon as the beautiful Daniella dances inside a ring of fire.

As her silent song reaches its climax, she drops to the ground and assumes the features of a wild animal. A group of searchers push through a wood until one man is viciously murdered. Suddenly, the vision has dissipated as the same girl awakens from this nightmare, hysterically convinced that she is to follow in her ancestor's paw steps, becoming a beast on the night of the full moon and living her dream.

Her fears are justified, for when her sister Irene arrives at their country estate with her new husband, his features are exactly those of the victim in Daniella's dream. And on the night of the full moon, her worst dread is realized when she tears at the poor man out in the garden. Even doctors and modern medicine cannot help her. She escapes from the hospital, leaving a trail of bloody bodies in her wake. Her only respite is a peaceful affair with a stuntman who finds her cowering beneath a hedge.

He nurses her back to health, but just when it seems she has recovered completely, three thugs kill the stuntman and brutally rape Daniella. Reverting back to her animal state, she slaughters the trio and races back into the forest. The authorities find her dancing within a circle of fire.

But her confinement has not laid the werewolf's soul to rest. Even as these words are written, a production called *Wolfman* is being mounted in North Carolina by producer/star Earl Owensby and director Worth Keeter. The hairy fellow's recent return to the screen in a few paltry productions over a span of a few years has nothing

84

on the resurrection of the eternal embodiment of the cold evil of Transylvania, however.

After popping up on screens year after year with hardly a pause, kept vital by *Old Dracula* (1973), *Captain Kronos: Vampire Hunter* (1974), and *The Satanic Rites of Dracula* (1975), among others, the infamous count and all his living-dead denizens are flooding the theaters and major movie studios again. Although his return to the top of the fads was officially heralded by a best-selling book and a Broadway revival, his theme was kept gruesomely alive by a well-made adventure called *Vampyres* (1974), which was re-released the following year as *Daughters of Dracula* (1975).

Marianne Morris and Anulka are the living-dead darlings Fran and Marian, who are murdered at the movie's opening by an unseen assailant (Dracula, himself perhaps?). From there on, they spend their time rising from the grave, taking off their clothes, making love, and drinking blood. Posing as hitchhikers, their victims include a playboy (Michael Byrne), a couple out on a camping trip (Brian Deacon and Sally Faulkner), and a nice guy named Ted (Murray Brown), who just barely survives, thanks to some leftover human lust within Fran.

The last we see of the lithesome bloodsuckers, they are

Yes, along with *Dracula's Dog* (1977), *Nightwing* (1979), and *Martin the Blood Lover* (1978), there's the *Vampire Hookers* (1978). Just goes to show: you can't keep a good blood-sucker down.

disappearing in the morning mist, racing the rising sun to their graves. Perhaps now that vampires are in vogue again, director Joseph Larraz and producer Brian Smedley-Aston might bring the girls back.

One thing for sure, the femme-fatale concept is a good one, or else why would Warren Publications be trying so hard to push the multi-million-dollar adaptation of their comic character *Vampirella* into production? Originally, Hammer Studios had the option on the screenplay about the extremely sexy outer-space vampiress who goes around in a cut-out bathing suit and high-heeled boots. By the time the project met delays, statuesque Barbara Leigh had been signed to flesh out the bloodthirsty female, and Oliver Reed was set as her co-star. The word from the Warren offices in New York is now the whole package will be independently produced, utilizing most of the same cast.

Her murderous male counterpart has been given rebirth in no fewer than five new projects based on or around Bram Stoker's classic novel, *Dracula*. First, Anne Rice wrote a darkly sensual novel about a young reporter finding and talking to one tortured bloodsucker, calling the atmospheric work *Interview with the Vampire*. Although highly touted by critics, it was only a moderate success in hardcover and paperback, leading to a movie sale but not an actual production.

It took the triumphant return to Broadway of the original 1927 dramatization of Stoker's work by Hamilton Deane and John L. Balderston to secure its production schedule. When the play originally appeared in this country, the part of the count was enacted by a veritable unknown named Bela Lugosi. In the 1977 reincarnation, the incisors are beautifully handled by Frank Langella, who adds an animal grace and tongue-in-cheek style after being told to make more like Lord Byron than a stolid Transylvanian.

His portrayal is immeasurably heightened by the stage designs of Edward Gorey, an artist whose deathly pen-and-ink drawings have earned him a large cult following. All his devices are in abundant evidence on stage. Skull-faced cherubs flutter above a victim's bed. Bats abound, as wallpaper designs, as pajama clasps, as pillows, even as clouds. More clouds turn the full moon into a death's head.

The vampire himself is a vision in black satin, his only other color being the white of his shirt and the deep red of his cape's lining. In the course of the play, bats zoom in and out, Dracula appears and disappears at will, crosses burst into flame, the vampire transforms into a bat and disintegrates before our eyes as a well-aimed wooden stake is driven home.

Frank Langella casts his spell over audiences as *Dracula*.

What Frankie can do, Georgie thinks he can do better! George Hamilton rules the night in *Love at First Bite*. . . **Thank you, Kelli Sturdevan-Garris: photo.**

This is the stuff movies are made of, and, indeed, both *Interview with the Vampire* and the Broadway *Dracula* are in the advanced planning stages. But others, who know a good thing when they see it, do not plan to be outdone. 20th Century Fox's European division has secured the talents of premiere German director Werner Herzog in mounting a remake of the classic silent vampire film *Nosferatu* (1923).

Isabelle Adjani, the beautiful actress of *The Story of Adele H.* (1975) and *The Tenant,* has been signed to play the girl who keeps the monster occupied until sunup to save her true love. Elsewhere, Richard Chamberlain has been pegged as another variation on the count in an, as yet, unspecified project. By far the most audacious concept is the work of Metafilm, a California-based independent company which plans to create a ten-million-dollar "definitive" adaptation of the original novel written and directed by Ken Russell and using the renowned expert, Leonard Wolf—author of *The Annotated Dracula*—as technical adviser. On the other end of the budgetary spectrum is *Love at First Bite* (1979) a Robert Kaufman–written comedy staring George Hamilton as a love-smitten Dracula chasing a high-fashion model in New York.

It seems, with all this vampiric excitement, producers won't be happy until they not only suck innocent young victims dry, but all possible patrons as well. It seems that the count is not down for it.

3 FANTASTIC SCIENCE

AS SOCIETY RUSHES into the future, it sometimes seems as all of earth's occupants are holding desperately on, the winds of progress tearing at them. Fabulous new developments for good and ill are being discovered daily. No sooner is an advanced method of surgery discovered than so is the knowledge that hair coloring can cause cancer. As soon as one space probe has reached Mars, another crashes to earth causing radioactive contamination.

As reality heaps possible horror after horror upon our heads, many find themselves running to the movies in search of a comforting vision of a possible tomorrow. For that, a new genre had to be instituted. Science-fiction, it seemed, had a tendency to concentrate on the world's shortcomings and inconsistencies, exaggerating them to serve as futuristic morality tales or warnings. So the concept of *science-fantasy* was born, exploding throughout the land with super-heroes and outlandish adventures.

Unfortunately, when a science fiction film is based on an ill-researched, unsubstantiated concept, or on an advanced idea that has no basis in scientific reality, it too is automatically relegated to the ranks of fantasy, since it has been deemed too unbelievable to accept. So a genre that was created to put the masses' minds at ease is slowly being infiltrated by the violent, the dour, and the dirty.

The latter is led in no uncertain terms by *Cinderella 2000* (1977), released in the spring but taking place in the year 2047 when everything is run by the Controller (Erwin Fuller)'s computers and love is outlawed unless okayed by the machines. Cindy (Catherine Erhardt) slaves for her wicked stepmother (Rena Harmon) and

Cinderella 2000.

stepsisters (Adina Ross and Bhurni Cowans) while longing for a true love to appear.

Instead, a fairy Godfather (Jay B. Larson) comes, who, after having some preliminary wand breakdowns, transforms the plain lady into a vision of loveliness, who no sooner gets to the Controller's masked ball than she is ravished by Tom Prince, the head-man's surrogate. Soon, the computer-loving man himself is turned on to the joys of love, and a new era begins.

The concept of outlawed love was not new in the realm of the "X" rating. About a year earlier, *Rollerbabies* (1976) took on the theme and took off as a satire of

87

Rollerball (1975), Norman Jewison's science fiction vision of sports as war. Once the idea that overpopulation has resulted in love being illegal, the main plot of the porno rolls. Robert Random (Alan Marlo) is a television producer whose career is based on an important contract with the Federal Exhibitionism Commission. It seems that certain physical acts can only be performed for the masses by licenced artists and Random has been sluffing in his duty to bring the public their favorite spectator sport. Just when it seems that his cancellation is assured, a friendly scientist (Philip De Hat) comes up with the idea for a roller derby where the object is to get together.

It Came From Outer Space (1953) got a subtle once-over from an "X" exploit in November of 1977 with *Invasion of the Love Drones*. But instead of controlling earthlings to repair their alien space ship as in the SF classic directed by Jack Arnold, here we have Dr. Femme (Viveca Ash) creating a race of love drones to start a world-wide orgy since their ship runs on physical energy. Jaime Gillis, Eric Edwards, and Bree Anthony also get involved in what was billed as a "Drones Films Release of a Sensory Man Production."

Hot on its heels was what Burbank International called "The $ens-uous (sic) Sequence to *Star Wars*." It was named *2069: A Sex Odyssey* (1977), hopefully giving both Stanley Kubrick *(2001)* and George Lucas grounds to sue. Leaving no genre stone unturned, the distributors also described the Willie Pribil–written, George Keil–

AN EROTIC SCIENCE FICTION FANTASY

Starring ALENA PENZ NINA FREDRIC GERTI SNEIDER RAUL RETZER CATHRENE CONTI HEIDY HAMMER MICHAEL MEIN HERB HEESEL
Directed by GEORGE KEIL Written by WILLIE PRIBIL Music H HAMMERSCHMID Produced by GÜNTHER KOPF

2069: A Sex Odyssey.

directed German import as "an erotic science-fiction fantasy."

Even a classic like *The Invisible Man* (1933) is not safe. *Henry's Night In* (197?) concerned a Casper Milktoast type who discovers exactly what fun he can have when a trunk he buys at an auction holds the secret of invisibility.

Originality in terms of content is about the only thing good about *Behind Locked Doors* (1976), the last of the sensual fantastic-science films, but the first of their cheaply vile counterparts. Two young girls (Joyce Denner and Eve Reeves) pay for their promiscuous ways when a seemingly gentle Mr. Bradley (Danial Garth) takes them in after their car "mysteriously runs out of gas." There they meet his sister Myra (Irene Lawrence) and the house handyman Freddy (Ivan Hager) as well as discovering that no transportation is available and the phone is "mysteriously dead."

After a fitful night, the girls, Terry and Ann, are rousted and "mysteriously" imprisoned in separate rooms where they are told of Bradley's main aim in life. After years as a mortician, seeing beautiful, but lifeless, bodies, he works toward the ultimate in love incorporated into one female body. Thus lectured, the girls are shown his previous attempts, preserved with naked perfection in the cellar dungeon.

Thereafter follows one experiment after another with greater concentration on flesh than flasks or formulas. Finally, the girls manage to escape through a secret passage. In a last-ditch attempt to retrieve them Bradley knocks over some lit candles which ignite some ancient drapes. As the flames rise, we see the supposedly lifeless bodies of Bradley's previous "guinea pigs" move toward him. Boxoffice International, tasteful as ever, was responsible for this eighty-minute effort.

Behind Locked Doors had nothing on World Wide Films' *House of the Living Dead* (1976) for subtlety, obviously. No sooner had young Lady Marianne (Shirley Anne Field) arrived in the South African veldt at the beginning of the twentieth century, than she is informed that her fiancee's brother has been kicked in the head by a horse and confined to the attic of the family estate, Brattling Manor.

Things do not improve. Her fiancee's mother reacts coldly to the girl who had traveled thousands of miles for a previously arranged marriage. The stable boy is found dead. A local witch doctor is killed. A policeman investigating the brutal murders is brutally murdered himself. The horse that kicked brother Brett is found mutilated in the manor's lily pond.

Meanwhile, Marianne is bothered by ghastly footsteps

Behind Locked Doors.

in the night, eerie organ music, and repeated warnings to leave the estate if she wants to avoid a grisly fate. The housemaid is not so lucky. Her grisly fate, sans warning, is to be tortured, then stuck at the organ console to take the rap for the little night music. Finally, Marianne is cornered by the man she thought was her fiancee (Mark Damon) only to discover that he is really the horse-kicked brother, who has been killing people left and right in order to keep their souls in bottles in the attic.

Why he wants to do this and how he managed to accomplish the scientific feat is never explained. Suffice it to say that there was method in his madness. For his next magic trick he had hoped to unite Marianne's soul with her real fiancee's after pushing his mother over a

balcony to her death, but thankfully a friend of the family, Dr. Collinson (David Oxley), arrives in time. After a fight, the souls escape from their glass prisons and cause the crazy brother to follow his mother in a death plunge.

The publicity release for the horrid little exercise proclaimed, "It drives you mad before it kills you!" Although this is misleading in terms of *The House of the Living Dead*, it could be safely said for *The Incredible Melting Man* (1978), an American International release which infuriated by undercutting all its initial promise.

Heralded as "The first NEW horror creature," this molten mass was once handsome astronaut Colonel Steven West, the first man on Saturn. His return is triumphant, but the aftermath is horrific because a space-contracted disease is causing his skin to melt. His doctor, Ted Nelson (Burr DeBenning) is confused when he cannot find a reason for the affliction, and his commanding officer, General Perry (Myron Healey) is perplexed when West escapes from the hospital.

The Incredible Melting Man.

Only after several gruesome deaths does Nelson diagnose the major side effect of the alien infection. Steve West must feed on flesh to regenerate his own corroding tissue. But even his mass-murderous repasts do not check the flow of West's degeneration. As the mutilated bodies and West's rage mount, the sheriff (Micheal Alldredge) is let in on the military secret and a posse is created for an intensive search of a wooded area where West is supposed to be.

By then the astronaut's mind has snapped. Although one eye is useless and his body is a barely-held-together mess, the affliction gives him super strength. When his pursuers finally corner him at a power plant, he neither recognizes his friends nor cares about them. One after another, they are dispatched, crashing down through a maze of pipes, electrocuted on the electrical wires, shot by their own men, until the still-living monster shuffles off, only to completely melt in the puddle of his own body.

Samuel Gelfman and Max Rosenberg are two experienced producers who collected a suitably inexpensive cast and crew for what could have been a meaningful and exciting little horror film. Instead, because of a variety of artistic complications, the movie turns ludicrously disappointing. Gelfman had previously mounted *Cannonball* (1976), a moneymaking car-chase movie with David Carradine, while Rosenberg was responsible for many of the best Amicus productions in conjunction with partners Milton Subotsky and John Dark.

Their primary mistake was to hire Rick Baker to do some extensively complicated makeup work, advertise the film as a special-effects-orientated entertainment—spotlighting Baker's work—then curtail any possible excellence Baker could attain. Originally, the young artist created a marvelously intricate set of makeups for the West character, utilizing four separate and distinct phases of melting so the man could become increasingly gruesome during the eighty-six minutes of the finished film.

Unfortunately, in the hands of writer/director William Sachs, most of Baker's work went for naught, since, in the two separate stages of editing, no coherent deteriora-

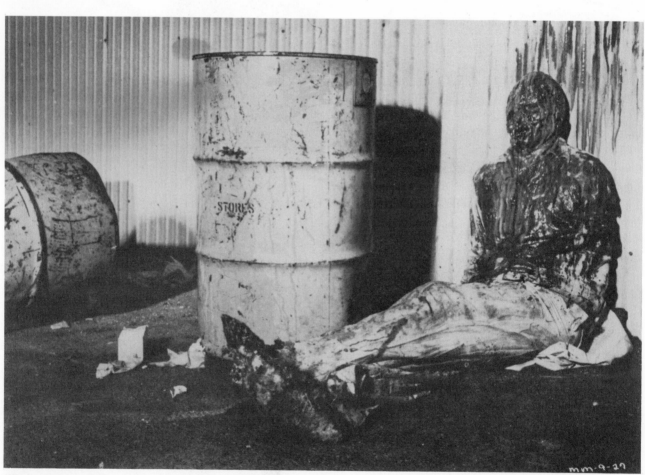

The sad finale of *The Incredible Melting Man* (© A.I.P.).

tion schedule could be established. West looked more or less the same throughout, without so much as an explanation. What explanations there were sounded lame and arbitrary since no one on screen or in the audience ever finds out what truly causes the affliction, what hampers it, whether it is communicable, or anything else. Initially, the director did not even want to show West before the disease hit him. He wanted what could have been an effective story or medical suspense film a la *The Andromeda Strain* to be merely an illogical excuse for excessive violence.

Strangely enough, even with this gory concept, *Variety* knocks the picture for "not being gruesome enough to measure up to monstrosity peaks." One reason for that could have been star Alex Rebar, who was rumored uncooperative when it came time for the extensive makeups. The only memorable moments the film possesses are when Baker's imagination and talent were given full reign and a moralistic scene where the corroding colonel begs for heavenly intervention while kneeling amid the crosses of a neglected graveyard.

The final production gaffe was perpetrated by an overzealous publicity staff who worked up a twenty-four-by-forty-one-inch poster, which borrowed a quote from the *New York Times*, stating, "Special Effects are at the heart of what movie making is all about . . . their unique quality cannot be duplicated in any other art." It then proudly proclaimed below, "Rick Baker, the new master of special effects, who brought you the magic of *The Exorcist* and gave you the wonder of *King Kong*, now brings you his greatest creation, *The Incredible Melting Man*."

When William Friedkin, *The Exorcist*'s director saw that poster on an associate's wall, he was reported to have walked over and angrily ripped it down and tore it to pieces. He and industry members knew that the actual genius of *The Exorcist*'s makeup effects was Dick Smith. Baker, essentially Smith's protégé and friend, only assisted the movie veteran.

Rick himself was horrified by this particular campaign, and he was the first to say, "Dick wanted some help so I first went out to do some work on the dummy whose head turns around 360 degrees. I really didn't do anything creative, I just did labor." Then, when asked if this unsatisfying movie and public-relations oversight would hurt his ever-growing career, he said lightly, "maybe."

Still, the producers expect enough box-office action to warrant their collaboration on several subsequent productions, although not definitely defined as yet, audiences can be assured of at least a few fantasy projects,

since the genre has never done Rosenberg wrong. Even when the man mounted three inexpensive, almost-exploitive adaptations of Edgar Rice Burroughs's adventure books, audiences flocked to them.

The first, and most poorly received, was *The Land that Time Forgot* (1975), presented by Rosenberg and Subotsky and helmed, as were the subsequent duo, by producer John Dark and director Kevin Connor. Here we have an uncomfortable mixture of effective physical effects, such as fine miniature work and a decent volcanic eruption, and lousy full-scale work. The various prehistoric monsters which populate the lost world of Caprona, the "Land" of the title, are made from rubber as well as other stiff and unrealistic materials. Their constantly unconvincing appearances do much to mar the enjoyment of the overall work.

A German U-boat sinks a British ship in World War I. The survivors, led by intrepid Doug McClure, board and take over the enemy vessel, setting the stage for an uneasy truce when they drift far into the region of the South Pole. There the patchwork group, comprised of John McEnery, Susan Penhaligon and Keith Barron, fight for their lives amid the savage splendor of the savage land where evolution goes wild. At the fiery finale Doug and Susan survive to etch out their lives in the mythical wilderness and prepare for a sequel.

Their turn would have to wait until *At The Earth's Core* (1976) had run its course, however. This version of Burroughs's justly famous tales of the land of Pellucidar, which exists at the center of the earth, was the second adaptation that reached the screen. Dark's and Connor's Pellucidar exists mostly at Pinewood Studios, where they put together the picture with bailing wire and string.

This production did not have even a few believable visuals or a script of the caliber of the one mounted by the noted science fiction author Michael Moorcock, that the first movie had. Instead, the crew was left with a screenplay by Subotsky (who had since left Amicus and American International to create his own Sword and Sorcery Productions) and special effects consisting of unconvincing rear-screen projections, obvious monster masks, and unwieldy monster costumes.

Thrust into this mess was Peter Cushing as the absent-minded professor, Abner Perry, and Doug McClure as his playboy partner, David Innes. The time is the early 1900s; the place is within the Iron Mole, a massive burrowing device on its way through the earth's inner layers. Once the pair emerge in the "central city," they discover a race of Mahars—vaguely prehistoric lizards with wings (actually actors in wire-supported rubber suits)—who exploit primeval humans with the

Two monsters do their version of the hustle *At the Earth's Core* (© A.I.P.).

help of the Sagoths—vaguely alien humanoids (actually actors wearing masks that resemble a cross between an ape and a mole).

David falls in love with Dia (Caroline Munro), a raven-haired slave beauty, and succeeds in freeing the people from the monsters' oppressive rule. A handy earthquake helps an awful lot as well. One of the film's saving graces was the fact that it took itself far from seriously, stressing humor and action more than any sort of realistic development of character or plotline.

The same concept made its way into the third Burroughs effort, *The People That Time Forgot*. Here, the keynote was fun. Since the picture had a larger budget; the actors were new, and for the most part, talented; and the plot was concerned more with heroics than monster confrontations; Connor and his cast could really enjoy themselves.

The plot revolves around one of McClure's friends gathering together a rescue party to fly over to Caprona. Along for the ride is veteran Hammer/Amicus character

actor Thorley Walters, as a crusty old geologist, and young, innocent Sarah Douglas as a photographer for the *Times*. Patrick Wayne, son of John and star of the third *Sinbad*, was the lead, who meets up with a spectacular Capronian accomplice in the stunningly amazonian form of singer Dana Gillespie.

Together, the four face the usual array of dinosaur mock-ups, including a flying pteranodon and a fire-breathing creature who attacks in a skull-lined cave that leads to the particularly violent Na-gas tribe of Neanderthal humans. Another handy natural disaster is brought in at the last minute to save all the good guys and gals, and, by a decent margin, this latest Amicus tale is the most colorful and consistently enjoyable.

Dark and Connor are not through with supernatural science tales, however. Production began in September of 1977 on a non-Burroughs-based fantasy adventure entitled *Warlords of Atlantis*. Although an original work, all the other ingredients which have made the previous trio successful return for another reworking. Doug

A Mahar attacks in *At the Earth's Core* **(© A.I.P.).**

Director Kevin Connor looks none too pleased about the script for *The People That Time Forgot* **(Courtesy of Amicus).**

Patrick Wayne gives one of his heroic smiles during a break in filming *The People That Time Forgot* **(Courtesy of Amicus).**

McClure also returns, this time as Greg Collinson, an American engineer and friend of Charles Aitkin (Peter Gilmore), who, with his father, a professor, hopes to find the legendary land of Atlantis at the close of the nineteenth century.

They succeed all too well, salvaging a large golden statue, only to be threatened by their greedy crew and the guardian of Atlantis: a monster octopus. The eight tentacles take the entire group to the shores of the fantasy world, where Atmir, the authority figure, guides them through the seven cities that are left. Numbers one and two are already beneath the waves and inhabited by unheard-of creatures. City three is in ruins, and the fourth, called Vaar, is being prepared against an assault that comes shortly after the expedition arrives.

Savage gill men imprison every human but Charles, who is brought before Elder Atsil in City Five where he discovers the Atlanteans' origin and the fate that they have in store for the group. The origins: Atlantis's original inhabitants crash-landed on a primitive earth in prehistoric times. Their true home is Mars. The fate of the group: to be turned into mermen in order to fight the

Thorley Walters gives it a stiff upper stick, Sarah Douglas looks for a way out, and Dana Gillespie tries to stay out of the way of a monster in *The People That Time Forgot* (Courtesy of Amicus).

Christopher Lee reigns over the lands within which *An Arabian Adventure* **takes place.**

many monsters surrounding the island, including fish creatures, flying snappers, giant, clawed Zaargs, and a mutant millipede named Mogdaan.

Will the human crew remain human and escape? Will Atlantis control earth's destiny? Will Amicus make another Burroughs adaptation or another original? The answer is "no." The producer Dark and director Connor mounted an old-fashioned Arabian Nights adventure called, logically, *An Arabian Adventure* (1979). The fantasy starring Christopher Lee, Peter Cushing and Mickey Rooney and has been described as the ultimate "flying carpet" movie.

Amicus isn't alone in terms of independent fantasy production or seabound adventure. Two wildly diversified works had appeared previously, incorporating seafaring cliches, the most eccentric of which was the Spanish-French corporation of what was ostensibly titled *Jules Verne's The Mysterious Island of Dr. Nemo* (1976). The production was eccentric in that it may have been an unknowing collaboration brought on by the American Cinerama Releasing Company.

Not only is the movie a muddled combination of *20,000 Leagues Under the Sea* and *Mysterious Island*, but the technical credits are formed by a duo, one of whom French and the other Spanish. The directors were Juan Antonio Bardem and Henri Colpi. The screenplay was by Jacques Champreaux and Juan Antonio Bardem. The directors of photography were Enzo Serafin and Guy Delecluze, the set design by Cubero Y. Galicia and Phillippee Ancellin. And so it went through-cameramen, sound men, costumers, and assistant directors.

So it was either that the different nationalities handled their own participants or someone pieced two foreign films together for stateside consumption. The latter seems the most likely since even the film development was handled by two color labs: the Eclair-Paris and Fotofilm of Madrid. It seems unlikely that a united crew would purposely send each half of the picture to a different country in the name of cooperation.

The plot of the complete film tells of a group of Union prisoners during the Civil War who escape in a hot-air balloon. Touching down on a deserted island, they fight a bunch of pirates who are trying to protect some recently buried treasure. Saving the day is Omar Sharif as Captain Nemo, who appears in The Nautilus and disappears in a volcano which destroys the island. The escapees survive the eruption, a hurricane, and a tidal wave, to be picked up by a passing frigate by the end of the picture.

The next undersea adventure up for consideration is *Beyond Atlantis* (1975), a quickie starring Patrick Wayne as Vic, a money-hungry island hopper who discovers a tribe that has descended from Atlantis when hunting for inordinately large pearls. His pals, Logan (John Ashley), East Eddie (Sid Haig), and a beauteous archaeologist, Kathy (Lenore Stevens), match wits with the goggle-eyed tribe's people: the normally eyed elder (George Nader) and his gorgeous daughter Syrene (Leigh Christian).

The landlubbers want the huge pearls the Atlanteans have, and the tribe wants Vic to mate with Syrene to insure the next generation—since the elders always mate with an "outsider." Both get what they want intially, but the jealous Syrene is accidently killed in a fight with Kathy, and the pearl chest is knocked overboard in the crew's haste to escape the island and vengeful residents. So ends another Dimension Pictures Release, helmed by Eddie Romero, who also coproduced with John Ashley.

Several other producers are making their reputations from creating fast, fresh, futuristic phantasmagoricals. Probably the leading American representative is Charles Band, who has given us the aptly titled *End of the World* (1977) and the more-ambitious *Laserblast* (1978) in rapid succession under the production auspices of Irwin Yablans and distribution control of the Manson Corporation.

In the business for more than twenty-five years, Manson is fairly selective about which movies it represents, a policy that is mirrored in the relative quality of Band's science-fantasy films. "Relative" quality because, in both cases, the plotline incorporates the gruesome as well as the fascinatingly effective. In the case of the former title, starring Sue Lyon and Christopher Lee, the gruesome was inherent in the story about an alien race disguising themselves as priests and nuns in order to destroy mankind.

The title, *End of the World*, makes good at the finale, where, on screen, the earth is destroyed from within, blowing pieces of continents and the seas all over outer space. It seemed that mankind's diseases were causing too much intergalactic trouble, so the large-skulled, blugy-eyed, tiny-eared aliens were dispatched to dispatch us, along with such other supporting players as McDonald Carey, Lew Ayers, and Dean Jagger.

CONCEIVED AND SPAWNED IN A WORLD BENEATH THE SEA.

FORGOTTEN BY NATUR

...INVADED B

MODER

MAN

Starring JOHN ASHLEY · PATRICK WAYNE
LEIGH CHRISTIAN and GEORGE NADER as "Nereus"
Screenplay by Charles Johnson • Produced by John Ashley and Eddie Romero • Directed by Eddie Romero
METROCOLOR PG PARENTAL GUIDANCE SUGGESTED A DIMENSION PICTURES RELEASE

Beyond Atlantis.

Even with such an impressive climax, Band outdid himself on the next project, completed in the astonishing length of three weeks, filming on location in California. *Laserblast* begins with two brown-encrusted, pointy-head aliens chasing a tiny-pupiled, green-eyed humanoid across a desert plain. The pursued raises a large weapon but the others shoot first. The victim is zapped into nothingness while the chasers are forced to flee themselves when a plane passes overhead.

Along comes Billy (Kim Milford), a much put-upon

Two model animated aliens appear as exterminators at the opening of *Laserblast* (© Manson Distributing).

youth from a nearby town. He finds the fallen combination of bazooka and rifle as well as a pendant that the dead alien had worn which seems to give the weapon its power. For, as Billy soon discovers, the laser only blasts when the medallion is worn. Unbeknownst to the lad is its equally as destructive side effects. As the teen exercises the new-found power, the pendant begins to become part of him and his complexion starts to turn a shade of blue.

Soon he finds himself unleashing the ray gun on everything in sight, including: his girl friend's granddad (Keenan Wynn), the doctor who tried to help him (Roddy McDowall), various cars, houses, and even a *Star Wars* billboard. The CIA and FBI are called in but to no avail since Billy has slowly become the spitting image of the initial alien victim, "possessed" eyes, sharp, pointy teeth, and blue skin. It takes the reappearance of the

original other-worldly executioners to end his spree of destruction.

This essentially simple plotline, filmed as cheaply as a lot of less-effective efforts, boasted some professional special effects which added immeasurably to the overall quality. Dave Allen, the creator of the actual *Crater Lake Monster*, supplied the animated-model aliens of the opening and climax, working several months in advance of the actual shooting schedule. The unobtrusive makeup designs were worked up by the husband-and-wife team of Steve and Ve Neill. The forehead, cheek, and jaw additions were painstakingly applied for 3½ hours every morning, but Steve proved that he wouldn't have Milford do anything he wouldn't do himself, by portraying the alien who was disintegrated in the opening shots.

Further special effects were handled by Harry Wolman; and the entire thing was controlled by director Andy Gallerani from a script by Franne Schacht and Frank Ray Perilli. Charles Band isn't through with the genre by any means. Turning from these violent visions, he is producing *Fairy Tales* (1979) with the same scriptwriters, Harry Tampa as director, and Irwin Corey and Martha Reeves in the cast.

Many other independent companies could learn a lesson from Band, most notably the makers of *Starship Invasions* (1978), who went through a "trial by title" from as far back as November, 1976. On Thanksgiving of the bicentennial year, it was proudly announced that the Montreal-based Hal Roach Studios had returned to filmmaking for the first time since Lamont Johnson's *The Groundstar Conspiracy* (1972). They were now responsible for what was billed as the most expensive Canadian film ever made, an 1.8-million-dollar science fiction whopper called *Alien Encounter*.

Starring Christopher Lee and Robert Vaughn, the advertisement pictured a pasty-faced, dome-headed alien in the foreground with what was undeniably a classic flying saucer in the background shadows. Soon after, *Variety* ran a full-page ad declaring that principal photography had been completed and the premiere was set for the spring of 1977. Spring came and went and the only new word surfaced on May 11. *Variety* ran a small news item concerning Columbia's injunction against the smaller studio.

Although the Roach representatives felt it was not so, Columbia wanted the film's name changed so there would be no question as to who had the *Alien Encounter* and who had the *Close Encounter*. Following that was another news blackout which lasted two months. Finally, Warner Brothers let it be known they would be handling the distribution of what was now called *War of the Aliens*. Nothing further was heard until another two months had passed and the west coast of the United States was bombarded by a half-million-dollar publicity blitz concerning a movie called *Starship Invasions*.

Slowly but surely, the film made its way east until New York was invaded in the first week of February, 1978. It was hardly worth the wait, unfortunately. Every penny of the $1.8 million showed in the lack of visual accoutrements, from everyday set decoration to the unimaginative

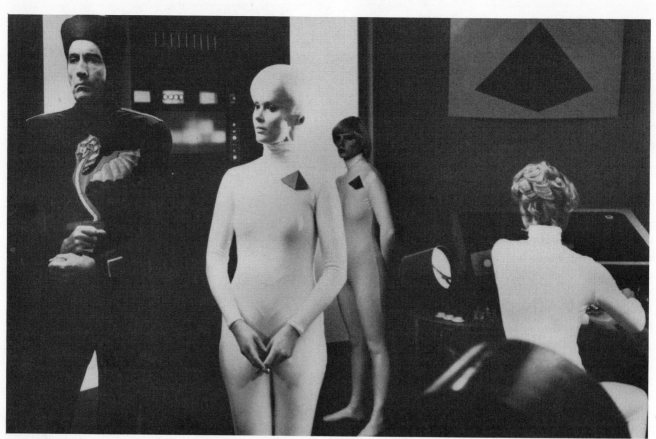

Christopher Lee looks about to utter, "Curses, foiled again" in the company of swell-headed Tiiu Leek during *Starship Invasions* (© Warner Brothers).

98

Robert Vaughn (far right) looks bullets at the photographer who snapped this backset shot of *Starship Invasions*. The flying saucer is actually two tons of inflatable rubber (© Warner Communications).

flying saucers, which usually looked more like pie pans hurled across screen than anything else. The plot concerned a fairly ancient set of overused cliches as well.

Chris Lee was Rameses, the leader of a sleek, blue-garbed pack of aliens in search of a new home— their own planet threatened by an unstable solar system. The so-called "Legion of the Winged Serpent" installs a suicide-inducing satellite in the upper atmosphere and zips over to the Bermuda Triangle where they must deal with the earth's long-time guardians, The League of Races. Composed of dome-headed, white-garbed good guys as well as a variety of nubile young ladies, whose costume budget must have been extremely low, they dwell in an undersea pyramid, protecting and monitoring earth's development.

The lines are drawn and the two groups of aliens go at each other in the Canadian skies. The human military only serves as an unknowing ally to the Winged Serpent, since they shoot down the heroes' spaceship. Anaxi (Daniel Pilon), one of the League's rulers, then finds himself requiring the aid of Professor Allan Duncan (Robert Vaughn, looking woefully tired and overweight), a UFO enthusiast and talk-show host and his friend

Malcolm (Henry Ramer), a computer specialist. With their help, the League's machinery is improved and the good guys win after a few outer-space dogfights reminiscent of the worst of the fifties drive-in fodder.

The general tackiness of the whole affair is difficult to overlook, even with the few interesting technical contributions concerning makeup and special effects. Though it took Maureen Sweeney four hours to install one skull addition to the swell-headed heroes, even in the publicity pictures the plastic additions could be easily discerned. Even though the producers went as far as patenting technical designer Warren Keillor's "Space Machine," its actual use was hampered by the lack of funds until the young special-effects man had to resort to "hacking apart turkey basters and pudding tins to make a whole series of lights to illuminate flying saucers," according to one Canadian newspaper.

Even with an array of shapely females, including the supporting role of Gazeth going to an ex-*Penthouse* magazine subject, Victoria Johnson, their actual use was superfluous, making the Devil's Triangle fight scenes look like first-cut day at the Playboy Mansion. Most responsible for the general lack of good cheer was director/writer/co-producer Ed Hunt, who has yet to be quoted as to his intent or postrelease reaction.

His is not the only laughable science fiction attempt, however. Compared with 20th Century Fox's December 1977 release, *Starship Invasions* seems to be first class. It was reported in the *New York Times* that executive Alan Ladd, Jr., although laudable for insisting that *Star Wars* be produced, thought real success would be garnered by the nine-million-dollar adaptation of Roger Zelazny's *Damnation Alley*. Comparing the two is like comparing caviar to tripe in retrospect.

Damnation Alley is all the more unfortunate since it was put together by a profitable studio with decades of experience. It is a further step back from intelligent fantasy work than the likes of *Starship Invasions*, *The Incredible Melting Man*, and *At the Earth's Core* put together. The basic problem, it turns out, is one that has been haunting Hollywood since year one: a team of producers who care not one whit for the original author's work.

Roger Zelazny, one of the most respected and controversial science fiction authors, wrote the novel on which the film is based in two weeks, and, although it is not considered in the ranks of his *Dream Master* and *Lord of Light*, it was deemed a fast and enjoyable read concerning an ex-Hell's Angel trying to survive in a nightmarish post-holocaust world. Jerome Zeitman and Paul Maslansky were the production team and immediately set about altering the book into more "acceptable family entertainment."

Hell Tanner, Zelazny's lead, became just Tanner (Jan Michael Vincent), a young military man who seems to ride a motorcycle only because it's "cool." Completely new in the film version are Denton (George Peppard, sporting white hair and an annoyingly incongruous black mustache), the "old school" hero figure who believes in discipline; Keegan (Paul Winfield), the "token black" who gets killed early on, taking the only enjoyable performance with him; and Billy (Jackie Earl Haley), the token delinquent who turns angelic because of family affection.

The other remnant of the novel, a female thug Hell picks up in the book becomes the French-accented girl named Janice (Dominique Sanda, unfortunately choosing this as her Hollywood premiere performance) in the movie, an ex-Las Vegas showgirl. Even the basic plot was detrimentally altered. Instead of Hell leading a medical convoy across the nation to plague-ridden New England, we have this team of cliched cuties traveling to Albany, New York for the want of something better to do.

Finally the producers got around to the title. If the first name of Hell had to be dropped, one can be sure they initially thought *Damnation Alley* too strong for the kiddie trade, so the title was originally changed to *Survival Run* and stayed that way until one week before premiere. The 20th Century Fox executives panicked when they saw what the finished film looked like and hastily changed the title back, hoping to attract the dyed-in-the-wool science fiction fans.

What finally appeared in movie theaters made both the studio and the filmmakers look ridiculous after all the talk about scientific accuracy and the wonderful new technological advance of "Sound 360," a technique that supposedly put the audience "inside" the action. Fox's answer to Universal's "Sensurround" was actually no more than eight-track stereo that was far from effective, and the "reality" of the situation was lost in the first five minutes of the Lukas Heller (surprising the producers didn't change his name as well) and Alan Sharp-adapted, Jack Smight-directed film. We are supposed to believe that Murray Hamilton (who speaks a total of one line in this film after editing), Peppard, and especially the rosy-cheeked Vincent, are in charge of deploying nuclear retaliation on a foreign attack.

The desert installation's war board shows at least thirty-five to fifty hits on the United States, after which we find Hamilton drinking himself to death, Peppard building something in the shop, Winfield acting as a guard, and Vincent racing around on his bike almost two years later, after the explosions have pushed the earth off its axis. Every awful ploy utilized in this scene is an obvious warning as to the travesty this film would degenerate into.

Vincent has a girl on the back of his motorcycle. Winfield even looks at her through binoculars. But when "giant" scorpions attack (obvious unmoving scale models combined with poorly processed photography to the point you can see through the insects in several instances), he drops her off his cycle for speed. It is then that Winfield notes that the girl was "really" a dummy all along. Ho, ho, ho, what a joke on him.

What stands in for action and irony here are cheap special effects and what amounts to an audience cheat. It was obvious that it was a female stuntperson riding with Vincent, so when the manikin is uncovered in close-up, all reality is shuttled. This is only the beginning. Constantly obvious shortcuts are employed to the audience's immediate recognition until a tangible aura of frustration is created. When the "Land Master" is revealed—a combination tank and Winnebago (a $300,000 construction job under the supervision of stunt coordinator Dean Jeffries)—the script calls for its exact

A *Damnation Alley* poster from Japan, where the film made most of its money. Well, there's no accounting for taste (© 20th Century Fox).

copy to follow, since Denton had supposedly built two. Instead, the filmmakers chose to use the same piece of film over again in place of shooting the unveiling sequence a second time.

They compounded this oversight by never showing the two vehicles together except in one obvious process shot. When giant flesh-eating cockroaches attack, again the scenes are so poorly composed that it becomes obvious that most of the creatures are models pasted on rugs which are pulled across the floor with ropes, leaving the way open for the single funniest line of the picture. Peppard gets on his C.B. and announces, "The town's infested with killer cockroaches!"

When a new island is created out at sea, the world is pushed back on its axis and a tidal wave is also created, smashing down on the Land Master amid the wreckage of an auto junkyard. In the next shot, however, the only vehicle shown under water is another obvious model of the heroes' transportation. The final straw and worst offense comes at the end. After enough explosive force and radioactive waste has been employed to wipe the world clean twenty times over, the sky suddenly turns blue, the water becomes clean, the air is clear, the grass is green, and trees are growing.

Just in time for a happy ending the troupe finds a pleasant community of paved roads, telephone poles, calmly grazing horses, and well-mannered, well-dressed citizens. If any of the audience had become an onscreen character, they would have figured they had just entered "The Twilight Zone."

The secret word for the entire endeavor was "obvious failure," since the film couldn't measure up even for those who aren't fantasy enthusiasts. It is a perfect example of this chapter's initial thesis that if science fiction is well conceived, it's successful; if stupid, it's fantasy. *Damnation Alley* was relegated to the ranks of such other acknowledged disasters as *The Ultimate Warrior* (1975) and *Who?* (1975).

Who?, released in the summer of 1975 but finished a year earlier, had a lot in common with *Survival Run*. Based on a novel by Algis Budrys, the Allied Artists production was somewhat shuttled during production by unimpressive writing and direction by John Gould and Jack Gold, respectively, and an uncooperative distributing staff, who did not see the film premiere in New York. *Who?* joined the ranks of many "lost" movies which were never even bought for television.

If it ever reaches the tube, a few million might get to see the espionage adventure concerning an FBI agent named Robers (Elliott Gould) assigned to discover the actual identity of an android delivered to America by East Germany after one of our top scientists was whisked away after a car accident. Now the United States has to find out if the metallized man is really the scientist or a dupe cleverly programmed by enemy agent Azarin (Trevor Howard).

The Ultimate Warrior went the same way of *Who?* and had some passing similarities to *Damnation Alley* as well. Also rarely shown, never televised, and set in post-holocaust America, this was an actioner, written, directed, and produced by Robert Clouse, starring Yul Brynner as an unnamed adventurer who enters a feud between two rival gangs after a series of plagues wipe out most of mankind.

Brynner sides up with a group run by Max Von Sydow in order to take Joanna Miles and an unmutated package of seeds through the destroyed subway system to "freedom." Along the way, he gets to kill dozens of people just to make the trip interesting. Another thing these generally unreleased films have in common is that they are not very good.

The same can be said for *Welcome to Blood City* (1977). The pair who brought the world *To The Devil, A Daughter* (1975)—director Peter Sasdy and writer Michael Winder—brought this British-Canadian co-production to the fore, utilizing American, English, and Canadian actors. An uneasy combination of *Westworld* (1973) and *The Ultimate Warrior*, it concerned Lewis (Keir Dullea), kidnapped by a fascist organization and mentally transported to "Blood City," where murder is a mark of social status.

Here, Sheriff Frendlander (Jack Palance) is immortal because of his twenty kills. As Lewis makes his gory way through the everyday life in his mind, his body is monitored by Katherine (Samantha Eggar), and the entire cerebral city is controlled by the Supervisor (Barry Morse). Soon, it becomes clear that all this razzle-dazzle is actually a recruitment test for the "Kill Master" plan, in which agents murder prominent political and military targets.

Lewis finds the world within his brain far more entertaining than reality, and the finale finds him back in Blood City without the audience knowing anything about the workings of Kill Master, how they got the brain machine, how the brain machine works, how Samantha Eggar can be in both places at once, etc. Many critics suggested that several minutes of its ninety-eight minute running time be chopped in order to fit in a television-time slot, since the technical credits aren't much better than video quality.

Rife with shortcomings, peppered with inconsistencies, and loaded with faults, the previous five films could learn some lessons from the official sequel to *Westworld*, American-International's *Futureworld* (1976). Although it too is loaded with action and special effects, the script and direction were mounted in such a way that the cast of talented actors had distinct characterizations and followed a logical progression.

Richard T. Heffron directed the script by Mayo Simon and George Schenck in order to create a largely entertaining adventure. No *2001* certainly, but it wasn't trying to be. It opens where *Westworld* left off, after a black day at the adult amusement park of Delos when all the individually programmed robots made a break for freedom by killing every human in the area except reporter Chuck Browning.

Played by Richard Benjamin in the original, he managed to defeat a robot gunfighter, played by Yul Brynner, and escaped alive. Some time later, Delos is reopened after a complete renovation and a huge publicity campaign to assure pleasure seekers that the hugh place was truly safe. Back too is Browning, this time portrayed by Peter Fonda and accompanied by a female partner, the spry, tough-minded Tracy Ballard (Blythe Danner).

Naturally, Chuck is far from satisfied when it comes to the reassurances of Duffy (Arthur Hill), the Delos mouthpiece who is assigned to show the reporters around. They are presented wonder after wonder in the four sections of the Disney-like establishment, but it is in Futureworld (actually filmed at the Houston Manned Space Center) where things start going awry.

There the pair discover that the park's technicians are also robots and an entire mechanical hierarchy has been set up under the direction of the white-haired, sharply featured scientist Schneider (John Ryan). They also find an ally in the black-bearded Harry (Stuart Margolin) a southern technician whose insider's knowledge is invaluable in fighting the real threat of Delos.

Interestingly enough, while *Westworld* was essentially a straight-forward fantasy more interested in playing on the audience's doubts about computers than developing logical explanations for what was pictured, it was up to *Futureworld* to make coherent sense out of both movies. Why should robots programmed for service suddenly kill? Only one logical reason: they were actually programmed to kill. *Futureworld* tells us flat out that murder was part of the original plan, but, because of a technical problem, the killings started too early.

The actual plan is to take over the world by murdering prominent, vacationing officials and replacing them with exact android duplicates. The same fate seems about to befall Browning and Ballard until, with the help of Harry, they manage to face off with their mechanical doubles after blasting Duffy, who turned out to be an android himself. Tracy and her double set up for a shoot-out in a left-over Westworld area. Chuck and his double battle to the top of a Futureworld rocket gantry. A shot rings out and one girl falls. A scuffle ensues and one man drops to his death.

The last day of the reporters' visit is the next morning. Schneider beams down proudly at what he thinks are the first of his bionic replacements as they prepare to leave. His composure is shattered when the sputtering mechanical duplicate of Tracy stumbles in and the supposedly robotic Chuck turns from the exit and gives the scientist a universally understood hand gesture. The newspaper people quickly leave the amusement park with flesh-and-blood authorities already closing in.

Here was a colorful, fast, bright, and satisfying film made with professional snap thanks considerably to the efforts of producers Paul N. Lazarus III and James T. Aubrey. Lazarus returned to the genre two years later with another exciting adventure that should have been straight science fiction, except for one morally vacuous point. It labeled NASA capable of murdering its own astronauts as a fund-raising ploy.

This horrid concept was the basis for *Capricorn One* (1978), an I.T.C. production, written and directed by Peter Hyams. Other than the incredibly detrimental central theme, the movie plays remarkably well. Astronauts Willis (Sam Waterston), Walker (O.J. Simpson), and Brubaker (James Brolin) are stopped practically at the lift-off of a Mars landing mission by the head of the manned space program, Dr. Kelloway (Hal Holbrook). It seems as if there's a fault in the life-support system, but the project can't be scrubbed because of governmental and budgetary pressures, so the decision is made to fake it.

The three hapless astronauts are brought to a desert studio and are blackmailed into going through the motions for the television audience, until the nationally televised mock-up of their reentry shows the capsule's heat shield popping off and the vehicle disintegrating. A sinking feeling suddenly comes over the group. If they are supposed to be dead, what plans do the men behind the hoax have for them? They don't wait to find out. Absconding with a private jet, they crash-land in the desert and set out to escape.

Meanwhile, a sharpie in Mission Control discovers that the signals that should have been coming from Mars were originating nearer than 1,000 miles away, and he tells this to investigative reporter Robert Caulfield (Elliott Gould). Because of his subsequent investigation,

These three intrepid astronauts are in for the nightmare of their lifetimes once they step aboard the aborted Mars spacecraft known as Capricorn One. Left to right: Sam Waterson, James Brolin, and O. J. Simpson.

government enforcers cause him to lose his job, ruin his reputation, and almost take his life. Finally, the unemployed, unkempt reporter gets a clue to the astronauts' position from the last phone conversation Brubaker had with his wife (Brenda Vaccaro). He hightails it over to the Midwest, where both Willis and Walker have been located and eliminated.

With the help of a wildly eccentric cropduster named Albain (Telly Savalas), Caulfield rescues Brubaker in a biplane with two rocket-powered helicopters on his tail. There follows a wild ride, which stunt coordinator Frank Tallman called one of the most dangerous and complicated aerial chases ever planned. The makeup people made life masks of Brolin, Gould, and Savalas to fit on the stunt flyers, so the action would be realistic, and audiences loved it, making *Capricorn One* the surprise world-wide "sleeper" hit of the year.

One distributor called it the most exciting movie he had ever seen. Happily, the cropduster drops its payload

of insecticide at an opportune moment, blinding the helicopters so that they crash. Brubaker is reunited with his wife during his burial ceremony at Arlington. Again, beyond the fact that the premise is damnable and the lesson of history—in that the real-life deaths of Apollo One's astronauts almost scuttled NASA rather than strengthened it—Hyams brought much quality and style to the proceedings.

Unfortunately, producer Lazarus's subsequent actions have done much to throw the integrity of the finished film in doubt. The prerelease publicity highlighted NASA's supposed cooperation in the making of the movie to the tune of unlimited technical assistance and 500,000 dollars worth of hardware. Information from the space agency shows that report to be false. The kind of hoax supposedly perpetrated by NASA in the film is being mirrored on a smaller scale by the filmmakers in reality.

No hoax was involved with *Embryo* (1976), a modern horror story written by Anita Doohan and Jack W.

Beauty Barbara Carrera brings out the beast in most
men, but this is ridiculous! From *The Island of Dr. Moreau*
with love (© A.I.P.).

Thomas, and directed by Ralph Nelson. Nelson, an able director who began his career with *Requiem for a Heavyweight* (1962) and *Lilies of the Field* (1963), has trod this ground before with *Charlie* (1968), and had much better results. Here, instead of a lyrical, affecting science-fiction tale of an operation that makes a retarded man into a temporary genius, he helms an out-and-out shock extravaganza wherein Dr. Paul Holliston (Rock Hudson) invents a rapid-growth hormone and uses it to develop a premature fetus into the ravishingly beautiful Victoria (Barbara Carrera).

Unfortunately, she has not developed mentally along with her body, so the doctor tries to shape her in the "proper" image only to open the way for medical and emotional horror. As the hormone begins to speed up, Victoria must pit her genius against time to save herself. Her solution includes having to get another premature fetus, while the only one available is in Holliston's pregnant daughter-in-law. Naturally, things do not turn out tremendously.

Although this production is filled with exceptional technical credits—music by Gil Melle, art direction by Joe Alves, makeup by Dan Striepeke and John Chambers, photography by Fred Koenkamp; and supporting performances by Roddy McDowall and Diane Ladd—the film does not deliver on its horrific premise, lingering on less-than-vital character interludes instead of socking the story home.

Carrera and makeup men Chambers and Striepeke were reunited, with far better results, a year later when American-International released the six-million-dollar remake of *The Island of Lost Souls* (32), now named for the original H.G. Wells novel *The Island of Dr. Moreau* (1977). Far from being a Bert I. Gordon rip-off, however, this is one of AIP's new high-quality genre productions which began, essentially, with *Futureworld* and will continue through the coming years with the likes of *Force Ten from Navarone*, *Avalanche Express*, and *Meteor*. This time out, though, producer Sandy Howard and Samuel Z. Arkoff took director Don Taylor; actors Burt Lancaster, Michael York, Nigel Davenport, Richard Basehart, and dozens of caged animals and deposited them on St. Croix in the Virgin Islands to film the engrossing little shocker about a nineteenth-century man who uses twenty-first-century knowledge incorrectly.

It tells the tale of Dr. Moreau (Lancaster), who saves the life of a young seaman named Andrew Braddock (York) only to use him in bizarre experiments on evolution. It seems that the sometimes patiently kind, sometimes violently egomaniacal doctor has developed a means to humanize animals, but only for a short period of time. His work in civilized lands led to misunderstandings, then hate, and finally exile, while his ongoing tests lead to confusion, pain, and death.

Braddock falls in love with Moreau's consort, Maria (Carrera), but is pegged as the doctor's ultimate experiment. If he can turn a human bestial, perhaps it will lead him to discover how to keep a beast human. The young sailor is waylaid, worked on, and caged, but manages to retain his humanity by remembering his childhood. The half-human animals take this moment to finally revolt against Moreau's iron rule by tearing him to shreds, then attacking the compound.

Braddock escapes with his love and both are rescued by a passing ship. At least that's the way it finally appeared in theaters. Originally, two other endings were filmed: one in which Maria is discovered to be one of Moreau's successful tests, and begins to revert back into a black panther; and another where the girl, pregnant, gives birth to a tiger kitten. The former was considered too depressing and the latter too ludicrous in the long run, so the movie ends on a seemingly rushed, haphazard note.

The artistic and technical prowess was far from

Michael York and one of the many "humanimals" get a directional hand from Don Taylor during the last fight in *The Island of Doctor Moreau* (© A.I.P.).

rushed, however. A major plus, beside the lush photography and location, were the performances by the two male leads. Lancaster is marvelous as the complicated scientist, on the one hand a civilized man hoping to further progress, on the other a sadistic teacher who sees himself as a god. York worked very hard to bring his character to life during the innocent-caught-in-strange-circumstances scenes but really shone in the aforementioned sequence where he tells a story about winter sledding in order to recall his humanity.

The real star of the production, however, was Chambers and Striepeke's makeup, which turned the likes of Basehart, Gary Baxley, David Cass and the Great John L. into a boar-man, bear-man, lion-man, bull-man, hyena-man, and many other less-distinct animal types. The designs were wonderfully realized, so much so that AIP decided to patent them under the title of "humanimals." The makeup applied to the actors consisted of foam latex pieces with a newly developed adhesive to make them heat and water resistant. The rest of their bodies were human combined with fur-cloth hair. These constructions really took a beating in the constant battles with real animals, including a central fight between the bull-man and a bengal tiger and the exciting finale where everything and everyone goes wild!

Things get pretty crazy during the course of the ten-million-dollar *Meteor* (1978) as well, scheduled for release in the Christmas season. AIP teamed up with Warner Brothers and the production team of Arnold Orgolini and Ted Parvin to get this show into production, garnering enough money to hire the top-flight director Ronald Neame and a star-studded cast including Sean Connery, Natalie Wood, Henry Fonda, Karl Malden, Trevor Howard, Donald Pleasence, Joseph Campanella, and Brian Keith.

Filmed in Los Angeles, New York, Germany, Tokyo, and Italy, the movie concerns, not surprisingly, a larger-than-usual meteor on a collision course with earth. This causes, also not surprisingly, a lot of trouble even before it gets close to hitting us. The stars battle earthquakes, tidal waves, fires and other natural disasters, all while trying to figure out how to avoid certain death, making this the ultimate disaster picture. Kind of a "Towering Poseidon Earthquake."

For a real disaster, audiences should look no farther than *Doc Savage: The Man of Bronze* (1975), if they could find it. Here was what fans hoped would be the first great American hero of the seventies. As soon as the news broke that George Pal would be the one to bring the famous adventurer out of the pulp pages and onto the screen, high expectations were raised. Both Doc and Mr.

Pal had admirable reputations and warranted such preproduction excitement.

Clark Savage Jr., AKA "Doc," was introduced to the nation in 1933, when Kenneth Robeson wrote the first of 181 Doc Savage adventures, creating a huge, muscular, brainy individual of bronze skin and golden eyes, dedicated to fight evil wherever he found it. The creators of Superman publicly acknowledge that the man of steel was based on the man of bronze. Indeed, Doc celebrated his forty-fifth anniversary, bringing wonder to the masses in March, 1978, while Clark Kent waited until the summer of 1978 to become forty. Almost bi-monthly since 1963, Bantam paperbacks have been republishing Savage's exploits, sometimes going into more than a dozen printings in order to supply his ever-growing number of fans.

The renowned George Pal, in the meantime, waited until seven years after Doc's initial appearance to make his way to Hollywood, producing a series of inventive "puppetoons," three-dimensional animations, for which he won a special Oscar. Following that, he began producing spectacular movies that would establish him as one of the primary creators of quality cinematic science fiction. *Destination Moon* (1950) was followed by *When Worlds Collide* (1951), then *War of the Worlds* (1953). *The Time Machine* appeared in 1961, while some of his more fanciful work included *Atlantis, the Lost Continent* (1960), *The Wonderful World of the Brothers Grimm* (1962), and *The Seven Faces of Dr. Lao* (1964). It seemed a gift of destiny that he and Doc would be united to thrill moviegoers.

Production information was anxiously awaited and eagerly distributed. First the news was that Pal and Joe Morhaim had written the script and that Michael Anderson, the Englishman who directed *Around the World in Eighty Days* (1956), *Shake Hands with the Devil* (1959), and *The Quiller Memorandum* (1966), was set to direct. But what the fans really wanted to know was who would play their hero? What actor could possibly fill the almost legendary boots of Doc Savage?

The answer came in the form of six-foot-four, two-hundred-and-ten-pound Ron Ely. His only other remembered role was that of television's "Tarzan", but Ely was nothing short of magnificent in this new larger-than-life role.

Everyone was extremely enthusiastic about the project at first. Casting went smoothly, garnering a wealth of solid acting talent from the theatrical world to play Doc's associates, the "Fabulous Five," and his initial nemesis, Dr. Seas—a bearded villain changed from the original novel's antagonist, Morning Breeze, a Mayan witch

Darrel Zwerling, Mike Minor, Eldon Quick, Paul Gleason, Ron Ely and William Lucking gather to discuss a Mayan threat in the beginning of *Doc Savage: The Man of Bronze* **(© Warner Bros.).**

doctor. Eldon Quick played William Harper Littlejohn, "Johnny," the geology and archeology expert. William Lucking portrayed Colonel John Renwick, "Renny," the engineer. Mike Miller was given the plum role of Lieutenant Colonel Andrew Blodgett Mayfair, "Monk," who's described as "only a few inches over five feet and yet over 260 pounds." Paul Gleason was pegged as Major Thomas J. Roberts, or "Long Tom," the electrical wizard. And Darrell Zwerling, late of *Chinatown* and *Capricorn One*, was Brigadier General Theodore Marley Brooks, or "Ham" the lawyer. A supporting actor, Paul Wexler, was elevated to become the major villain, Captain Seas, and the cast was filled out beautifully by Robyn Hilton as Sea's blond moll and Pamela Hensley as a native South American lovely.

Filming went well and the production received fine publicity. George Pal's optimism ran high to the point where he was quoted as saying, "I'm sure we're going to make several Doc Savage pictures. After the first one is successful we'll make another one, and then we'll sell the series to television." Already two sequals had been planned—*Doc Savage: Arch-Enemy of Evil* and *Doc Savage in Atlantis Country*. Pal even went as far as putting several minutes of the next adventure at the end of *The Man of Bronze* and having the words, "Watch for the next thrilling adventure of Doc Savage," blaze across the screen.

Warner Brothers reacted to Pal's enthusiasm by creating merchandising plans that started with postcards, bumper stickers, posters, buttons, and statues. Wall-sized displays popped up in California, and full-page ads were taken out in trade papers declaring: "His body . . . a physical phenomenon. His mind . . . a mental marvel. His fight . . . to right all wrongs. His name . . . enough to strike terror into the hearts of the most-hardened criminals!"

However, when the executives saw the movie, the doubts began. Immediately, more than twenty-five national sneak previews were arranged, and the audience reaction confirmed the studio's fears. *Doc Savage: The Man of Bronze* was hastily pulled from national distribution. Only a few dedicated fans fast enough and willing to travel to less-populated areas managed to see the film when it first came out.

Since that time, it has played on cable television and was televised twice on NBC, each time hastily edited to fit in a two-hour time slot. George Pal's dream of introducing a "real hero" was dashed. His Savage movie turned out sadly camp and slow, marred by static direction and an uncomfortable plot. Only in two spots did the Savage magic take hold. The postcredit sequence of an assassination attempt and subsequent chase was wonderfully realized with grand special effects and Ely's strong presence. The shipboard fight scene, which comprises the center of the movie, is well structured and dazzlingly performed, again especially by Ely, whose mastery of the oriental arts as well as good-old American fisticuffs is thunderously satisfying.

By and large, the other members of the cast are satisfactory but are continually undercut by direction that has them simply delivering lines to each other in static two shots or close-ups. The basic, and fatal, flaw of the production seems to be its confusing plot and premise. Very little is portrayed realistically in the period recreation; supporting players are ill-defined and given arbitrary characteristics—like a henchman who sleeps in a giant crib for no reason at all—and Seas never develops into a promising threat.

The climax is disappointing at best, nonexistent at worst. The two main antagonists face off for a series of bouts using international fighting techniques, actually labeled at the bottom of the screen. A cute idea on paper becomes frustrating to viewers who want serious action and adventure. These coy techniques only serve to diminish Doc Savage's heroic stature, as if the filmmakers are making fun of him, a thought his many fans could not stand!

However, *Superman* (1978) fared much better in the hands of producers Ilya Salkind and Pierre Spengler, an international team responsible for the success of the light-hearted *The Three Musketeers* (1973), *The Four Musketeers* (1974), and *Crossed Swords* (1978). There should be little doubt of its success given the quality of the production crew and the size of the budget, reported nearing the fifty-million-dollar mark.

It all started almost five years ago when Ilya, then twenty-nine-years old, was having a meal with his father,

Christopher Reeve strikes a familiar pose across the New York skyline. It's a bird, it's a plane, it's *Superman* (© Warner Brothers)!

Alexander, the European film producer. They were trying to figure out a suitable follow-up to the Musketeer movies, when Ilya remembered the comic books he loved so much as a child. Now there was a thrilling concept—the first big-budget recreation of an actual American legend. Alexander, having rarely left Europe, never heard of the Man of Steel. But after a little talk, he gave his blessing. *Superman* was going to be made, and it was going to be made big!

So the younger Salkind started mounting the production and immediately ran into difficulties. Every writer he approached seemed to be rendered ineffective by the size and scope of the project. Major and minor authors gave up in the face of Superman's legacy. Finally help came from an unexpected source. Mario Puzo, the author of *The Godfather,* decided to tackle the superhero head-on, pounding out a one-hundred-and-fifty-page-plus "bible" on the way the film should go. He took the four or five retellings of the Superman legend from the comics and television, opened them up, aired them out, and put together a new story like a jigsaw puzzle. He made psychological sense out of a lot of original inconsistencies.

The primary one is described by Salkind in an interview. "What is the motivation? What is the mission? He's the ultimate good guy, he'll help anybody, right? Even Batman has a good reason which Superman doesn't have at all. Superman's just there."

Puzo gave him a reason to be on earth, as well as elaborating on many other humanistic details to the point that the Smallville section—the scenes showing Superman growing up—has become the heart of the new film according to many involved. But that was all Puzo could do. Once he established the framework, he found himself unable to flesh out the screenplay.

For that, the literary talents of David Newman, Leslie Newman, and Robert Benton were used. These three, apart and together, were responsible for the creation of *Bonnie and Clyde* (1967), *Bad Company* (1972), and *The Late Show* (1977). They, with a little after-the-fact consultation by Tom Mankiewicz, put the final touches on a huge shooting script which was to become *Super-*

Marlon Brando as Jor-el—the "S" is his Kryptonian seal, the one that his son naturally assumes on Earth—prepares to relegate villains Zod, Non, and Ursa (Terence Stamp, Jack O'Halloran, and Sarah Douglas) to the Forbidden Zone at the opening of *Superman* (© Warner Brothers).

110

man, parts one and two. Salkind and Spengler were planning to produce, essentially, one four-hour picture that would be separated and shown one year from each other—the same thing they did with the *Musketeers*. However, the best laid plans . . . but more on that later.

Rights were secured and the casting process began. In order to get sufficient monetary backing, Salkind knew he had to get big thespian names, so the search was on for a star lead. After checking out Burt Reynolds, Robert Redford, Sylvester Stallone, and Bruce Jenner, Ilya changed his tactics. He decided to surround the Man of Steel with stars but get a capable unknown for the major role, thereby insuring quality.

Everyone now feels that an established star as Superman would have guaranteed artistic disaster. The first to sign up was Marlon Brando, attracted by a major role requiring only three weeks of work and a salary of two-million dollars. This price tag was well worth it,

since it was Brando's presence that got the production ball rolling. In rapid succession, other acting greats were secured to flesh out the comic characters.

Gene Hackman becomes Lex Luthor, the ultimate villain; Valerie Perrine is Eve, Luthor's moll; Susannah York is Lara, Superman's Kryptonian mother; Brando is Jor-el, his father; Terence Stamp, Sarah Douglas, and Jack O'Halloran become three Kryptonian villains— Zod, Ursa, and Non; Glenn Ford is Pa Kent; Trevor Howard and Harry Andrews become elders of Krypton; Jackie Cooper is Perry White; Marc McClure is Jimmy Olsen, and E. G. Marshall becomes the President of the United States. Originally, Peter Boyle was cast as Luthor's henchman, but previous committments kept them from recreating some of the acting magic they displayed in *Young Frankenstein* (1975), so Ned Beatty was called in to play the small-time mobster Otis.

Slowly but surely, the casting continued for the pivotal

Director of Photography Geoffrey Unsworth intends to capture every nuance of Krypton's destruction in this backset shot from *Superman* (© Warner Brothers).

roles of Lois Lane and Clark Kent, not to mention his mighty alter ego. After the hundreds of young ladies were narrowed down to seven, Margot Kidder was finally chosen for the important role. As for Superman, a 6'4" television and stage actor named Christopher Reeve was picked for his talent and ability. Any uncomfortable similarity between the young man and the television Superman, George Reeves, stops at their names.

Chris makes a svelte, cleft-chinned, younger man of steel and has the unenviable job of bringing to life a three-dimensional humanoid alien capable of controlling unlimited power for the first time. There is no running and jumping into the sky in this incarnation. When the new Superman wants to fly he just takes off, straight up like a shot.

And speaking of flying, Salkind and Spengler had to collect quite an array of behind-the-scenes talent who could create incredible wonders for the man to do and us to believe. Initially, Guy Hamilton was set to direct, a bit of news that shocked superhero fans. Many considered the English director responsible for cheapening the James Bond character in recent years, an allegation we shall examine shortly, but their minds were put at rest when Hamilton was forced to back out of the production because of tax problems.

The two young producers then contacted everyone from Coppola to Spielberg to take over the reigns, but it was American Richard Donner, whose one claim to feature fame came from *The Omen*, who got the nod. Along with him came Stuart Baird, the editor who also did the honors on *The Omen;* Geoffrey Unsworth, a forty-seven-year veteran with titles like *2001, Cabaret* (1972), and *Murder on the Orient Express* (1974) to his credit, became the director of photography.

The never-stopping John Barry became the production designer, after achieving notoriety from *A Clockwork Orange* (1971) and *Star Wars* (1977). He chose a futuristic, gem-studded concept for the overall design of Krypton and the Fortress of Solitude, using a large picture book on minerals as his guide. Then came the special-effects people, a five-team crew sometimes numbering over 600. Flying effects were controlled by Wally Veevers and Dennys Coop. Mechanical effects were produced by Colin Chilvers, who threw things around for *The Legend of Hell House* (1973) and *The Rocky Horror Picture Show* (1974).

Les Bowie and Derek Meddings handled the model work; Roy Field took on the optical effects, the same as he had on three of the James Bond pictures and so many others he has lost count; and John Richardson devised the action effects, like explosions and a subtly difficult

When Gene Hackman as Lex Luthor points, director Richard Donner usually looks. The arch-enemy of *Superman* is not to be ignored (© Warner Brothers).

race with a train, using the experience he had garnered on *Straw Dogs* (1972), *Rollerball, A Bridge Too Far* (1977) and others.

Stuart Freeborn was called in for makeup effects, installing Gene Hackman's bald cap, Jack O'Halloran's beard, and producing exact-double dummies of the major stars for the various special effects teams. Soon, the whole shebang got so massive that the production duo felt the need to bring in director Richard Lester as a third producer, in charge of coordinating the various crews.

The first film pictures Krypton's destruction and Superman's arrival on this planet; his growth in Smallville, and his moving to Metropolis; his meeting and subsequential love affair with Lois Lane; his secret identity and his Antarctic Fortress of Solitude; and, finally, his confrontation and battle with arch-enemy Lex Luthor.

The second movie details what happens when Lex manages to free three superpowered criminals from the Forbidden Zone. The crew shot in New York at the height of the 1977 heat wave, moved up to Calgary, Canada which served as Kansas, then traveled over to Pinewood Studios in Iver Heath, England in order to finish the interiors and complete the myriad special effects. And what interiors, what special effects! Constantly Superman is talking to his father beyond the grave, Jor-el's face appearing in the Arctic sky. The Fortress of Solitude is a gigantic set of ice crystals which rise out of the north Atlantic seas. Lex Luthor's lair is a subterranean train station, and, in the course of the picture, the Man of Steel catches a 747, stops an earthquake, flies around the world in ninety seconds, saves the Golden Gate Bridge, gets batted through a skyscraper, and prevents a worldwide catastrophe.

Naturally, such an audacious and complicated movie deserves as much time as needed to insure high quality, but originally the producers and Warner Brothers, the home studio, decided the premiere should coincide with the comic Superman's fortieth anniversary, so release was set for June of 1978. The filmmakers' deadline was March!

Not surprisingly, word came in late January of that year that the special effects would probably not be completed in time, so the production postponed its public appearance until December of 1978, a fact that disappointed theater owners who had already scheduled the major blockbuster. But the delay heartened others, who appreciated the crew's dedication to the final

product, a quality that was missing on *King Kong*, *Logan's Run*, and other so-called "motion picture events." Salkind and Donner, who had been with the project for so long, were not going to let it out of their hands until they knew it was the best it could be.

It finally opened on December 10, 1978, and reaction was immediate and overwhelming!

Such an anticipated and expensive project was just part of a cycle. A cycle starting with *Star Wars* and continuing with new productions, all announced shortly after the space fantasy's success, and *Superman*'s shooting schedule started. Milton Subotsky, the ex-cohead of American International was reportedly frustrated by his inability to mount productions of his personal favorites, so he moved to England and opened Sword and Sorcery Productions, Ltd., which initially

Director Richard Donner prepares Marc McClure (Jimmy Olsen), Jackie Cooper (Perry White), Margot Kidder (Lois Lane), and Christopher Reeve (Clark Kent) for a New York –based scene of *Superman* (© Warner Brothers).

went after the *Conan* books. Ed Pressman, an American producer, secured those, but Subotsky retaliated by optioning Lin Carter's series of *Thongor the Barbarian* paperback novels.

Thongor, like Conan, is a mightily muscled, lusty, and able barbarian, wont to come up against a great variety of sorcerers and monsters. But Subotsky, unlike Pressman, is having major difficulty getting his project off the ground. All that is known presently is that he is considering Dave Prowse for the lead, that noted model animator Tony McVey has made three, winged "Lizard-Hawks," and actual model animation will be under the direction of Barny Leith, a veteran of British television.

Stateside, Pressman has assigned muscleman Arnold Swarzenegger at least five Conan pictures, the first of which has already been written by Roy Thomas, a Marvel Comics editor, and Ed Summer, the film's coproducer. At last report, John Milius was the front running director, but nothing is certain at this writing. Meanwhile Dino De Laurentiis knows a good thing when he sees it, so his money spoke louder than words when he secured the movie rights to refilm the adventures of Flash Gordon in conjunction with an animated television feature being prepared by Filmation, Inc. Absolutely nothing else has been finalized except the projected budget—$20,000,000—and a list of possible screenwriters, directors, and stars.

All of these producers: Pal, Salkind, DeLaurentiis, and Subotsky, have been quoted as saying they consider their respective creations to become going concerns. That is, characters capable of returning in sequel after sequel, until they become full-scale series. And the character they always seem to mention in comparison, the success they always aspire to, is the James Bond series.

Starting with *Dr. No* (1962), a movie costing less than one million dollars and starring an unknown named Sean Connery, over the next four years, the brainchild of novel writer Ian Fleming and producers Harry Saltzman and Albert Broccoli, became a powerful cinematic force. Through *From Russia With Love* (1963), *Goldfinger* (1964), then *Thunderball* (1965), the series concerning the British secret agent with a license to kill got bigger and bigger, snowballing its box-office success with incredible merchandising returns until, by 1967, there was 007 toys, books, posters, pens, clothes, beer, and cologne.

Songs were written about him—"Double O Soul"—TV shows tried to emulate him—"The Man From U.N.C.L.E."—and other moviemakers tried to steal a bit of his thunder—James Coburn as Derek Flint and Dean Martin as Matt Helm. But no one seemed to be able to copy his exacting brand of sex appeal, humor, flash, and daring. By the time *Thunderball* premiered, Sean Connery *was* James Bond and the 007 phenomenon was reaching its peak.

Then something happened. Something extremely subtle but telling in the thrust of the Bond films from then on. The fourth 007 opus concerned evil Ernst Blofeld's organization, Spectre, stealing two atom bombs in order to blackmail the world. In January, 1966, less than one month after its premiere, two atomic bombs were actually lost off the Spanish coast. Reality had finally caught up with James Bond. Up until then, although filled with thrilling action, outlandish sets, and insidious plots, the criminal doings were in the range of possibility.

Dr. No tampered with early space launches. Erna Klebb and Red Grant of *From Russia With Love* wanted a code device. And *Goldfinger* hoped to plunder Fort Knox. All earthbound, all within the realm of reality. The next Bond film following *Thunderball* was *You Only Live Twice* (1967), wherein space capsules were swallowed by a larger craft and the villain's headquarters were in a dry volcano. In the course of the story, Bond pilots a

The heartily manly scot, Sean Connery as James Bond (*Diamonds Are Forever*—© United Artists), versus. . .

114

mini-copter outfitted with machine guns, bombs, and heat-seeking missiles; and climbs down the side of the bad guys' headquarters using suction cups. It was all fairly action-filled and colorful fun. But not, by any stretch of the imagination, realistic. Bond had taken his first full-fledged step out of espionage adventure into action fantasy.

The following year saw Connery leaving the series to prove his worth as an actor and an Australian named George Lazenby replacing him for *On Her Majesty's Secret Service* (1969). Lazenby, an ex–car salesman and model, was unsatisfactory in the acting and presence department, although his action scenes are probably the most thrilling of any Bond picture, thanks to the direction of Peter Hunt, the original editor of the previous five 007's.

Hunt also opted for a more realistic approach to the movie, eliminating all the gimmicky trappings for a straight and strong story line. Unfortunately, too many were turned off by Lazenby and an unwanted serious romance interest, so, although the film turned a profit, it did not do the business expected, and Hunt was released and all semblance of reality went with him. Following was *Diamonds Are Forever* (1971) and the return of Sean Connery. Desperate for a major success, the producers agreed to pay one-million dollars to a charity of Connery's choice to get him back, then hired the director of the most successful Bond, *Goldfinger*'s Guy Hamilton, to helm this America-based adventure.

Together, the two fashioned what is probably the most disagreeable and unintelligible Bond ever made, filled with exact lookalikes, kidnapped millionaires, a Las Vegas space center, homosexual henchmen, car chases, illogical murders, nonsensical plot twists, awful acting, and a diamond-powered laser satellite. It was terrible dross in comparison to the past Bond glory, but it made money, thanks to Connery's participation, so the ongoing Bonds retained the fantasy aspects.

Guy Hamilton stayed on and Tom Mankiewicz was pegged to write the new movie *Live and Let Die* (1973). For this, the producers also had to find another new 007, since Connery had thoroughly destroyed his Bond image with *Diamonds* by being overweight and unattractive, and Lazenby let it be known that *On Her Majesty's Secret Service* would be his first and last Bond (a decision that certainly relieved the producers). The man finally decided upon was one of the original people considered for the part among Rod Taylor, Patrick McGoohan, Lee Marvin, and Richard Burton,

For the eighth in the series, Roger Moore, late of television's "The Saint" and "The Persuaders," lost twenty pounds and cut his hair to start his reign as the new James Bond. He was indeed new, displaying an English ruthlessness and charm in juxtaposition to Connery's manly Scot. Sadly, the filmmakers created a plot line in which Moore had less to do than a manikin.

Again the story was muddled and illogical, filled with so many inconsistencies as to be incomprehensible. Basically, it told of an underworld boss who uses voodoo to control his Jamaican minions. Somehow Bond gets involved with the intrigue, following the trail from New York to New Orleans until he does in the criminals and gets the girl. Along the way he meets up with Baron Samedi, ably embodied by Geoffrey Holder, who is the voodoo chief and just can't seem to die, even though Bond hurls him into a coffin of snakes and blows a lookalike apart with a magnum.

This immortal aspect is thrown away along with the other supernatural overtones in exchange for the degradation of the 007 character and the embarrassment of innocent bystanders which passed for humor in this outing. During a chase with Bond in a one-engine plane and the villains in cars, 007 sends a reluctant passenger to the hospital suffering from shock, a situation he laughs

The cool, Britishly brittle 007 Roger Moore. From *The Spy Who Loved Me* (© United Artists).

115

off in the next scene. During the climactic boat chase, a bayou-side wedding is disrupted, destroying the seven-tiered cake in the process. The director's sense of fun included showing the bride bursting into tears.

The following 007 exercise transferred this lack of concern directly to Bond until the evil villain appeared to be more attractive, civilized, and entertaining than our hero. *The Man With the Golden Gun* (1974) put Moore through more demeaning situations, a move that was considered so sacrilegious to his dedicated fans that an organized campaign was started to get director Hamilton off the series. Thankfully, this ninth film in the series made less money than its predecessors. It became clear that the audience did not appreciate having their hero demeaned.

The plot here concerned the energy crisis and kung fu, as a million-dollar hit man named Scaramanga (Christopher Lee) races Bond to the ultimate solar-cell device. It was an uncomfortable combination of low humor and unsustained action. The high points were nonexistent, the fights were few and the final confrontation weak, confusing, and predictable. It was then that Saltzman decided to be bought out by the more industrious Broccoli. And once that maneuver was consummated, the producer decided that it was about time all the stops were pulled back out and the 007 brand of tightly plotted, fantasy super-heroics returned.

Toward this end, the most expensive James Bond movie thus far planned—fourteen-million-dollars—was mounted. Lewis Gilbert, the director of *You Only Live Twice*, was signed; and Richard Maibum, the screenwriter for the best of the Bonds, was teamed with Christopher Wood, a forty-two-year-old writer who had greater respect for the 007 character than the previous director. These three worked up an entirely new plot for the tenth film in the series: *The Spy Who Loved Me* (1977). Even though this was nothing new to 007 collaborators—*Live Twice* and *Diamonds* were *totally* new stories—this time it was from Ian Fleming's express orders. Upon selling the movie rights originally, the author requested that *The Spy's* plot be changed simply because he felt it his worst book.

From the original novel, concerning a young American woman's rescue from two thugs by James Bond, was fashioned quite possibly the best Bond film—assuredly the best Roger Moore Bond at any rate. Meticulous care was lavished on the movie, from the high budget to the shooting schedule: a hefty five months of filming all over the world. The spectacular opening ski sequence of the epic was filmed on Baffin Island, twenty miles north of the Arctic Circle (it is immediately noticeable to

Director Lewis Gilbert grimaces and bears it as explosion after explosion rips the two-million-dollar set. The rest of the crew carefully checks the "corpses" at the finish of *The Spy Who Loved Me* (© United Artists).

long-term fans the new concern for 007—the previous Moore films the precredit sequences dealt with the villains; Bond was lamely introduced later).

It is in the small town of Pangnirtung where 007 is called by M—using a ticker-tape device in Bond's watch—to return to London, since two nuclear submarines have disappeared. Naturally, the agent is in the midst of a romantic tryst with a blond skier (Sue Vanner) in a mountain cabin. Casually, 007 redons his sporty ski outfit as the girl cries, "But James, I need you!" With a casual, "So does England," he's off.

Ah, but the girl is actually a Russian spy sent as a diversion to a team of ski-bound assassins. There follows a crystalline chase with a "helpless" Bond zipping across and under ice bridges, and the enemy blasting away with their submachine guns. Suddenly 007's ski pole sprouts a trigger and he whirls about. There's a blast of gunpowder and the pole's steel tip smashes through the leading Russian's chest.

Bond moves off unerringly toward the edge of a cliff. The climax of the scene is literally breathtaking. Rick Sylvester is actually the fellow who skied off the edge and plummeted down thousands of feet before opening the parachute with a Union Jack emblazoned across it. The effect was stunning and many critics felt sure that there would be nothing else in the film that could live up to it. Happily they were wrong.

Bond is briefed on the situation at the Faslane Submarine Base on the southwest coast of Scotland, which was an actual Polaris submarine location. The producer considered it a "small miracle" that permission was granted to film there, but it just goes to show the Bond series's influence. Meanwhile, back at the plot, the Secret Service finds a lead to the missing British and Russian subs in the person of Fekkesh (Nadim Sawalha), an Arab who possesses some information on the secret tracking device used to run the undersea vessels to ground. So Bond sallies forth to Egypt where the crew happily took advantage of natural locales, like the Ibn Talun Mosque, the Gayer-Anderson Museum, three temples of Ancient Thebes, the Nile River, and the Great Pyramids of Gizah, where 007 first meets his Russian counterpart, a beautiful female spy—naturally—Anya

Jaws (Richard Kiel) gives 007 a sun roof during *The Spy Who Loved Me* (© United Artists).

Amasova (Barbara Bach), who's also after the tracking device and the missing subs.

Both are beaten by a seven-foot-two-inch tall fellow named Jaws (Richard Kiel) because his teeth are dentures of interlocking steel. His size and power become an effective running joke as Bond dispatches him to "certain death" time and again, only to wind up facing him a little later. First, the two agents battle the giant for Fekkesh's microfilm, then leave him under the rubble of a collapsed desert excavation. The microfilm's incomplete clue leads them to the Italian Island of Sardinia where a shipping magnate named Karl Stromberg (Curt Jurgens) anchors his spider-shaped headquarters in the middle of the Tyrennean Sea.

There, they meet up with Jaws again on the bad end of a gun, when Bond's new "Q" supplied car is chased by a Kawasaki "900" motorcycle equipped with a teleguided explosive sidecar, a Ford filled with gun-wielding thugs, and a Bell Ranger helicopter piloted by Stromberg's moll (Caroline Munro). Naturally enough, Bond's auto is no normal car. The Lotus Esprit is especially equipped to deal with each threat. Good old-fashioned driving causes the sidecar missile to hit the rear of a tractor-trailer truck, then a combined jet of liquid cement and oil blinds the other car, which plummets over a cliff and into the roof of a small shack (seconds later Jaws emerges from the front door brushing off his coat), then as the machine-gun-equipped helicopter bears down on them, Bond drives the car across the seaport's docks and into the ocean, much to Anya's horror in the passenger seat.

Suddenly the wheels move up and in, slats slide across the windshield, fins appear, and the car is merrily tooling along underwater at a top speed of 7.2 knots. This device was built and equipped exclusively to the producer's specifications by the Florida-based Perry Oceanographic Company, installing a periscope, special propulsion and rudder units, radar screen, harpoon guns, and a missile launcher, all built into the Lotus's body. One missile takes care of the helicopter, harpoons eliminate several frogmen, and a floating mine destroys a Stromberg mini-sub which arrives to investigate.

These underwater sequences were shot by Lamar Boren, a noted sea cinematographer in the waters of the Bahamas. However, it is the Sardinian beach where Bond drives up, causing an immediate sensation. Forever the gentleman, he casually drops a small fish out the front window before driving back to his hotel. This last attack is the final straw. The secret services of Russia, the United Kingdom, and the United States decide to cooperate in order to combat the Stromberg threat. He is evilly planning to blow up the world with the

James Bond's specially equipped Lotus Esprit is filmed in Bahamas waters at the beginning of the submarine attack during *The Spy Who Loved Me* (© United Artists).

kidnapped submarine's missiles so his dream of an undersea world can be realized.

Bond and Anya are dropped onto the deck of the United States submarine *Wayne* to find the Nordic shipping magnate's massive oil tanker, the *Liparus*—which has never docked since its original launching. Before too long it finds them, and in an astonishing maneuver, its bow opens and swallows them up. Bond and company find themselves in a huge hollowed-out hanger, lined with Stromberg's own private army and flanked by the two other missing submarines.

This fantastic concept was given a vital reality—as were the other opulent sets—by production designer Ken Adam, who conceived and controlled the birth of this

The two-million-dollar set inside the largest sound stage in the world—the "007 Stage"—is taken down the hard way at the climax of *The Spy Who Loved Me* (© United Artists).

Here's the actual storyboard for the final battle between Bond and Jaws and a rare chance to see how the actual scene compares (© United Artists).

particular history-making set. The first stumbling block he faced was that there was no sound stage big enough to hold it. Said producer Broccoli, "Build it." So on the back lot of Pinewood Studios, the Specialist Builders of Uxbridge constructed the United Artists and Eon Productions joint-owned "007 Stage," the largest in the world.

Within its tall white walls the *Liparus*'s hold was built, then destroyed when Bond released the naval prisoners and led the attack on their captors. Although Bond successfully impregnates the operations room and prevents World War Three, Stromberg and Jaws escape back to the spider headquarters with Anya. Bond single-handedly gains entry, kills Stromberg, battles Jaws, and rescues the Russian spy just before American torpedoes destroy the villain's lair.

But Jaws, like Darth Vader, will be back. Although the intrepid agent bounces a PPK bullet off the metal teeth, then uses an industrial magnet to dump the monster into a shark's pool, the last we see of the brute, he's swimming off into the ocean to return when James Bond himself returns in *Moonraker* (1979), which started production in August, 1978.

Producer Broccoli has publicly labeled the series highly stylized fantasy and he wants to retain the 007 heroics in the midst of the bizarre sets, villains, and situations. Toward that end he worked on story ideas with Tom Mankiewicz, who then turned over the plot to Christopher Wood, who fashioned the actual screenplay. *Moonraker* has officially become the most expensive 007 film, budgeted at 25 million dollars. The plot is filled with space stations, space shuttles and more action than several of the previous Bonds put together. Roger Moore, who never looked better and proved himself a tough 007 in the latest success returned for the eleventh feature, although he has admitted that the work is always strenuous and often dangerous.

Several times during *Spy*, "mock" explosions were

Star Moore, co-star Lois Chiles, and director Lewis Gilbert, aiming to deliver more action, more thrills, and more fantasy than ever for *Moonraker* (© United Artists).

real enough to send him flying across the room and set his clothes on fire. Not bad for a man in his fifties. Another returnee is Lewis Gilbert, who got fine notices for his admirable control of the chaotic goings-on. His directorial hand was fast, tight, sure, and light, always stressing the more stupendous aspects of the script without getting cloying or obvious. The finished film is wildly opulent but never lost sight that the main strength of the series lies not in its gimmicks but in the strong character of James Bond.

Another strong character was that of George Patton. His inner strength could be matched by Henri Charriere, the man known as Papillon throughout the world. The only other thing these two have in common is that their screen stories were directed by one of the last of a breed which includes David Lean and Cecil B. DeMille—Franklin Schaffner. Schaffner, after garnering television experience and helming two small, but well-received, movies—*The Stripper* (1963) and *The Best Man* (1964)—became known as a "big movie" director after finishing *The War Lord* (1965). His subsequent titles include *Planet of the Apes* (1968) and *Nicholas and Alexandra* (1971). His newest work takes one of Ameri-

ca's best leading men and one of the world's greatest actors and pits them against each other in the midst of a political and sociological nightmare. Schaffner has just finished making *The Boys From Brazil* (1978), starring Gregory Peck and Lord Laurence Olivier.

Kenneth Ross wrote the screenplay from a novel by Ira Levin, who's not new at this kind of thing. His previous work includes *Rosemary's Baby*, *The Stepford Wives*, and the Broadway hit, *Deathtrap*. While those three are about a witches' coven, automated loved ones and theatrical mass murders, *The Boys from Brazil* is about Mengele (Peck), an ex-Nazi, who has recreated the exact environment that Hitler grew up in for ninety-four boys he has tampered with genetically. Nazi hunter Lieberman (Olivier) becomes involved when these boys' fathers start dying mysteriously and en masse.

Hitler's father died when he was twelve, so Mengele and his associate Seibert (James Mason) must make sure that the fathers of their boys do the same. Intrigue piles on intrigue, murder follows murder until the heroic faction pieces the conspiracy together. Into this plot Schaffner has mixed some of the world's great supporting talent, including Michael Gough, Walter Gotell, Linda Hayden, John Rubenstein, Uta Hagen, and Lilli Palmer.

This is all being mounted under the auspices of Sir Lew Grade and ITC Entertainment, who are becoming to large-scale adventure films what Walt Disney Productions is to family entertainment. Another one of their film properties is Clive Cussler's novel, *Raise the Titanic*, in which oceanography troubleshooter Dirk Pitt is assigned to do just what the title says in order to secure a rare ore substance suspected of being in the sunken liner's hold.

In the year 1988, you see, the President of the United States has created the Meta Section, whose duty it is to implement impossible schemes, the most successful of which is a fool-proof defense system which would make war obsolete. This would be possible if they could get their hands on enough byzanium, the only supply of which was reported to be aboard the Titanic. Initially this movie project was awaiting production for more than nine months while original producer/director Stanley Kramer got prepared. Recently, Kramer left the helm, so the duty of *Raising the Titanic* fell to Jerry Jamieson, and the sure-to-be-expensive and exhaustive special-effects work got under way.

Already completed and awaiting release on the ITC schedule is *The Medusa Touch* (1978), reportedly an excellent tale of terror by mental control. Richard Burton plays John Morlar, a man who is getting back at society by using a strange extrasensory power to kill. Lee Remick is psychiatrist Dr. Zonfeld, who is trying to

Gregory Peck (left) and James Mason star in The Boys From Brazil, and they're just the bad guys! The good guys include Lord Laurence Olivier (© 20th Century Fox).

control his destructive tendencies, and Lino Ventura, a French actor with experience dating back to 1954, plays Inspector Brunel, a detective who becomes involved when Morlar's skull is bashed in by a mysterious intruder.

Slowly but surely Brunel tracks down the clues until he comes to the conclusion that while Morlar's body hovers near death, his brain is alive and well and planning a horrible revenge. Among the rest of the able cast are other French and English notables like Michael Hodern, Marie-Christine Barrault, and Gordon Jackson of "Upstairs, Downstairs" television fame.

Two more English productions which promise to be interesting are still in the preproduction stage. Ridley Scott will be making a projected four-million-dollar science-fiction thriller called *Alien* at the London-based Shepperton Studio, while Frank Yablans, the brain behind *The Fury*, mounts *The Demolished Man*, one of the most famous science-fiction novels ever written. Alfred Bester won one of his three science-fiction-

novel-of-the-year awards for this work, which John Farris is busy trying to adapt to the screen. It tells the story of Ben Reich, who attempts to commit the perfect murder in the year 2301, a murder in a society where the police are telepathic.

Although written in 1951, the work is still fresh, still exciting, and still challenging to its director, Brian DePalma. Given his past record, he might just be the man to bring it off. He is inventive, audacious, and almost always intriguing. That isn't to say he's always successful, however. His 1975 contribution to the fantastic science genre was all that and more but just didn't catch the fancy of audiences. What the young director did was combine *The Phantom of the Opera*, *Woodstock*, *The Portrait of Dorian Grey*, *The Devil and Danial Webster*, *Hair*, and *Psycho* to come up with the rock musical/horror movie, *The Phantom of the Paradise*.

Paul Williams plays Swan, the head of a record company who keeps a portrait in the closet which grows

121

William Finley proves to be a real swinger as _The Phantom of the Paradise_ (© 20th Century Fox).

old instead of him, thanks to selling out to the Devil years earlier. Into his den of iniquity comes Winslow Leach (William Finley), a mild-mannered composer whose rock cantata is stolen and drugs planted on him. He is subsequently busted and lanquishes in jail plotting revenge while Swan auditions singers for the opening of his new Paradise Theater where Leach's cantata will be the main event.

Winslow manages to escape prison and gets within Swan's recording facilities, only to get his head caught in a record-pressing machine, to get shot, and to fall into the river. But he's not dead yet. Work continues on the Paradise and the opening attraction until a black-leather-garbed, hawk-masked phantom takes up residence among the rafters. From that vantage point, the changed Winslow spies Phoenix (Jessica Harper), a willowy singer whom he's instantly enamored of. But Swan's evil ways lead to a premiere night no one would forget, if they were alive by the end of it.

The rock show reaches its peak with an onstage electrocution and climaxes with a deadly free-for-all with the freaked-out audience dying and loving every minute of it. Even backed by fine reviews from _Time_, _Playboy_, and _New York_, the film was not a financial success, nor was it particularly easy to make. Originally it was to be called _Phantom of the Fillmore_, the Fillmore being a

famous New York rock theater of the sixties. But Bill Graham, the real-life manager, wasn't too pleased about the encroachment. Hence the Paradise was born, under production designer Jack Fisk, who also repeated the favor on De Palma's _Carrie_.

Another interesting note is that _The Phantom_'s set dresser was Fisk's wife, a Texas blond who was to make it in front of the cameras by the time of _Carrie_—the latter title's star, Sissy Spacek. Another actor who has come a long way is Kevin McCarthy. Back in 1956 he starred with Dana Wynter in Don Siegel's _Invasion of the Body Snatchers_, from the novel by Jack Finney. It, too, was unsuccessful at the time of its release and each participant went their own way.

Finney went on to write _Time and Again_ and _The Night People_, Siegel went on to helm _Madigan_ (1967), _Dirty Harry_ (1972) and _The Shootist_ (1976), while _Invasion of the Body Snatchers_ went on to become one of the undisputed classics of the horror genre, garnering a large cult following. Suddenly, Kevin McCarthy found himself before the cameras again, twenty-one years later, playing essentially the same character in the new United Artists production of _Invasion of the Body Snatchers_ (1978).

The new scriptwriter, W. D. Richter, and the young director, Phillip Kaufman, were quick to advise that their movie was not a remake, per se, but more of a continuation. Donald Sutherland plays the leading role against Leonard Nimoy's supporting portrayal of a doctor "taken over" by alien beings. These beings take the form of large pods which manifest into human shape then take over the person they resemble when the victim is asleep.

In the original, McCarthy just manages to convince the authorities the threat was real, but, in the follow-up, he is torn to pieces by an angry mob as society itself is ripped asunder by the outer-space threat. Donald Sutherland and Leonard Nimoy star in the intelligent horror film premiering December 22, 1978.

Abundant thrills and chills can be found in the steady output of the Walt Disney Studios. Ever since their first animated feature in 1937—_Snow White_—and their first live-action movie in 1950—_Treasure Island_—the studio that bears Disney's name has been producing and releasing successful westerns, adventures, musicals, comedies, and fantasies. But out of those only a very few could fit into the category of fantastic science.

Following in the footsteps of the "Witch Mountain" duo, however, came _The Cat From Outer Space_ (1978), a worthy successor to the likes of _The Absent Minded Professor_ (1961) and _The Computer Wore Tennis Shoes_, made by an experienced team of Disney veterans. The coproducers were Ron Miller and Norman Tokar, who also directed. Miller started with the Disney studio in

1957, slowly working his way up until he now supervises all the film and television production. Tokar began in 1962 with *Big Red* and directed twelve other films before *The Cat From Outer Space*, producing several others along the way.

The primary human cast was also experienced in the ways of the studio, many having done up to six other Disney-studio features. The plot here concerns Zunar J5/90 Doric 4-7, or, in English translation, Jake the Cat (Rumple the Cat), getting stuck on this planet when his beetle-shaped spaceship breaks down. All the feline needs to return to his mothership is six cubits of Org-12, which happens to be $120,000 worth of gold. All he has is thirty-six hours before rendezvous will be impossible, and his only assistance will be his telepathic power and a collar which causes levitation.

NASA finds the ship and team-leader Dr. Heffel (Hans Conreid) assigns Dr. Bartlett (Sandy Duncan) and Dr. Leak (McClean Stevenson) to investigate at the Energy Research Lab. It is only after the others are stumped and offbeat physicist Dr. Wilson (Ken Berry) is brought in that Jake makes his presence and predicament known. The three earthlings band together in order to raise the $120,000 but they are continually foiled by Olympus (William Prince), a millionaire intent on ruling the world, and his spy Stallwood (Roddy McDowall).

Ken Berry can't believe he's co-starring with a cat. *The Cat From Outer Space*, to be exact (© Walt Disney Productions).

After a hectic round of betting on the horses and in the pool halls, the gold is gotten, the ship is prepared, but Bartlett and her cat Lucy Belle (Spot the Cat), whom Jake has fallen in love with, are held captive by Olympus. Jake heroically foregoes return to his own planet to save his pussy love, and all ends well as the villains are arrested, Bartlett and Wilson get together and the president announces that Jake is a foreign dignitary and should be treated as such.

The movie ends with Jake becoming a United States citizen, playfully making the judge levitate during the pledge of allegiance. Rounding out the cast are Harry Morgan, Ronnie Schell, Alan Young of *Mr. Ed* fame, James Hampton, and Rick Hurst. Rounding out the crew are animal trainers Rudy Cowl and Don Spinney, and Ted Key, noted for his creation of the Saturday Evening Post's continuing cartoon maid, "Hazel."

Speaking of comic strips, the success of *The Cat from Outer Space*, as well as Disney's upcoming *The Black Hole*, and American International's *The Adventures of Stella Star* and the reappearance of the Italian import *Star Pilot* as well as dozens of other upcoming pictures, can be, in part, traced back to 1971 and a young man fresh out of film school on the west coast. A man who had filmed a short documentary on the making of *McKenna's Gold* (1967), watched the filming of *Finian's Rainbow* (1968), assisted director Francis Ford Coppola on *The Rain People* (1969), then went on to work up several feature ideas of his own.

Among them was a space fantasy, one originally envisioned as a remake of *Flash Gordon*. But when the rights were unavailable to his poor bank account, he continued his science-fiction research and made an extension of his University of Southern California student film, *THX-1138:4EB*, for Warner Brothers. Released in 1972, minus the "4EB," and starring Robert Duvall, it did poorly at the box office. Still nursing concepts of a tried-and-true space opera, the young man hustled out his next picture, an inexpensive quickie populated by then unknown actors, made by eighteen people in less than a month. It was called *American Graffiti* (1973) and among those unknowns were Richard Dreyfuss and Suzanne Somers.

While that went on to garner millions for Universal Studios, the young director sat down in January, 1973 to actually write his science-fantasy. He continued to write—eight hours a day, five days a week—for a little longer than three years, winding up with four possible plot lines, a mediocre budget, an experienced crew, and a contract with 20th Century Fox. The young man was named George Lucas, and his unfinished screenplay was entitled *Star Wars* (1977).

Peter Mayhew lurks within the carpeting and patented
facial mechanics of makeup master Stuart Freeborn, who
created Chewbacca the Wookie along the same lines as his
previous "Dawn of Man" apes in *2001* © 20th Century
Fox).

From then on it was to be seven days a week, sixteen hours a day as Lucas struggled to imbue his film with a little of his original vision. Alan Ladd, Jr. was the intrepid executive who backed George and his friend/partner/producer Gary Kurtz with 20th's board, which must have thought the creative team absolutely bonkers when Lucas explained he wanted to make a children's movie. He felt that kids today had no one decent to emulate. Television taught them nothing about imagination.

In an interview he said, "We had a whole generation growing up without fairy tales." So he wanted to mount one which he envisioned costing more than $15 million. Twentieth's board said less. Lucas said eight. They said seven. Lucas said no way. Eight million was decided upon, a price tag which was to rise two million more. Immediately, the creative team began to gather a nucleus of talent to realize Lucas's plot line from a variety of *Star Wars* drafts.

Ralph McQuarrie was hired to visualize the basic characters, costumes, props, and sets. Ben Burtt was pegged to start conceptualizing alien languages and futuristic sound effects (a chore which won him a special Oscar award), Alex Tavoularis began story boarding and Colin Cantwell was assigned the job of designing the initial spacecraft models. John Barry was signed as production designer and told to get that real "lived in" feeling to everything, then Joe Johnston came in for detailed story-board concepts. Lucas finally settled on Gil Taylor as director of photography because he wanted the same sort of documentary feel Taylor gave *Dr. Strangelove* (1964) and *A Hard Day's Night* (1964).

All of a sudden work got underway even before anyone seemed to understand what was going on. The chaos was a combination of two basic things. The first was the unsettled shooting script. One of the preliminary plot lines involved all the main characters on a planet of Wookies, and even in the script they finally used, several major concepts were constantly changing. Secondly, even up until its premiere, Fox never considered *Star Wars* more than a gamble of possibly passing interest. They felt it was going to be a harmless quickie which might make back its investment—a curiosity piece at worst, a cult favorite at best.

Meanwhile, *Star Wars* was growing like *The Amazing Colossal Man* (1956). John Stears was in on mechanical effects, responsible for the creation of a dozen robots and assorted weaponry. Stuart Freeborn became the head of makeup and related duties like creating Chewbacca, the 7½-foot Wookie. John Mollo came on to design the extensive costumes, among which were for the stormtroopers, Sand People, and the infamous Darth Vader.

The interiors were being built at the EMI Elstree Studios outside of London because it could provide nine large sound stages to hold simultaneously the thirty sets envisioned by Barry's crew, and because it was close to the myriad other geographical locations necessary. On the basis of his past record and present integrity, Lucas secured the acting talents of Alec Guinness for the pivotal role of Ben Obi-Wan Kenobi, an accomplishment all the more impressive considering the fact that the role, at the time, was of a doddering old fool who becomes strong in the face of doom, then saves the day at the last moment.

As filming went on, Guinness fleshed out his part, convincing Lucas that he should be a majestic gentleman rather than an absent-minded professor. The other roles were embodied almost exclusively by newcomers or genre greats. Mark Hamill played the leading role of Luke Skywalker; Carrie Fisher, whose one other role consisted of seducing Warren Beatty in *Shampoo*, got the nod as Princess Leia; Harrison Ford, who had been appearing on screen since 1965 and supported the likes of Elliott Gould and Gene Hackman, received the plum part of Han Solo, the swaggering space swindler.

Peter Cushing came from a forty-year career as one of the great horror stars to play the coldly vicious Grand Moff Tarkin, the commander of the Death Star. Next came the "costume" characters; four main roles which were played undercover, so to speak, and have turned out to be the most celebrated of all. The previously mentioned Wookie was played by Peter Mayhew; R2-D2, the "rolling refrigerator" was filled with Kenny Baker, a professional small person; C-3PO, the prim golden robot was played by Anthony Daniels; and Darth Vader, the dreaded Lord of the Sith, was played by Dave Prowse—a 6'7" muscle builder, exercise coach, ex-British heavy-weight-lifting champ, and actor—coming from experience playing the Frankenstein Monster three times, and the bodyguard in *A Clockwork Orange*, among other things.

As he remembers it, he was offered both the roles of Chewbacca and Vader. Asked for descriptions, his employers pictured the Wookie as a giant teddy bear and Darth as the major villain of the piece. Quoth Prowse, "You know what you do with Chewbacca, don't you?" In the long run, naturally, Prowse was wise. Although Chewie is lovable, the heavy-breathing, masked monster has become *the* cult figure of the film; a fact that has also led to problems for the tall actor.

This problem was nearly shared by Anthony Daniels,

Alec Guinness (seated left), Mark Hamill (seated right), and Anthony Daniels as C-3PO (seated in back) discuss pressing matters of the day with storm troopers in *Star Wars*. Their land floater is actually a three-wheel vehicle with either the wheels matted out or the device hung on wires or on a crane off screen.

the embodier of C-3PO. Though R2-D2 just "beeped and booped" in an exacting language created by Ben Burtt, and Chewbacca just growled, Daniels and Prowse spoke throughout the picture and both had English accents, a fact that worried director Lucas. He wanted C-3PO to be a little more "oily." He wanted a con man and he was getting a neurotic. The shorter actor lucked out, however. After testing thirty other voices, Lucas stuck to Daniels's foppish impersonation.

Prowse, on the other hand, wasn't as fortunate. Although he delivered Vader's lines throughout and conferred with Lucas on a plan to retape his dialogue later then metallize or robotize it, he discovered later that James Earl Jones had redubbed his role without prior

contact or discussion. Although he appreciated Jones's contribution, he felt that he could have done as good a job, and felt just the tiniest bit slighted that he was never given the chance.

These were not the only problems, though. Lucas, by nature a personal filmmaker, had an albatross around his neck—a huge production brimming over with personalities. Gil Taylor wasn't interested in making another pseudodocumentary, leading to many a hard day's night between him and the director. Taylor was captured by the possible colorful flash the movie could impart. Because of his vision, the finished work combined slashing action with dreamy hues, which turned out to be a winning effect.

Han Solo (Harrison Ford—center left) and Luke Skywalker (Mark Hamill—right with poncho) watch the rebel fighters readied during the last half of *Star Wars* (© 20th Century Fox).

Meanwhile, Lucas had contacted John Dykstra, a past student and assistant of special effects master Doug Trumbull, in the hopes of acquiring a special-effects man who would cooperate extensively with the director and not try to push his own view as to what was or wasn't possible. Lucas, essentially, wanted to be in charge of everything, which led to further difficulties and on a film of *Star Wars* size.

Dykstra took on the challenge of creating the 365 special effects shots necessary to supplement the live action, but, not surprisingly, professional conflicts arose. For while Dykstra knew what he and his crew were capable of, Lucas knew what he wanted and was upset when he didn't get it. The special effects crew grew with the same speed as the other production sections until Dykstra bought a warehouse in Van Nuys, California and instituted The Industrial Light and Magic Corporation.

This group included Richard Edlund as director of photography, Grant McCune as miniature maker, Bob Shepard as production-shop head, George Mather as special effects coordinator, Robbie Blalack as optical-department organizer, Adam Beckett on laser and other related animation, and Richard Alexander, Bill Shourt, Don Trumbull, and Al Miller Electronics on design and construction.

Invented from the camera down and the floor up was the Dykstraflex, a device which enabled the crew to film the complex space battles using a camera on tracks under the control of a computer. As the crew moved slowly but surely through each necessary effect, the live-action shooting schedule continued at the same pace. What was originally set as filming period of a little over a two months took over a month longer to complete.

First the crew descended on Tunisia, filming desert

scenes in Tozeur, and Luke Skywalker's homestead sequences in Matmata. What doubles as the young man's dwelling is actually the Hotel Sidi Driss, a dwelling much like any other in that area—a hole in the ground surrounded by caves and tunnels. On location the group was plagued by bad weather and sand. Those who portrayed robots were continually exhausted from their heavy costumes and the irritant of grainy residue in their every joint.

The first major alteration of the script came then when a scene involving a village of Jawas, those little desert scavengers, was cut out. After 2½ weeks, the crew went back to Elstree, where the Barry-created sets awaited and the real difficulties began. Halfway through filming, Lucas made a monumental scripting decision. In order to give the movie a needed dramatic thrust, he decided to kill off Ben Kenobi.

Originally, during the climactic fight between Obi-Wan and Vader, Ben managed to escape and live to see the heroic end, but Lucas wound up gently informing Sir Alec that he was becoming a supporting lead. Guinness took it well and immediately began strengthening the film with new perceptions of his role and convinced the director that the concentration should be on "The Force." Then the central scene of the spaceport cantina had to be filmed, a sequence Lucas wanted to be a classic of its type.

Freeborn was about halfway toward completion of the thirty-odd alien makeups necessary when he was taken ill for the first time in his long career, missing both the end of *Star Wars* and his next assignment, *A Bridge Too Far*. The scene was filmed minus most of the color and style wanted, a situation that haunted Lucas to the extent that he asked Alan Ladd, Jr., after the principal photography was completed, to let him supplement the scene.

The time and money supplied were six weeks and twenty thousand dollars, a veritable drop in the bucket. But they got as supervisor of this second unit Rick Baker, who, with his crew of five sculptors and model animators,

Alec Guinness and Dave Prowse face off in a much-choreographed, much-rehearsed fight scene in *Star Wars*. Those "light sabers" are actually long revolving wooden dowels covered in reflective tape (© 20th Century Fox).

created dozens of full-scale monsters to be edited into the scene. The musicians were Baker's, the aliens at the tables were his, and, surprisingly, the alien "hit man," Greedo, was given his vocal movements by Baker and his crew. While Freeborn actually created the creature, set to eliminate Han Solo for squelching on a debt, Baker built in the mechanics to move its mouth and ears to the language developed by Ben Burtt and a Berkeley college student. In a month and a half, the makeup crew delivered. "Which is pretty good," Baker admits, "considering that thirty days isn't enough to do one of them correctly."

Meanwhile, the live-action material was finished, although at one point the crew had to move over to Shepperton Studios, twenty miles away, to film a "rebel hanger" sequence on the, then-largest sound stage (the new largest sound stage, as previously reported, is the 007 Stage at Pinewood) where *2001* was filmed. It was then time for the special effects to be finished, since both the studio and Lucas were aiming for a summer of 1977 release. Lucas and producer Kurtz had originally pieced together a black-and-white "dogfight" sequence out of old WWII movies to act as inspiration for the special-effects people as they pieced together the final attack on the Death Star.

Optical was heaped on optical, model. bunched on model, matte on matte until Lucas had a working print consisting of over 340,000 feet of live action and just about as much special effects. In March of 1977, composer John Williams took his one year of concepts and got together with the eighty-seven-piece London Symphony Orchestra to begin a series of fourteen sessions necessary to record the ninety minutes of movie music to be patched onto *Star Wars*.

The final product was given its soundtrack at the Samuel Goldwyn Studios using the Dolby System of noise

The closing shot of *Star Wars*. Let's hear it for C-3PO, R2-D2 (Kenny Baker), Luke Skywalker, Princess Leia (Carrie Fisher), Han Solo, and Chewie (© 20th Century Fox)!

Spielberg and John Williams seem to be talking at once about *Close Encounters'* musical score, a beautiful piece of music which was crudely edited for an Arista Record release.

reduction. In late May 1977, the film descended upon America. George Lucas sat exhausted and depressed, waiting to be trounced. He felt the film a quarter of what he wanted it to be and fully expected to be brought to task for each of its shortcomings. The initial response was immediate and overwhelming.

Star Wars was a hit, garnering long lines outside the theater and rave reviews. Lucas's glorified pastiche of the swashbucklers he loved as a kid given an science-fiction coating worked on every level, going on to receive ten Academy Award nominations, create a full-fledged cult, and became the biggest grosser of all time, beating out *Jaws* at the beginning of 1978. It must have been ironically gratifying for Lucas to know that because of his success, Dino De Laurentiis put up the big bucks to secure the Flash Gordon rights, those that George wanted to begin with.

Many, in the meantime, were infuriated by Lucas's lack of scientific detail and the fact that this obvious derivation of mistreated past classics was such a phenomenal success. But most of these people were placated, in part, by the next fantasy blockbuster to premiere just six months later. About a year before *Star Wars* was to be released, a crew of 114 people began filming in South Dakota what was destined to become one of the most controversial, most beautiful, and certainly the most secretive film of its kind.

The director of the movie *Star Wars* had eclipsed in box-office returns, *Jaws* (1975), created a new masterpiece much in the same way Lucas created his fantasy extravaganza—one piece at a time. After television experience, directing one segment of "The Night Gal-

lery" premiere; a famous episode of "The Name of the Game" called "L.A. 2017", written by Philip Wylie; and the spectacular television movie *Duel* (1971), the young director named Steven Spielberg began writing a script entitled *Close Encounters of the Third Kind,* while editing his first feature, *The Sugarland Express* (1973).

Spielberg approached the production team of Michael and Julia Phillips in 1974 when he was preparing *Jaws*—they were basking in the success of their *The Sting* (1973) and producing *Taxi Driver* (1976)—and asked if they wanted to mount a movie about "flying saucers and Watergate." According to the production notes, the producers' enthusiasm was immediate as was Columbia's, the studio which decided to back the project (the overwhelming success of *Jaws* probably had something to do with it).

By the time the production was about to begin, Spielberg had selected the nucleus of his crew. Vilmos Zsigmond, one of the best known cinematographers in the business because of his stunning work on *Deliverance* (1972) and *Obsession* (1976), was the director of photography. Douglas Trumbull, by far the most famous special-effects man today, was the visual-effects coordinator. The production designer was Joe Alves, who was responsible for finding the memorable locations and creating the unforgettable sets. The cast was signed through a variety of maneuvers.

Doug Trumbull, the king of modern special effects (© Columbia).

Spielberg sent the script to Richard Dreyfuss, who had become a passionate fan of the director the moment he saw *Jaws*. Which is odd considering that Dreyfuss was in the fish story and hated it until its release. However, with *Close Encounters*, the actor desperately wanted the leading role of a middle-aged electrical worker, Roy Neary, caught up in extraterrestrial events. Spielberg replied by rewriting the part for Dreyfuss.

The part of a French UFO expert, loosely based on real-life expert Jim Lorenze, was reserved for international director Francois Truffaut after Spielberg saw him perform in his own *Day for Night* (1973). Nervously, the American director called the French director to offer him the role. After reading the script, Truffaut accepted. After all, he was writing a book on the actor's condition, so how better to understand the thespian's problems? Teri Garr was picked as Dreyfuss's wife after the producers saw her in *Young Frankenstein* (1975). She more or less repeated her *Encounters* role as John

Denver's wife in *Oh, God*. Cary Guffey, who plays a four-year-old in the film, was discovered during a national talent hunt at a Georgia nursery school. Melinda Dillon, who played the boy's mother, was cast after 400 other actresses were auditioned—one week before shooting started.

Suddenly, filming began and a cloud of secrecy descended on the crew like an iron fire curtain. Inside that shroud, it was much like *Star Wars* in the sense that no definite decisions concerning several integral plot points had been made. Meanwhile, the residents of Gillette, Wyoming, and Bay Minette, Alabama, were shocked to find their towns invaded by film folk dragging along up to two thousand extras to enact evacuation scenes. That was the last any regular member of the American public saw of them. The crew receded into two airplane hangers on a demilitarized air force base in Mobile, Alabama.

What happened within those walls became one of the

Richard Dreyfuss questions Spielberg on a dramatic point as Francois Truffaut and Bob Balaban await. A backset look at CE3K (© Columbia).

131

Top: The first view of a *Close Encounters* UFO. Melinda Dillon and Cary Guffey are suitably awed even though, before the special effects were put in, they had nothing to react to (© Columbia).

Bottom: The extraterrestrials—children dressed in suits and extensive makeup designed by the likes of David Ayers and John Chambers (© Columbia).

132

Top: The "Dark Side of the Moon" technicians face the wonder and mystery of the Mothership in *Close Encounters of The Third Kind* (© Columbia).

Bottom: The indescribable Mothership, conceived by Steven Spielberg, realized by Doug Trumbull and admired by millions (© Columbia).

most sought-after secrets since Project Manhattan in World War II, especially after word came from merchandisers who had seen a Doug Trumbull special effects reel. It was enough, to coin Trumbull's own description, "to knock your socks off!" *Encounters* became one of the most eagerly awaited movies of all time. The excitement was communicable, the rumors were nothing short of phenomenal, and the media outlets were desperate to know more.

Spielberg wasn't about to tell them. By nature a perfectionist, constantly changing the script as he felt it warranted; he was sure any outside interference or misleading prepublicity, especially in this case, would do untold damage to the finished film. Reporters and Columbia's publicity department began to make idiots out of themselves trying to second guess the actual production. Security police cordoned off the Mobile

location while Doug Trumbull toiled in secrecy at Marina Del Rey, California in a 13,500-square-foot building, where he and his crew from Future, General, Inc. installed a wood shop, paint shop, camera shop, miniature shop, model shop, metal shop, lighting shop, optical shop and editing shop.

Extensive experiments went on in their sound stages, all under the direction of Trumbull who was creating Spielberg's concepts. Richard Yurucich supervised the photographic teams; Matthew Yurucich, his brother, headed up the matte-painting team; Bob Swarthe guided the animation department; Greg Jein handled the miniature model constructions; and the special effects crew was rounded out by Don Jarel and Bob Hull, who controlled the optical and matte photography.

Meanwhile, Spielberg was having his own problems trying to control his ambitious script. Changes needed to be made daily, and the sets necessary to realize the director's vision called for a new degree of realism. Joe Alves came through continually, finding the Devil's Tower in Wyoming and designing the "dark side of the moon" set where the final confrontation between man and alien was to take place.

The director sent his actors through their exhausting paces again and again, usually having them react to empty air or colored lights when a spaceship should be there. It was recently reported that the marvelous reactions culled from little Cary Guffey were elicited by an extra jumping around in a bear suit, but Spielberg has not commented. Teri Garr, Melinda Dillion, Richard Dreyfuss, and assorted extras cavorted on the "Harper Valley bend" set, where the aliens first appeared, without the bear's aid. Dillon and Dreyfuss hiked up the Devil's Tower set all day, sometimes as long as sixteen hours.

The huge final-confrontation set, with its lightboard, organ, and surrounding rocks, was built inside one hanger and swathed in blue screens, so the intricate effects could later be achieved. Finally, some last scenes were filmed in various American locales using William Fraker as director of photography since Zsigmond's tenure had run out, and he had previous commitments. Douglas Slocombe served in the post when Spielberg traveled to India to film a scene with Truffaut as some final-character development.

Meanwhile, special effects work continued and the rumors flew. Colin Cantwell was hired to try some computer effects, but they didn't fit in. John Chambers and three assistants did some finishing touches on an alien makeup design by David Ayers. Bob Baker worked up some alien creatures which were first edited out then returned to the final print. Carlo Rimbaldi created his first successful American creature with the smiling hydraulic robot seen at the end of the picture.

Entire scenes were scuttled in the headlong rush toward release, some because of complexity, one because of pretentiousness. The ludicrous scene was kept in the novelization of the film and concerned Dreyfuss's reaction to his wife's breast, while the complex sequences all came during the last forty minutes, which, if shot as originally conceived, would have been much longer. It called for levitating female aliens, undulating cubes, a ballet of UFO's and golden "pixie dust" exploding across the encampment.

By October of 1977 Spielberg, had a version of his film in the can, but, as a last test, sprung it on an unsuspecting Texas audience to see what further tightening and improvements he could achieve before the November New York premiere. An editor of *New York* magazine managed to get in and wrote a scathing two-page review which predicted the film's utter failure. This move showed three things. One, that the press was utterly desperate for any kind of information on the ground-breaking feature: two, the *New York* writer proved himself totally unprofessional and woefully short-sighted; and three, the anticipation for the film had reached a fever pitch.

Spielberg did some final trimming with editor Michael Kahn of a scene where Dillon runs into a horrifying scarecrow while chasing her son, and eliminated Jiminy Cricket singing "When You Wish Upon a Star" just before the closing credits. Then he gave the go-ahead to hold the premiere at the Ziegfeld Theater in New York. Most of that audience was stunned, some were disappointed, but none were bored. Spielberg had a major success on his hands, and Doug Trumbull had come through with flying colors, in more ways than one.

Although some of the UFO's were actually no more than colored lights, *Encounters* had the finest special effects in the history of motion pictures, bar none. Their subtlety and complexity have led many less-versed in movie magic to take them for granted, but their brilliance and realization were nothing short of staggering to anyone with even a rudimentary understanding of filmmaking. Some were deceptively simple, such as the "zero gravity" in Dreyfuss's truck cab created by whirling the cab section in a studio, and the "billowing clouds" which precede a UFO's appearance created by injecting white paint into a tank of clear water, but most were so detailed and extensive that they defy description.

For instance, the initial appearance of the "mothership" was done using a three-by-four-foot ship

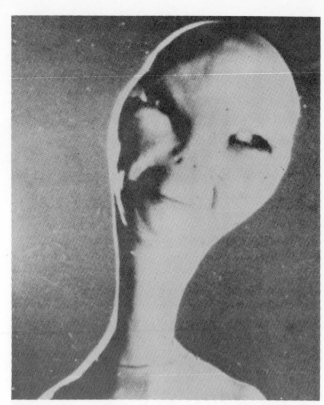

The Carlo Rimbaldi hydraulic robot alien (© Columbia).

model rising above a five-foot mountain miniature, a matte-painted landscape, a front-projected "star field", and a live-action matte insert. Although *Encounters* had one hundred fewer special effects than *Star Wars*, theirs was the greater achievement, since many of them were much longer and less obvious.

The reviews came in and were, for the most part, highly favorable. In fact, Ray Bradbury in the *Los Angeles Times* called it, "the most important film of our time. We were waiting for it before we were born." Most critics weren't that effusive, and as time went on and its initial power began to fade, many began to viciously attack both films: *Star Wars* as useless, meaningless drivel, and *Encounters* as pretentious wishful thinking. However, the audiences did not desert these optomistic visions, and time will probably hold both movies in good stead.

Indeed, by the looks of things, we haven't seen the last of either. *Star Wars II* has begun production with a script by Leigh Brackett based on the first chapter of a ten-chapter George Lucas-written opus. Mark Hamill, Carrie Fisher, and Harrison Ford are back in harness under the sharp directorial eye of Irvin Kershner in the first of a projected series lasting until at least 2001.

And in-between his producing chores on *I Want to*

Hold Your Hand (1978) and direction of *1941*, Spielberg has been seriously·pressured to consider heading up a sequel to *Encounters;* one he had left a lot of room for in the original. What happened to Roy Neary after the mothership took off? Where are they going? Will they ever be back? Who were those little guys, anyway? Will we ever know the answers?

4   TELEVISION

IT ALL STARTED officially in 1925, when Englishman John L. Baird made the first demonstration of a wireless television set. Four years later he would begin the daily duties of the British Broadcasting Agency—the BBC. The Americans would beat him by one year, since E.F.W. Alexanderson began triweekly programming in the spring of 1928. The bold new medium was off and running, but it would be twenty years and a world war before its sociological impact would be truly telling.

At the time of the second world war, home televisions numbered in the thousands. Within half a decade, their number was in the tens of millions. The populace was captured by this new kind of magic. To begin with, game shows, westerns, comedies and variety shows monopolized the viewers hearts, culled from a variety of sources, but mostly from radio, movies, and the vaudeville stage.

Strangely enough, the first fantasy-based show was a product of—and named after—the new medium. In 1949, Richard Coogan stepped into his mountain lair to begin his short tenure as "Captain Video and His Video Rangers:" The Guardian of the Safety of the World. At first, the thirty-minute program was mounted as a continuing serial, but with the beginning of the new decade the lead changed—Al Hodge became the new captain—and within three years the concept changed to a weekly adventure called "The Secret Files of Captain Video." During its seven-year run, the captain also spawned almost a dozen imitators and variations.

The most immediate was Commander Buzz Corey, as played by Ed Kemmer of "The Space Patrol." The show started in September of 1950 and was almost as popular as "Captain," running a total of six seasons and telling of the missions of the Rocket Ship X-R-Z as it protected the members of the United Planets. While both Video and Buzz had their assistants—in the former case Don Hastings as the Video Ranger and in the latter Lyn Osborn as Cadet Happy—1950 also saw a space cadet getting his own show and equal popularity. Frankie Thomas began his six-year reign as "Tom Corbett: Space Cadet." Aboard his spaceship, The Polaris, it was his job to protect the Solar Alliance, and his dream to become a full-fledged member of the Solar Guards.

Strangely enough once again, the original "real McCoy," "Buck Rogers," didn't make much of a splash on the tube. Played by Kem Dibbs and appearing for only one season in 1950, the show followed the original plotline of a twentieth century man waking up in the twenty-fifth century after having been stuck in suspended animation. His compadre, "Flash Gordon," did not do much better when he reached the small screen in 1953 in the form of Steve Holland. Managing to be syndicated for only a season, the show wasn't even as popular as the three Buster Crabbe "Flash Gordon" serials, which had also reached the tube by that time.

The networks soon found themselves resorting back to the more-successful concepts. Cliff Robertson and Jack Weston began their long careers aboard the rocket ship Beta in 1953 as "Rod Brown of the Rocket Rangers" and his companion, Wilbur Wormser, commonly known as Wormsey. Along with Bruce Hall as ranger Frank Boyle, they, like all their predecessors, scoured the universe to right wrongs and battle evil. The same went for Steve Elliott of "The Atom Squad" (1953). Played by Bob

Hastings, Steve and his assistants were more earthbound and found less to fight about then "Captain Z-Ro" aboard the ZX-99, blasing off into time and space.

This fifteen-minute show had a difference in that Roy Steffins as the captain, and his assistant Jet (Bobby Trumbull) usually attempted to alter time to help those in need. Not so in "Rocky Jones, Space Ranger." His job remained constant and cliched: protect the United Solar System against bad guys. Embodied by Richard Crane and incarcerated aboard the Orbit Jet, Rocky zipped around from 1954 to 1955, ushering out the age of the outer-space enforcer.

The television stations just didn't have the money or time to copy the movie makers' visual abilities. There was no way any of these fantasy shows could live up to one difficult sequence in *Destination Moon* or even *War of the Worlds*, so the networks moved slowly back into their old standby—the situation comedy. So many of these have come and gone on the box that the fantasy overtones have appeared fairly regularly.

The earliest being, of course, the warmly received *Topper* (1953), based on the more warmly received trio of theatrical films starting in 1939 with Roland Young as Topper and, in the first movie, Cary Grant and Constance Bennett as his two friendly ghosts, George and Marian Kirby. For the series, however, Leo G. Carroll played papa to the two bon vivant spirits, Robert Sterling as "that most sporting of spirits," and Anne Jeffreys as the "ghostess with the mostest." For about three years poor Cosmo Topper had to put up with the other-worldly antics of his invisible houseguests and their alcoholic dog, Neil. Since then, the group has returned fairly regularly as reruns.

Fantasy in "sitcoms" didn't turn up again until almost a decade later with another series that stole some thunder from a film series. *Francis the Talking Mule* first appeared in 1950 and went through seven pictures with Donald O'Connor and Mickey Rooney. "Mr. Ed," the talking horse, appeared in 1961 and went through five seasons with Alan Young as Wilbur Post, an architect who moved into a new ranch house complete with the verbal horse left by an unnamed previous owner. Most of the humor derived from Post's complicated attempts to keep Ed's voice secret. The frustrating role led to Young's self-exile from show business for years.

Next in line was an other-worldly visitor played by Ray Walston on the popular "My Favorite Martian," who crashlanded on CBS in 1963 and stayed around Tim O'Hara (Bill Bixby)'s apartment for three years, raising Tim's blood pressure whenever he raised his antennae. After such a thankless part, Bixby was nearly exiled as

well, but some fine performances on "The Courtship of Eddie's Father" (1969) and "The Magician" (1973) brought him back to network prominence.

1965 saw the reuse of two old ideas—the human voice in non-human surroundings and the ghostly visit. "My Mother the Car" had Jerry Van Dyke as Dave Crabtree, buying a car which is actually the reincarnation of his mother. The dramatic thrust of the program has Van Dyke defending the antique auto—a 1928 Touring Porter—against the ranting of his family, who wanted a station wagon, and the greediness of Avery Schreiber, as Captain Mancini, who wants the auto, with Ann Southern's voice for his car collection.

The ghostly appearance was managed by Tommy Smothers in "The Smothers Brothers Show," but that was about all he did right for the entire two-season run as an apprentice angel coming back to earth to garner his wings with the help of his exasperated living brother Dickie. The pair, who first gained fame from their musical-comedy nightclub routines, would garner far more success with a popular and controversial variety show in 1967. The sitcom success they hoped for was achieved instead by a witch the year before and a genie the year after.

Elizabeth Montgomery looks positively dowdy in this shot from "Bewitched" (© ABC).

"Bewitched" began its eight-year run in 1964 with Elizabeth Montgomery as Samantha, a blonde witch who falls in love with "Dagwoodish" Darrin Stevens (Dick York, later replaced by Dick Sargent), a human advertising executive. The two are married much to Sam's mother Endora's (Agnes Moorehead) rage. The humor came from Darrin's fanatical attempts to stop his wife from using her supernatural powers and Endora's attempts to stop him. Before the show's run was complete, most of the witch's family was introduced, played by the likes of Maurice Evans, Marion Lorne, Bernard Fox, Alice Ghostley, and Paul Lynde.

The genie began her alternate reign on another network and worked her magic for five years under the title "I Dream of Jeannie." The "I" of the title was astronaut Tony Nelson (Larry Hagman), who found a bottle dating back to biblical times on a South Sea Island. Upon opening it, Jeannie (Barbara Eden) appears out of a cloud and professes eternal servitude to him. Thus the major conflict is established on this Sidney Sheldon created show. Two minor conflicts are the discovery of Tony's helpmate by his bumbling friend and associate Roger Healey (Bill Daily), and their constant run-ins with NASA psychiatrist Alfred Bellows (Hayden Rorke).

1965 was also a year in which the "battle of the network monster comedies" took place. When "The Munsters" appeared on CBS in late 1964, ABC retaliated with "The Addams Family," based on Charles Addams's famous cartoon characters. Neither won, as it were, since both were on the air exactly two seasons, premiering and disappearing within six days of each other.

"The Addams Family" consisted of Morticia (Carolyn Jones), a raven-haired beauty dressed in a spiderish gown; Gomez (John Astin), her hot-blooded hubby; Uncle Fester (Jackie Coogan), a bald-headed nut; Grandmama (Blossom Rock), a knife-wielding old crone; Ophelia Frump (also Jones), Morticia's sister; Esther Frump (Margaret Hamilton), their mother; Cousin Itt (Felix Sila), the four-foot ball of hair; Lurch (Ted Cassidy), the gigantic butler; Thing (credited as "Itself"), the family's helping hand; and the children— Wednesday (Lisa Loring) and Pugsley (Ken Weatherwax).

"The Munsters" consisted of Herman (Fred Gwynne), seven feet of clumsy Frankensteinian parts; Lily (Yvonne DeCarlo), his faintly vampiric wife; Grandpa (Al Lewis), an out-and-out bat man; Eddie (Butch Patrick), their pointy-eared werewolf son; and Marilyn (Beverly Owen, then Pat Priest), their "normal" niece. The never-changing humor of both shows consisted of regular society's reaction to the beastly brethren, since the

John Astin and Carolyn Jones pose with a preliminary version of Cousin Itt on "The Addams Family." The final "Itt" had floor-length locks (© ABC).

Addamses had Cleopatra, a man-eating plant, an octopus named Aristotle, and a black widow spider named Homer; while the Munsters had Spot, a fire-breathing dragon who lived under the stairs, a bat named Igor, and a raven in the clock which quoted Edgar Allan Poe.

Fantasy comedies took a vacation for the next two years with the appearance of "It's About Time" (1966) and "The Second Hundred Years" (1967). The former title was notable only in its ability to switch concepts when necessary. In its first season, the show concerned itself with two astronauts, Mac (Frank Aletter) and Hector (Jack Mullaney), who smash up their ship in a time warp and get dumped into prehistoric times where cave people Gronk (Joe E. Ross) and Shad (Imogene Coca) help them adjust. The "Flintstones"-like humor soon grew tiresome so the producers allowed the spacecraft to be repaired, and, quicker than you can say station break, the show now concentrated on the cave people's adjustments to modern civilization. Even with its adaptability, "It's About Time" quickly faded from sight.

"The Second Hundred Years" also concerned time, but traded chameleon-like changes for easy-going boredom. Luke Carpenter (Monte Markham), an eighteenth-century prospector is frozen in suspended animation by an Alaskan avalanche. Years later he's thawed out by the Air Force and put in the custody of his sixty-seven-year-old son, Edwin (Arthur O'Connell). The stories, not surprisingly, concerned the young-old man's adjustment to the late 1960's. Also not surprisingly, it was cancelled rather quickly.

The end of the decade held some respite with the moderately successful, moderately entertaining "The Ghost and Mrs. Muir" (1968), based on the movie of the same name starring Gene Tierney and Rex Harrison in 1947. On the tube was Hope Lange as Carolyn Muir who moves into an estate once owned and now haunted by Captain Daniel Gregg (Edward Mulhare). He makes a charming associate for the widow, her son (Harlen Carraher), her daughter (Kellie Flanagan), and her dog (Scruffy). Charles Nelson Reilly contributed strident, face-twisting comedy relief as the captain's spineless nephew. The audience stayed with it for a little over two years on two different networks.

The only other show worth its comedic salt was the short-lived, but award-winning, "My World . . . And Welcome to It," based on the "drawings, stories, inspirational pieces, and things that go bump in the night" of James Thurber. For the 1969 show's purposes,

William Windom and Joan Hotchkis try to muddle through life on "My World . . . And Welcome to It" (© NBC).

Thurber became John Monroe (William Windom), who retreats from life by allowing his cartoons to become real and his imagination to reign. The show was filled with animation and dream sequences, the direction was tight, the acting was exceptional, the series was awarded an Emmy, and the show was cancelled after its first season.

The seventies could deliver nothing that topped it. "The Girl With Something Extra" starring Sally Field and John Davidson showed up in 1973 and was about a girl who could read minds. It lasted one season and didn't even go into repeats. Nineteen seventy-five's "Good Heavens!," starring Carl Reiner as a helpful angel, did not have a season; instead, six shows were dropped indiscriminately into the ABC schedule wherever needed.

The first show that could be called a fantasy adventure was "The Stranger," wherein Robert Carroll would rescue those in need, then disappear without mentioning his name, his price, or his purpose. He appeared in 1954 and disappeared after two months on the air. Other than he, about the only other fantasy adventures outside the realm of the superheroes and the English imports were those of "The Immortal" and Michael Rhodes, the man with the Sixth Sense.

"The Immortal" was Ben Richards (Christopher George), who had a different type of type "O" blood which made him impervious to aging. But in order to reach a ripe old age he had to keep out of millionaire Jordan Braddock's (Barry Sullivan) and Dr. Matthew Pierce's (Ralph Bellamy) hands. They want a total transfusion while Richards just wants to be free. Introduced in a television movie during 1970, "The Immortal" also introduced two other series conflicts: one, Ben is in love with Jordan's wife (Carol Lynley), and, two, Ben has a brother who might also have the super blood. Hoping to garner a "Fugitive/Run for Your Life" audience, Paramount, the show's producer, and ABC, the network in question, blew up the interesting pilot film into a weak and short-lived series. "The Sixth Sense" suffered the same fate as "Good Heavens" in that it was shuttled around the time slots a bit before dying a natural death. The hero was played by Gary Collins, and he dealt with anything-but natural deaths in his network tenure during 1972.

Two years later, another television movie—this time one of the highest-rated of all time—was developed into a less-than-successful series with a single-season run. "The Night Stalker" was the original film title and was itself followed by "The Night Strangler." The first dealt with a modern-day vampire hunted down and defeated by an investigative reporter played by Darren McGavin. The

139

second dealt with McGavin in the same role undoing another immortal killer.

Although the movies were written by Richard Matheson and directed by Dan Curtis, the series that was borne from it was coproduced by McGavin himself and renamed "Kolchak: The Night Stalker" during a season that also boasted "Kodiak" and "Kojak." Suddenly, the hero became the hunter and the various denizens of the horror world became the hunted. In the one season Kolchak roamed the Chicago streets, he did in zombies, werewolves, vampires, robots, aliens, demons, spirits, ghouls, and even a reincarnated Jack the Ripper. But his weekly successes did not seem to turn on the viewers.

This is not a charge one could level at producer Irwin Allen. The only reason his putative science-fiction titles aren't categorized with the likes of *The Invaders* (1968) and *Star Trek* (1966) is that he always introduced glaring

fantasy aspects to the point that they could not be ignored. "Lost in Space" (1965) was mindlessly enjoyable throughout its three-year run, what with walking carrots, elves, and all other forms of creatures, but watching the last two seasons of the four-year "Voyage to the Bottom of the Sea" (1964) was like viewing a fever dream. Each week a new, incongruous monster was introduced, laws of time and space were shuffled, juggled, or shuttled altogether, and situations changed faster than the commercials.

As far as "The Time Tunnel" (1966), about two time travelers, was concerned, although the heroes usually found themselves in the past, occasionally they'd get stuck on a spaceship heading toward Mars, meet up with Nero's ghost, race across a million years, fight aliens, and rescue a kidnapped associate from the year 8433. "Land of the Giants" (1968) wasn't must better in terms

The Robinson family and Dr. Smith from "Lost in Space" (from the left, Marta Kristen, Jonathan Harris, Angela Cartwright, Guy Williams, June Lockhart, Billy Mumy, and Mark Goddard).

of reality, although the adventures of a future spaceship's crashing onto a world of colossal humanoids was a little more "down to earth," even though various episodes dealt with invisibility, more elves, brainwashing, more outer-space aliens, and dinosaurs.

Allen's shows were like anthologies of monsterdom, a form which has proven popular in thirty years of television's widespread growth. In 1949 "Lights Out," a video translation of the famous radio show, appeared with Frank Gallop as the host. The show lasted three years offering mysterious fantasy, suspenseful fantasy, and the supernatural. Two years later, no fewer than two shows offered the same weekly chills: "Inner Sanctum" had Raymond (Paul McGrath) as the unseen narrator, and "Out There" was a thirty-minute program featuring stories adapted from science-fiction pulp magazines.

"Tales of Tomorrow" made it a 1951 threesome, but was stronger in the hard science department than the previous duo. The eeriness continued unabated as Alfred Hitchcock made his corpulent way onto the tube with "Alfred Hitchcock Presents" (1955), weekly tales of murder, mayhem, and the mysterious, which ran for ten years on two different networks. His ironic and sardonic comments before commercials were worth viewing no matter how good or bad the individual episode. His presence insured his decade of video output a special place in television's history.

One of the "Ebonites," a race of invading aliens in the "Nightmare" episode of "The Outer Limits."

The big news came in 1959. Not one, but two shows hit the jackpot of quality television programming. Each had an individual style, each was haunting and hard-hitting and each has made television history. They are the two giants of the supernatural: "One Step Beyond" and "The Twilight Zone." The former appeared for three seasons with the friendly looking John Newland as narrator and director of the episodes. Newland was everyone's wise old uncle—someone you'd go to whenever you wanted a good rip-snorting scary story delivered in detail.

Along the way, lots of great actors appeared in the episodes depicting occurrences "one step beyond" reality, including Patrick O'Neal, George Grizzard, Louise Fletcher, and Warren Beatty. Most of the tales were reportedly based on fact and dealt with spirits and psychic phenomena. Newland would appear at the beginning and end of the show, like Hitchcock, to deliver the last nugget of thought-provoking information.

If Newland was the kind of man you'd want along on a camping trip to tell stories around the campfire, Rod Serling is the kind of man you'd want at a family reunion to scare your mother-in-law to death. His dark demeanor and unforgettable voice have laced millions of people's nightmares since the opening episode of "The Twilight Zone" until long after the last segment aired five years later. From the opening strains of its theme song till the last credit rolled, the show had the ability to transport you beyond the limitations of your home and the technical abilities of television. Serling wisely chose not to stand apart from his show but actually exist within the story, narrating from just beyond the character's view. Here was the colossus, the king, the highest a supernatural, or *any*, show could go. "The Twilight Zone" transcended both its genre and its medium.

Some great writers and directors were given their initial experience by the show, including Charles Beaumont (*Seven Faces of Dr. Lao* screenplay); Richard Matheson; George Clayton Johnson (*Logan's Run* coauthor): Earl Hamner, Jr. ("The Waltons" creator): director Richard Donner; Ted Post (*Magnum Force* (1973) director); Lamont Johnson (*The Groundstar Conspiracy* (1972) director); and Don Siegel. Nineteen sixty-one was another highlight of anthology programming, with two out of three shows becoming historic landmarks as well. The dud of the trio was "Great Ghost Tales" with Frank Gallop as host, but still it involved such acting talent as Robert Duval, Lee Grant, and Kevin McCarthy.

The biggies were "Walt Disney's Wonderful World of Color" and "Way Out." Disney himself hosted his show, an ever-turning carousel of stories that have made the

Dennis Hopper (left) gets a sudden glimmer as to who the shadowy figure that has been advising him how to control millions is in the "Twilight Zone" episode "He Lives."

Disney name tops in the family field. Cartoons, musicals, human interest, nature—all the aspects of our world and the universe beyond—were done in the tight, colorful Disney style, all imbued with a sense of wonder and vivid imagination. Vivid was also the word for "Way Out." Lurid can also safely be used. Writer Ronald Dahl served as host for the David Susskind-produced series, which didn't last long but cemented itself in the memories of many a viewer with its wit, imagination, horror, and gore, all supplemented with the talents of makeup director Dick Smith.

Since then, things have been pretty dry in the medium. Both Newland and Serling returned to the genre with less-than-stunning results. In 1971, Jack Laird produced "Night Gallery," thinking he knew more about creating entertaining scare stories than Serling did. The result was an hour-long mishmash made up of two or three playlets and lasted three seasons. Even though the concentration was on campy ironies, weak jokes, and uninspiring tales of retribution, the series managed to shape such future top talent as Don Taylor, John Badham *(Saturday Night Fever* (1977) and *Dracula* (1978) director), Jeannot Swarc, and Steven Spielberg.

Newland returned in 1977 with glasses, white hair,

Antoinette Bower and Richard Basehart do the old "Adam and Eve" number during the last season of "The Twilight Zone" in an episode entitled "Probe 7—Over and Out."

142

and video-tape for "The Next Step Beyond," a surprisingly flat half-hour pilot for Worldvision, Inc. It was another tale of psychic experience, this time an autistic boy rescuing a helpless young girl from a tidal wave, but it didn't create many waves in the critical or rating departments.

The last four gasps came within eight years of each other from a variety of sources. ABC brought forth "Journey to the Unknown" (1968), a British show with a good theme song, good acting talent, and that lifelong bane of television programs: bad writing. Because of that, the show lasted five months. Another English show, this time hosted by Anthony Quayle, appeared in 1973 and hardly lasted the season. Called "Evil Touch," it too suffered from the dreaded lousy scripts, replacing mood for substance, and soon succumbed to the malady.

But the networks weren't giving up. For three months in late 1972, a show called "Ghost Story" appeared, hosted by Sebastian Cabot. It was the era of *Tales from the Crypt* (1971) and *The Vault of Horror* (1972), with Ralph Richardson and Peter Cushing playing variations of death, so the portly television actor took on the persona of Winston Essex to introduce the various supernatural stories. When this device went for naught, Cabot was dropped and the show was retitled "Circle of Fear," managing to last six months more on the screen.

Sinking fast, the anthology managed to make a limp comeback with producer Quinn Martin ("The F.B.I.," "Barnaby Jones," etc.)'s "Tales of the Unexpected" (1977). William Conrad lent his sotto voce voice to the proceedings, but nothing, save better writing, could help. The show was unceremoniously yanked from the schedule in less than three months.

Speaking of Yanks, the British seem to be able to do

Alexandra Bastedo, Stuart Damon, and William Gaunt take a moment out from their battles as "The Champions."

everything better than we do. Their television fantasy imports prove that even when the show's concept is silly or the scripting is awful or the acting is passable, the overall program is still intriguingly watchable. For instance, a show that tells about three secret agents who gain super powers from an ancient race in the Swiss Alps is pretty farfetched, isn't it? But that is what "The Champions" (1967) was all about.

Stuart Damon, Alexandra Bastedo, and William Gaunt were Craig Stirling, Sharron Macready, and Richard Barrett, the operatives of the super-secret spy organization, Nemesis, who went around leaping in slow motion long before their American bionic brethren. They also survived gunfights, fisticuffs, and car chases with casual ease.

But even the English can't survive awful writing. The primary case in point is "Space: 1999" (1976), a show that seemed to have everything going for it: an experienced producer, Gerry Anderson, who also mounted all those great Saturday-morning marionette science-fiction adventures; a great special-effects man in Brian Johnson and an equally impressive special effects budget; a good cast headed by Martin Landau, Barbara Bain, and Barry Morse; a great publicity budget; and world-wide programming sales that were the envy of almost everyone in the media business.

The writing killed it. There was nothing the actors, directors, or special effects people could do to improve upon the horribly illogical scripts, which developed insubstantial or moronic characters, misguided and unscientific plots, and adhered to a wrong-headed concept. First of all, the idea that the moon would be in one piece after being thrown out of orbit by massive explosions of nuclear waste is very suspectable, so, when the ideas brought forth after that just got worse, viewers expecting good science-fiction or even tight story-telling switched the channels in droves.

The problems that plagued the production are rumored to be the sole responsibility of some mispicked technical help and some on-set egotism, but the final public blame lies on Anderson's shoulders. Even the fact that it was one of the most expensive and opulent shows ever

Martin Landau, Barbara Bain, Barry Morse, Nick Tate, and the rest of the "Space: 1999" cast prepare to make a take.

144

"Space: 1999" special effects wizard Brian Johnson holds two of his detailed ship models before the vertical version of Moonbase Alpha.

produced is no excuse for scripts that always seem to solve an alien problem by blowing them up. It was a shame, in a way, since Anderson's previous live-action outing, "U.F.O." (1972), was far more successful in imparting intriguing plot lines and concepts.

Writing was certainly not a problem for the "big three." The shows in question were not only excellent, but extremely telling in their value to the mass medium. The story of the first began in 1961 when a series called "Police Surgeon" showed up on English television. There was a mysterious character named Steed who remained a mystery until after an actor's strike cut short the program. When the show resumed in 1962, Steed was back with a first name, a new partner, and a whole new concept. Steed (Patrick Macnee)'s first name was John, the partner was Catherine Gale (Honor Blackman) and the concept was that they were two British operatives battling outlandish threats to world security under the moniker "The Avengers."

We here in the States didn't get to see them at work until after Mrs. Gale resigned and Steed teamed up with Mrs. Emma Peel (Diana Rigg) in 1966. The new pair would bash away at all sorts of baddies (including Christopher Lee and Donald Sutherland), the individual episodes often containing all sorts of fantasy ingredients, until Emma's long-lost husband Peter was found up the Amazon. Steed got a new partner in the more voluptuous, but less attractive, Tara King. Tara (Linda Thorson) was chopped chuck to Emma's filet mignon, but neither were chopped liver. Steed and company got to fight evil for three years in the United States on ABC. Britain profited from their exploits for more than a decade, thanks to the reappearance of Steed in 1976 in the company of "The New Avengers" with Joanna Lumley and Gareth Hunt. The "Avengers" avenge on!

The second marvelous English program to create a stateside sensation slowly started infiltrating the American psyche in 1971 with a movie compilation of their best work but really hit it big in 1974 when public television began rerunning their half-hour antics, originally broadcast in England starting in 1969. Suddenly, "Monty Python's Flying Circus" was a reborn rage. Here fantasy was king—anything could, and did, happen. Sixteen-ton weights fell out of nowhere, suits of armor would hit people over the heads with chickens, naked men would play organs, and all sorts of weird episodes would take place—some of the more famous being: the "dead parrot" sketch, the television game show "Blackmail," "Hell's Grannies," and the science-fiction sketch where vanilla puddings from outer space turn all English people into Scots in order to win the Wimbledon tennis tournament.

The English crew sets up another incredible special-effects shot on Gerry Anderson's *Stingray*.

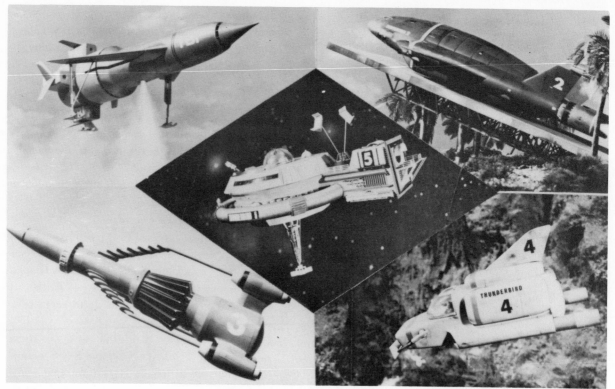

The five spaceships that comprised the Gerry Anderson Thunderbirds.

A rare glimpse of Gerry Anderson's UFO in its natural habitat: outer space.

John Steed (Patrick Macnee) has lost three partners previously. He has no intentions of losing Purdey (Joanna Lumley), one half of *The New Avengers*.

It seems as if "The Prisoner" (Patrick McGoohan, right) has finally won a victory over "The Village" and Number Two (Eric Portman) . . . but has he? From the "Free for All" episode.

MY PARTNER theGHOST

there's something different about this pair of private eyes . . . one of them is **DEAD**

murdered while on a case, Marty Hopkirk comes back as a **GHOST** to help his partner catch his killer

a DIFFERENT kind of detective series

An ad for the latest in a long line of British imports.

The final show of the terrific trio is considered by many to be the greatest television series ever made. In the summer of 1968, "The Jackie Gleason Show" was replaced by the series entitled "The Prisoner," which ran for sixteen weeks in the United States and was unusual in two major aspects. First, the series had a beginning, middle, and end. Second, it was unlike any other program in the history of television. It had influences that could be traced to James Bond, "The Fugitive," and even Flash Gordon, but it was completely unlike any of them.

The plot concerns an initially unnamed individual who resigns from an unnamed government agency. Upon returning to his flat, he is gassed and wakes in "The Village," a self-contained resort establishment which serves as jail for the man, now dubbed "Number Six." Until he gives up his thoughts of escape and tells his warders why he resigned, he will remain the prisoner. For the next four months, Number Six did battle with a variety of managerial "Number Twos" until he is proclaimed an individual in the last episode and makes good an escape.

Along the way, the show offered such fantasy paraphernalia as a huge white ball, known as "Rover," which would capture escaping villagers; a machine which controlled dreams, mind transfer, body transfer; limitless surveillance devices; and advanced brain-washing techniques. Since its original run, a "Prisoner" cult has grown to the point that it was rebroadcast on CBS in 1969 and again in 1978 on the Public Broadcasting System (PBS). Some interesting notes concerning the mysteries of the program: at one point, and at one point only, Number Six is addressed as "Drake," the name of Patrick McGoohan's character in the "Secret Agent" (1965) series, and The Village itself is actually the Hotel Portmeirion in North Wales. "The Prisoner" remains the most intriguing, thought provoking, trying, and reward-ing television experience ever made.

As far as imports go, the last two we shall examine are completely different exercises, one showing that occa-sionally the British can do as badly as we, and the other a delightful combination of the ridiculous and the sublime. The former description fits "My Partner the Ghost," a show that appeared in 1973 as a late-night filler. Kenneth Pope played Marty Hopkirk, a private eye who got croaked and came back to avenge his murder. His human detective partner, Jeff Randall (Mike Pratt) remains his business associate during their subsequent adventures.

The latter description fits what has become a British tradition, as sacred and tasty as afternoon tea. "Dr. Who" is the name of the program that has become a

George Reeves comes in for a rough landing in a rare action shot from *Superman*.

legend across the Atlantic. The show was bought up by Time/Life Films in 1970, and had a short run on PBS in 1973 and 1975, but the Who saga has been running for more than a decade in England. The Doctor is a member of the Time Lords, a group of gods controlling the various mechanizations of time, but whose creed prevents them from helping those in need. However, our hero takes off in his TARDIS (Time And Relative Dimensions in Space) which looks like a telephone booth, to do battle with evil wherever he can find it. Because of this, the Time Lords have alternately exiled him, expelled him, and damned him, but have continually needed his services as monsters galore threaten all the galaxies.

Originally a cantankerous eccentric, "Dr. Who (William Hartnell) regenerated his body into that of an even more eccentric scientist, a sort of cosmic hobo (Patrick Troughton), who played the flute and wore garish outfits. Following a variety of new adventures, the Time Lords exiled him to earth, bringing on another transformation. He became a tuxedoed, white-maned hero figure (Jon Pertwee), who was bolder and more the man of action. Finally the Doctor had to save himself from an overdose of alien radiation, manifesting into an even younger, curly-topped, bulging-eyed redeemer of the wicked (Tom Baker).

He battles still on the BBC and Time/Life is still hoping to start an equally voracious following in the United States. A small sidelight is that the hero got his earth name when he first appeared and people wanted to know what to call him. "Doctor," he said. "Doctor who?" they replied. And it has stuck ever since.

It is not as if we don't have our own share of champions. American sets are constantly filled with super-powered heroes, ready, willing and able to meet any insidious foe—within budgetary considerations. The first, and, most agree, the best, was "The Adventures of Superman," premiering in 1953. The Man of Steel had come from a successful past. From the greatest comic character ever created—by Jerry Siegel and Joe Shuster—to three successful serials—*Superman* (1948), *Superman vs. Atom Man* (1950) and *Superman and the Mole Men* (1951)—his audience was already large and eager when he reached the tube.

Their anticipation was put in the right hands. The larger-than-life hero, who flew, slugged, and x-rayed his way through 104 episodes was played by George Reeves. He was a young actor who had changed his name from George Bessolo on the urging of Jack Warner—who was using him as Brent Tarleton in *Gone with the Wind* (1939). Reeves, an ex-boxer, coming from fifteen years of acting experience, handled the role with professional style and vigor, attacking the weak, static scripts as if they were high art, until his psyche and Superman's were fused. You couldn't mention one without the other.

For over a decade George Reeves *was* Superman and audiences everywhere thrilled to his exploits. Unfortunately, given the limitations of the still-young medium, the Man of Steel wasn't called on to do much more than jump out windows and crash through walls. The villains, for the most part, were bumblers rather than cold-blooded killers, and the shows rarely had more than a superficial urgency. However there were some notable exceptions. *The Stolen Costume* (1953) had Superman exiling two crooks who uncovered his secret identity. *The Defeat of Superman* (1953) had him succumbing to kryptonite, *Panic in the Sky* (1953) had Clark Kent getting amnesia while a meteor hurtles on a collision course with earth, *The Wedding of Superman* (1955) had Lois dreaming about just that, and *Divide and Conquer* (1957) had Superman splitting in two.

With his success it was surprising that more producers didn't try adapting superheroes to the little screen. About the only other comic character to make it to fifties television was "Mandrake the Magician" (1954). Coe Norton played the twentieth-century wizard while Woody Strode played Lothar, his servant. Together they fought crime for less than a season and have disappeared completely. Even some television historians don't know that this show existed.

The major superhero glut waited until 1966 when "Batman" became the biggest hit ABC television had in years. Originally, the prerelease commercials seemed to be promising an all-out atmospheric adventure. With a close-up of one spinning Batmobile wheel, a sonorous voice intoned, "The wheels are humming . . . the Batman is coming." But when the show premiered, audiences saw and loved a "camp" extravaganza of sloped camera angles, overdone dialogue, and onscreen sound effects.

The dual role of Bruce Wayne and his secret identity was enacted by Adam West, a southern California actor with seven years screen experience in such films as *Tammy and the Doctor* (1963) and *Robinson Crusoe on Mars* (1964). His ward, Dick Grayson, was Burt Ward, a

newcomer to the business. They managed to fool around for three seasons until their concept ran dry and audiences became bored with the overdone shenanigans. About the only interesting aspects of the unrealized potential of "Batman" were the scheduling and guest-villain appearances.

Originally, two episodes were scheduled in one week, so "Batman" was essentially a two-part, one-hour weekly show with a "cliff-hanger" at the end of the first installment ("Tune in tomorrow . . . same bat-time, same bat-channel"). The guest list read like a Hollywood Palace party. It became the "in" thing to appear as one of Batman's many nemeses. Among the most notable: Frank Gorshin as The Riddler, Burgess Meredith as The Penguin, Cesar Romero as The Joker, Art Carney as The Archer, Vincent Price as Egghead, Liberace as Shandell, Otto Preminger as Mr. Freeze, Cliff Robertson as Shame, Tallulah Bankhead as The Black Widow, Ida

John Hamilton (Perry White), George Reeves, Jack Larson (Jimmy Olsen) and Noel Neill (Lois Lane) get together for a cast shot of "The Adventures of Superman."

149

Lupino as Cassandra, and Maurice Evans as The Puzzler.

After awhile, however, fans found the show unbearable. It rarely delivered any real thrills and never established a whit of involvement. Unbearable too were the trio of copies that were created in its wake. "The Green Hornet" was an ABC-spawned companion to the Caped Crusader which didn't survive in the camp wasteland "Batman" created. Van Williams played Britt Reid, the manager of the Daily Sentinel, who took on the disguise of The Green Hornet to fight modern-day organized crime. He had a gas-shooting gun, an armored car called "The Black Beauty," and a partner named Kato (Bruce Lee), who was also his karate-skilled butler and chauffeur. They struggled through the 1967 season while the other networks unleashed supposed satires of the comic-book heroes as competition.

"Captain Nice" was NBC's idea, putting supporting actor William Daniels at the fore as Carter Nash, a lovable chemist who mixes up some "Super Juice" which enables him to battle evil. Naturally, this causes some problems for his mother (Alice Ghostley) and his girlfriend (Ann Prentiss). CBS's incredibly original idea had a "Power Pill" give weakling Stanley Beemish (Stephen Strimpell) super powers for one hour at a time. His being "Mr. Terrific" in turn caused difficulties for his partner (Dick Gautier) and his boss (John McGiver). Neither show gave the public any sleepless nights. Both lasted less than a season, going off the air within six days of each other.

A Japanese curiosity piece appeared at the same time. Called "Ultraman," it concerned a Scientific Patrol Headquarters pilot who melded with the psyche of a generous alien and acquired all manner of super power, the foremost being the ability to grow to giant size in order to battle the various monsters who commonly attack the Orient. Those who watched could always be assured that they would see twenty minutes of mass destruction by a particular creature, then Ultraman would show up to bop the beast for ten minutes and save the day. Afterwards he took off for parts unknown.

There was an eight-year wait before a new superhero

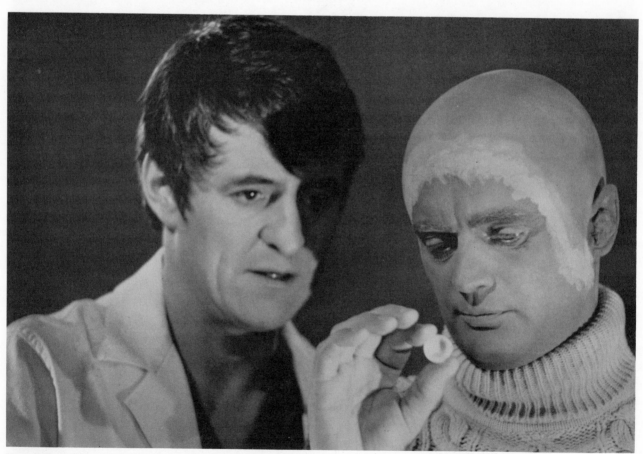

David McCallum (right), with bald cap, is made up completely blue on a soundstage so he can disappear on screen through the magic of "blue-screen" special effects. From "The Invisible Man."

150

would blast into national homes, but it was well worth the wait since the initial arrival heralded a deluge by 1978. The mid seventies saw the return of "The Invisible Man," which originally blanketed the airwaves in 1958 as another English import. Strangely enough, the part of Peter Brady, the clear individual of the title, was played by a mystery man who was always credited as "?" In the 1975 American version, David McCallum took on the thankless role. Thankless because if the audience couldn't see you . . . well . . . they can't see you. What good was your presence? This truism rang out the series which disappeared almost as fast as its star. The same went for "The Gemini Man" two years later, the star of which used a temporary man-made invisibility to fade away.

Faring better in the longevity department was "Wonder Woman." An uninspiring television movie starring Cathy Lee Crosby appeared in 1975 but was a lackadaisical update of the feminist World War II heroine. Crosby hardly filled out her costume—considerably altered from the original—while both the script and the direction lacked conviction. The initial concept's time had come, however, and the gal returned in the statuesque form of six-foot Lynda Carter and "The New Original Wonder Woman." This 1976 period piece, developed by Stanley Ralph Ross, put the punch back into the story, also restoring the lady's original powers, her golden lasso, and her transparent jet.

This second television movie was optioned further by ABC, which plopped it into various time slots during 1977 but refused to give it a clear-cut network berth. It was up to CBS to do that when they bought the show for the 1978 season. It also transported the whole kit and caboodle into modern times, so every week Carter can parade around in low-cut, clingy dresses, filmy nightgowns, and revealing bathing suits until her associate Steve Trevor (Lyle Waggoner) gets into trouble. Then she spins about, lightning flashes, thunder rolls, and she's decked out in her star-spangled mini-leotard and boots, ready to battle evil and midriff bulge. Her success heralded the coming of a new troupe of CBS superheroes.

The first to appear was "The Amazing Spider-Man," fleshed out by Nicholas Hammond as Peter Parker, a mild-mannered student who's bitten by a radioactive spider and takes on the arachnid's powers. He can now climb walls, beat up villains, and, with a little mechanical assistance, shoot webbing. This too was originally a made-for-television film by the Charles Fries Organization, but with the decent rating it garnered, in the spring of 1978 it was extended into a twelve-episode series.

The same happened to "The Incredible Hulk." Uni-versal had bought the rights to five Marvel Comics superheroes and the gamma-ray created green giant was the first to reach screen translation. On Friday, November fourth, to be exact, the film, produced, written, and directed by Kenneth Johnson, was shown and became a small-screen triumph. The experienced television producer had neatly eliminated all the comic's weak devices, inconsistencies and campiness, turning what could have been ludicrous into an effective two-hour fantasy tale. David Bruce Banner (Bill Bixby) is desperate to discover why some people can tap inner strength during times of crises, and he couldn't when his wife succumbed in a flaming car wreck. This research leads the young doctor to, one, discover that the atmospheric gamma radiation is high on the days when miracles could be performed, and, two, bathe himself in millions of gamma rays.

Now, whenever his emotions are at a fever pitch, he turns into a seven-foot-tall green muscle-bound monster who knocks down a lot of walls and throws a lot of people around. The initial movie got an excellent rating, so a sequel was immediately released which did just as well. "The Hulk" followed "Spider-Man" onto the weekly schedule, but premiered prior to the wall-crawling wonder, and, again, got terrific ratings.

CBS knew a good thing when it scheduled it. The executives have instructed Universal to prepare "Captain America," and "The Human Torch" for possible production. They were going to mount "The Sub-Mariner" as well until NBC beat them to the punch by releasing "The Man from Atlantis" as a 1977 television movie, then as a short lived series. Pat Duffy played Mark Harris, a strange and powerful merman discovered and aided by Belinda Montgomery as Elizabeth, an oceanographer. The pilot film was high-quality fare, interestingly establishing Mark's confusion, semi-amnesia, integrity, and power.

Also introduced was his number one nemesis, Mr. Schubert (Victor Buono), an eccentric millionaire interested in establishing an underwater kingdom and destroying society above sea level. All in all, the opening installment was involving, fast and enjoyable. Following it were two more ninety-minute movies which weren't as fast or involving but just made it on the enjoyable level. All three did well enough to warrant a weekly series. Then the show just fell apart. All in the intriguing concepts introduced in the pilots were jettisoned for irrational action. Even Duffy's charisma couldn't keep "The Man from Atlantis" afloat beneath the weight of the leaden scripts. It sank from network sight, taking any chance the "Sub-Mariner" production might have had.

Lynda Carter strikes a humbling pose for the first season of "The New Original Wonder Woman." Believe it or not, but the outfit just got smaller and smaller.

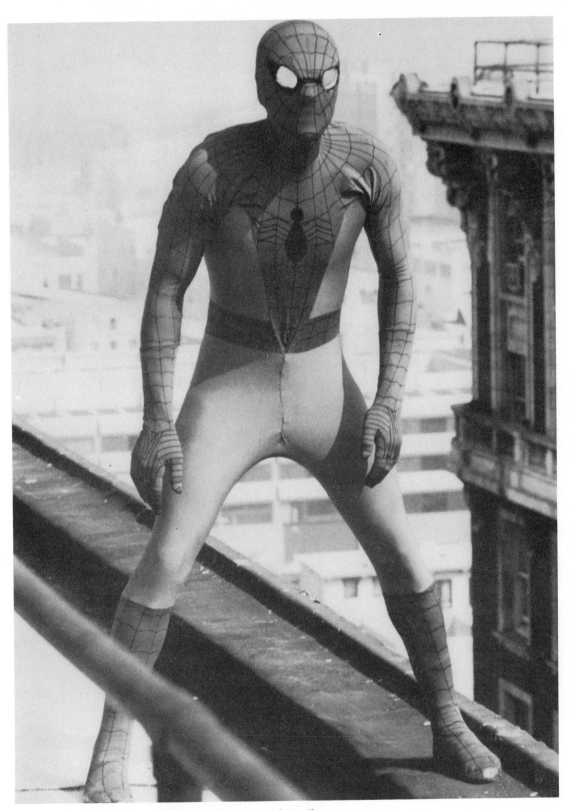

Nicholas Hammond is ready for anything except his tailor as *The Amazing Spider-Man* (© CBS).

Don't get Bill Bixby (left) mad. If you do, he'll probably turn into Lou Ferrigno (right)—*The Incredible Hulk* (© CBS).

Pat Duffy as Mark Harris: "The Man From Atlantis." His webbed hands, along with several other intriguing concepts, were ignored once his weekly series began.

Thankfully, there are other shows, hardly categorizable, that have delivered on their fantasy premises. "Between Time and Timbuctu," based on the stories of Kurt Vonnegut and written by the man himself, appeared on PBS in the mid seventies and was about the only inventive, audacious television film worth its imaginative salt. Its success and subsequent cult following led the way for three shows that are still running at the time of this writing, and all three are eminently watchable.

The first started as a minor phenomenon on a variety of variety shows. Since then, they have burst into a major conspiracy of inventive mirth, taking over the world with a high-flying combination of old jokes and futuristic presentations. By its second year on television, "The Muppet Show" (1976) was seen in 163 American cities and 103 other countries, making it the most-watched

Bob and Ray, radio and television comedians yuk it up as news commentators during PBS's "Between Time and Timbuktu."

program in the world—with an average 300 million viewers. It also managed to garner the most-impressive guest list in recent years. Just a few of those they have signed are Peter Sellers, Zero Mostel, John Cleese, Steve Martin, Julie Andrews, Elton John, Rudolph Nureyev, and many others of the same ilk.

Besides the everyday fantasy aspects of a show almost completely populated by hand puppets, it has creatures that defy description, including The Great Gonzo, Sweetums, talking French breads, and the merry inhabitants of the planet Goosbaine. For folks who want to revel in fantasy, they need look no further than "The Muppet Show."

In the first year and a half of its run, the Muppets also appeared on NBC's "Saturday Night Live" (1975) as alien worshippers of the Mighty Favog. Unfortunately, their work on the satiric show was mostly improvised and didn't benefit from later editing, so they were soon eliminated. But "Saturday Night" continued, its fantasy aspects held in good stead by "Jeopardy: 1999," a game-show satire; a Star Trek satire which was later republished in *Starlog* magazine; and the recurring adventures of "The Coneheads," an outer-space family who make their way in earth society by telling everyone they're from France.

The third and final uncategorizable show benefits from liberal doses of fantasy also. "Second City Television" is a half hour comedy that proports to show a fictional television station's (SC-TV) regular programming day. Led by head writer and coproducer Harold Ramis, the improvisational group that includes Andrea Martin, John Candy, and Dave Thomas lampoons every aspect of television, including commercials and station breaks. One such ad recently told of an upcoming SC-TV movie called "The Exorcist of Oz." If insanity is your bag, you would be well served to watch "The Muppet Show," "Saturday Night Live," and "Second City Television" religiously. Nowadays, they may be the only consistent quality available on the small screen.

In recent months, video fantasy has taken a nose dive unprecedented in shoddiness. This fact is all the more surprising in that *Star Wars* supposedly started a cycle towards high quality/high budget productions, and the television movie is a perfect place to test fantasy themes. It has been since 1971 when ABC introduced "The Movie of the Week," ninety minutes of mystery, comedy, or science fiction.

In its first season alone, it gave us "The House that Wouldn't Die," with Barbara Stanwyck, "Crowhaven Farm," with Hope Lange, the aforementioned "The

"Pigs in Space," Muppetmania's newest and zaniest science fiction serial, stars (from left to right) Dr. Strangepork, Commander Link Hogthrob and the always vivacious Miss Piggy.

The continuing "Muppet Show" saga of "Pigs in Space" is populated by Dr. Strangepork, Commander Link Hogthrob, and First Officer Miss Piggy.

Elliott Gould (center with cigar) confers with "Saturday Night Live's" "Conehead" family (from the left Laraine Newman, Jane Curtin, and Dan Ackroyd).

violent power at the family's rustic home, but even it could not favorably compare with "Duel," which Spielberg did for ABC the following year.

Working from a script by Richard Matheson, based on Matheson's original short story which appeared in *Playboy* magazine, the director fashioned what is probably the best shock/terror television experience of recent years. Instead of sharks or aliens, traveling businessman Dennis Weaver has a run-in with a tractor-trailer truck which escalates into a veritable "car wars."

Meanwhile, CBS ran a curiosity piece called "Gargoyles" (1972), starring Cornell Wilde as a vacationing gent who stumbles across a race of ancient monsters who plan to do in mankind. Although fairly amateurish, the script was punched home with solid conviction and the creatures themselves (made up by Ross Wheat and Ellis Berman) were worth the price of admission. The rest of 1972 was pretty soggy, with the fairly unsuccessful "Sandcastles"—a videotaped love story beyond the grave—"Haunts of the Very Rich"—another short story adapted from *Playboy* with a good cast—and "Poor Devil"—ostensibly a comedy about a devil trying to earn his horns by ruining human lives. Sammy Davis, Jr. was

Immortal," and, best of all, "The Point," Harry Nilsson's animated tale of a boy seeking individuality in a society of pointy-headed people, directed by Fred Wolf and narrated by Dustin Hoffman. And there was more to come, some good, most fair, some awful.

NBC had started the ball rolling with "Fame is the Name of the Game," then released "Fear No Evil" in 1969, with Louis Jourdan as occultist David Sorel out to save a girl's soul from her dead boyfriend's spirit. This one was really pretty neat since Jourdan made a believable hero and the supernatural overtones weren't ludicrous. The second Sorel film, "Ritual of Evil," appeared in 1970 and wasn't as successful as the first but delivered a diverting two hours.

Which is more than can be said for ABC's like contributions: "Satan's School for Girls" (1973), where Pamela Franklin got experience for *Suspiria* by fighting evil influences within Roy Thinnes; or "She Waits" (1971), with Patty Duke getting possessed. Thankfully, there were some other gems in the early clinkers, what with two films directed by Steven Spielberg at the opening of his career, "Something Evil" (1970) hit CBS with little Johnny Whitaker getting taken over by a very

Jonathan Frid cut an imposing figure as Barnabas Collins, TV's only daily vampire, on the horror soap opera "Dark Shadows."

the demon in question and Christopher Lee made a rare Unites States Television appearance as the Devil.

The next year, made-for-television films concerning fantasy were hard to come by and lousy when they came. "The Cat Creature," "Don't Be Afraid of the Dark," and "The Picture of Dorian Grey" were about the only things worth mentioning, and those just barely. "The Cat Creature," although written by Robert Bloch and directed by Curtis Harrington as their homage to old-style horror movies, was curiously devoid of style or shocks. John Newland directed "Don't Be Afraid . . .," but without much interest, and "Dorian," was a Dan Curtis special, a feat he was to repeat with 1975's "Dracula" and "The Strange Case of Dr. Jekyll and Mr. Hyde," both starring Jack Palance.

Curtis's highly successful horror soap opera, "Dark Shadows," had just finished its five-year run on ABC, so Dan was concentrating on film fare from then on. Harrington returned to the form as well in 1974 with "The Dead Don't Die," which had a plot reminiscent of *Ruby*. Does an army of mobster zombies sound familiar? Taking their places alongside this attempt was "The Stranger Within," Richard Matheson's derivation of all those Satan-spawned babies with an alien-spawned kid; and "Scream of the Wolf," another effort from the prolific Dan Curtis.

The big news of 1974 also came from Curtis with the title "Trilogy of Terror." The initial two segments were penned by William F. Nolan, who did the honors on *Burnt Offerings* too, and are only of passing interest. Richard Matheson wrote the third story in the anthology telefilm—the "devil doll" sequence—which saved the show. A momma's girl buys a tribal doll, for her latest amour, which comes alive and spends ten minutes trying to kill her. The apartment-bound battle is frighteningly effective and Karen Black, who starred in all the segments, was highly commended for her performance.

Things really began to corrode after that. The Bermuda Triangle was the going thing in 1975, and a couple of television movies were worked up around it, one with Doug McClure and Kim Novak, the other with Sam Groom and Fred MacMurray, both terrible. "The Werewolf of Woodstock" had a great title and that's about all. Even the aforementioned "Dracula" wasn't so hot. And it just got worse. The undiluted dreck that has been reaching the airwaves for the last three years went from the bad to the ridiculous.

It all really started with "Look What's Happened to Rosemary's Baby" (1976), starring Steven McHattie and Ruth Gordon—who won an Oscar for her role in the original theatrical feature. "Look What's Happened" is the kind of picture one watches in awed rapture because one can't believe the awfulness of what one is seeing. Besides being boring, it was incomprehensible. "The Possessed," on NBC, starring James Farentino, was an out-and-out copy of *The Exorcist* with the only attraction being the cast's charisma and Joan Bennett spewing nails from her demonized mouth. "Fantasy Island," "Return to Fantasy Island," and the subsequent weekly series starring Ricardo Montalban were pedestrian in their mediocrity and weren't supernatural in the least. "It Happened One Christmas," a Marlo Thomas production, only made *It's A Wonderful Life* (1946), the Frank Capra film it was based on, all the more rewarding to see again. It is a shame to simply dismiss any of these movies, since each had its good points, but neither is it fair for these films to force the viewer to search for the good points, which all the preceding titles did.

However, these last five might as well have been *The Sound of Music* (1965) for the relative quality of the upcoming five pictures. These clinkers must rate the hall of infamy for their obviousness and crudity. "The Man With the Power," on NBC, was a gigantic missed opportunity. The stupidity with which they approached the tale of a boy with a human mother and an alien father

Marlo Thomas smiled her way through "It Happened One Christmas." Critics did not (© ABC).

was astonishing. "The Bermuda Depths," originally made for theaters, but unable to acquire distribution, was a Rankin/Bass live-action production put on television with all its bounteous banality intact. It concerned a mermaid, a mermonster, and a giant turtle in a hokey love story and a murky plot. "Cruise into Terror" was even soggier. It had Frank Converse, Christopher George, John Forsythe, Hugh O'Brian, Stella Stevens, and Lee Meriweather in a hackneyed script concerning a mini-sarcophagus which bears warning to the coming of Satan's son. The whole thing was as creaky as the boat they were on.

At least "Cruise" was slightly original. "The Initiation of Sarah" was such an obvious rip-off of *Carrie* that it was stunning. Some scenes were almost lifted shot by shot and restaged for this sorry excuse for entertainment. How the likes of Kay Lenz, Shelley Winters, Tisa Farrow, Morgan Fairchild, Kathryne Crosby, and Tony Bill were enticed into this inconsistent schlock boggles the imagination.

And speaking of crude, stupid, banal, hokey, incomprehensible, hackneyed, creaky, rip-off, inconsistent and schlock, we come to "The Dark Secret of Harvest Home," a multihoured "novel for television Big Event," which was truly worthy of every insult imaginable. It was five hours of what can stand with the likes of *Damnation Alley* and *The Sentinel* as the worst viewing experience of the past decade. It tells the disjointed, unsubstantiated story of Nick Constantine (David Ackroyd), a New York cartoonist who moves into the quiet New England town of Cornwall Coombe (actually filmed in Ohio) with his beautiful wife (Joanna Miles) and beautiful fifteen-year-old daughter (Rosanna Arquette). From there on, little makes sense and even less is followed through.

The finale is a foregone conclusion before the first hour is over, and plot twists come and go without so much as a single clarification. Irrationality abounds, implication stands in for reason, and there are story holes that you could airlift the 245th Panzer Division through. The dark secret of "Harvest Home" is actually how NBC had the gall to televise it and how Bette Davis, Rene Auberjonois, Richard Venture, and Donald Pleasence got involved in it.

In the face of such junk, the average becomes bearable, as in the case of the two-part "The World Beyond." The stories told of a sportswriter who is legally dead for a few minutes, then brought back to life. During his demise, however, he created a connection to the spirit world, and the dead contact him occasionally to help those living kin in need. Granville Van Dusen played Paul Davis, the lead, in both pilots, each sixty

Kim Basinger (right) continues to guest star and model but Ernest Borgnine is about to become "The Ghost of Flight 401."

minutes long. The first was superior, although it too was basically an atmospheric combination of *Psycho* and *The Exorcist*. The spirit of a dead boy mummified upstairs takes over his stepsister supernaturally for evil doings until Paul forces his mother to commit suicide, taking him with her. The second show had a golem made from sticks and mud going after his creator's sister. Although also moodily mounted, it suffered from too arbitrary a solution—salt disintegrates it; the reason given: none—and a ludicrous-looking mud man.

About the only three decent recent fantasies were either ignored or based on fact. The latter classification suits "The Ghost of Flight 401," which was a best-selling paperback before it was made into a respectful and engrossing NBC movie produced by Emmet Lavery Jr. and directed by Steven Stern. A good cast, including Ernest Borgnine, Kim Basinger, and Eugene Roche, added to the story of flight officer Dom Cimoli (Borgnine) who died in the 401 plane crash but returned constantly as a spirit to warn subsequent flights of possible malfunctions. His friends and associates get together at the climax to lead Cimoli onto a higher plane in order to reach peace.

159

Gig Young and Robert Culp as the Sherlock Holmes and Watson of the supernatural discover the mummified body of Pam Rose prior to the climax of Gene Roddenberry's "Spectre."

The Devil never had it so good. These are but three of the demons sent to lure Robert Culp and Gig Young to their dooms during "Spectre" (from left, Vicki Michelle, Angela Grant, and Penny Irving).

Next was the highly enjoyable, though familiar, "Spectre," produced by Gene Roddenberry, directed by Clive Donner, with makeup by Stuart Freeborn, and starring Robert Culp and Gig Young as a supernatural Sherlock Holmes and Watson. It was sadly underrated and unrecognized as the best fantasy pilot produced in recent memory. The same could be said of director/writer/producer Phil DeGuere's intelligent mounting of *Dr. Strange* in September, 1978. Even with a cast including John Mills and Jessica Walters, and excellent special effects, the CBS network didn't advertise it with any enthusiasm. Less than ten million people watched, making it a failure in the ratings. A sad fate for a show that certainly outshone the likes of "Quark"—a lukewarm science-fiction satire—or "The Return of Captain Nemo"—Irwin Allen's revival of a great character reduced to his lowest common denominator. While we can always depend on Dan Curtis to whip up something like "The Curse of the Black Widow" (1977), with Patty Duke Astin turning into a giant spider when riled, surely the rest of modern television can come up with something that rivals the fantasy heights of Ernie Kovacs or "The Prisoner." The public television stations are constantly introducing exciting fare, like the BBC-imported "Dracula," starring Louis Jourdan. So maybe, just maybe, between the "Love Boats," "Little House on the Prairies," and killer cops, the major networks can raise a show where imagination counts more than commercials.

5   CARTOONS

IN *Willy Wonka & the Chocolate Factory*, Gene Wilder as Willy sings a song about the joys of "pure imagination." While he may have been referring to his life style and magical establishment, he might as well have been singing about the art of animation, where the creations live or die on the strength of the artist's imagination—and, of course, the director's firm hand and the producer's budget.

The art form started in the early 1900s as an extension of the motion picture industry. Cartoons could enable creators to realistically picture things actors were incapable of, as in Windsor McKay's famous *Gertie the Dinosaur* (1909). Three years earlier, Stuart Blackton had introduced the form with *Humorous Phases of Funny Faces* (1906) and several subsequent styles: the humanization of inanimate objects—*The Magic Fountain Pen* (1909)—and the fairy tale—*The Smoke Fairy* (1909). McKay, a newspaper cartoonist, continued his animated ways with *How a Mosquito Works* (1910) and *Little Nemo* (1911), while the American animation industry officially began around him.

The two major studios at the time were those of Raoul Barre, which would continue in one form or another until 1927, and John Randolph Bray, which branched off into three lucrative forms which have continued up to the present day. While Barre was producing Rube Goldberg cartoons and teaming with Charles Bower, who animated *Mutt & Jeff;* and Bray was releasing *Farmer Alfalfa*, World War One training films, *Quaky Doodles' Family*—and giving experience to young filmmakers Paul Terry and Max Fleischer—Pat Sullivan opened his studio to produce the first full-scale animation star—"Felix the Cat."

Sullivan began by animating Charlie Chaplin cartoons in 1914, then gave the directorial reigns over to Otto Messmer, who was by and large the genius behind Felix's silent-era success. It may come as a surprise to those who have seen the more recent "limited animation" Felix cartoons, with the cat stridently battling super villains with the help of his magic bag, that the original feline was fantasy personified—existing in his own world of imagination. Felix could, and would, do anything to facilitate his needs. The most famous single sequence was one where the hungry cat looks down into the water from the end of a wharf. A question mark appears above his head to signify wonder—a punctuation mark that Felix uses the next second. He grabs the bottom, sticks the black hook upside down into the bay, and pulls out a fish.

Felix used everything in his cartoons: his pointy ears were put together to make scissors, his tail a hand-held whip, exclamation marks as clubs, and the line of the horizon as rope. The "Felix the Cat" cartoons, ranging from 1919 to Sullivan's death in 1932 (from personal tragedy and drink) were glorious silent black and white exercises in mood and movement, the likes of which are still unique and eminently enjoyable.

At about the same time of the cat's movie appearances, three major animation landmarks were being instituted. Branching off from Bray-Hurd Process Company was The Paul Terry Studio, also known as the Talents Inc. & Famous Studio. This intrepid fellow would go through more incarnations than Dr. Who before producing the

Art Babbitt, one of the animation greats—among his credits are Geppetto in *Pinocchio*, the Queen in *Snow White*, and the Mushroom Dance in *Fantasia*.

series of characters he is most famous for today. First he put out "Farmer Alfalfa," then as he changed to "Fables Pictures" (1923), and "Aesop's Fables" (1927), he produced just that: *The Goose That Laid the Golden Egg* (1921), *Fable of the Pharaoh's Tomb* (1923), and *Bugville Field Day* (1925), among others.

Then, in 1929, his company became Audiocinema with the coming of sound, adding Frank Moser and J. Coffman to the production fold. With the help of such animation greats as Art Babbitt & Tex Avery, he instituted "Foolish Fables" and the familiar "Terrytoons." Nineteen thirty-two saw Moser-Terry Inc. instituted and characters like "Oil Can Harry" & "Cubby Bear" coming to the fore. Finally, in 1936, Terrytoons Inc. was established and the real stars of the studio took center stage: "Heckle & Jekyll" and "Mighty Mouse."

The former pair were two talking magpies who seem loosely based on "Amos & Andy," but have characteristics all their own. One talks like a "boid from de Bronx",

while the other has a high-pitched English accent and a tendency to utter "I say, old boy" a lot. The others favorite pronoun was "chum" and together they would usually make mincemeat of two dogs—one dumb hound and a tough bull dog. The height of their fantasy influences came when the two realized they were actually cartoon characters and spent the rest of the episode drawing themselves out of impossible situations.

Mighty Mouse, on the other hand, stayed pretty much the superhero who appeared at the last minute to save the lass, but went through several physical and costume changes before he became the muscle-bound mouse we know today. In his original cartoon, he became empowered by hiding out from cats in a "super" market overnight—all the super food giving him untold-of abilities. Still, he seemed kind of scrawny for awhile. Later he went through two distinct subject-matter changes. There was a series where he would participate in famous fantasy environments, like that of the days of Aladdin, volcanic South Sea isles, and an "operatic" period which would be mounted as a chapter in a continuing serial with all the dialogue sung. The other major difference was that the character had a rather torrid onscreen love life, a subject most other cartoons shied away from. Hardly a Mighty Mouse ended without him being showered with kisses.

Elsewhere, Walt Disney instituted his company in 1919 and had a prolific career before *Snow White* appeared in 1937. With Rudolph Ising and Ub Iwerks, among others, he created the Laugh-O-Gram Films Corp., which put out shorter versions of *Cinderella* and *Alice in Cartoonland*. When the company went bankrupt in 1923, Iwerks, Roy Disney, and Walt went to L.A. to begin again, while Ising teamed up with Hugh Harman in Kansas City to produce "Arabian Night" Cartoons before rejoining the fold in 1925 as Disney hit his stride again with "Oswald Rabbit", produced by Charles Mintz, who was then the head of Associated Animators. Harman-Ising split again in 1928, and Mintz took Oswald over to Screen Gems, but Disney countered by creating "Mickey Mouse."

Then came an age of innovation and achievement unparalleled in animation history. Nineteen twenty-nine saw "Silly Symphonies" being made in Technicolor by special arrangement, and the introduction of "Minnie Mouse." "Pluto" the dog, was created in 1932. *Goofy* and *Donald Duck* in 1936. Disney was smart, structured, and progressive. His cartoons, even in the early days, mirrored those characteristics. Jeff Rovin in *The Fabulous Fantasy Films* evoked the marvel and wonder of Disney's films and a little later this volume shall return to

A marvelously evoked moment from *Pinocchio* inside the whale.

an examination of the studio's latest work.

Meanwhile, back in 1921, Max Fleischer had left the Bray-Hurd company to begin his own studio and the "Out of the Inkwell" series. Max was a little less smart and structured than Disney, but he was as much the genius and as progressive. Out of his works came established techniques, the most known of which is the rotoscope, Fleischer's patented device to draw over live actors, achieving new styles of realism. But in the beginning, the watchwords were experimentation and entertainment.

"Out of the Inkwell" introduced "Koko the Clown," a crazy guy who lived in Max's inkwell, and, when released, got in all sorts of outlandish predicaments and created untold mischief, most often in conjunction with live-action objects. The height of his complications was in *Koko's Earth Control*, wherein the clown and his dog, "Bimbo," discover a lab where there's a switch marked "Danger. Beware. Do Not Touch. Earth Control. If this Handle is Pulled the World Will Come to an End." Unfortunately, Bimbo can't resist and indeed, the world

Walt Disney.

164

Grim Natwick, a pioneer animator, is known as one of the most talented, generous, and renowned in the business. He is largely responsible for *Betty Boop* and *Snow White* herself.

comes to an end with a flurry of lightning, visual thunder, earthquakes, and live-action disintegration.

Following Koko's success was Bimbo's emergence as a leading character in a series of "Screen Songs," where the musically inclined audience would "follow the bouncing ball" in order to sing along. They continued from 1927 to 1937, introducing along the way the category of "Talkartoons," which, in turn, introduced the character of "Betty Boop," in 1930. She really hit it big in 1932, and along with Bimbo, faced the likes of *The Old Man of the Mountain* (1933), *Popeye the Sailor* (1933) and all manner of monsters. If Mighty Mouse had torrid love interests, Betty's was conflagrations. Her chastity was in constant danger and her onscreen nubileness was renowned. One of her early cartoons even incorporated "R" rated animated pawing and near nudity.

Three months after Popeye's guest shot in Boop's cartoon, his own series started, one that would last longer

and be far more telling in the industry. Before Famous Studios of Paramount Pictures took over the character in 1942, the spinach-swallowing sailor introduced some great fantasy episodes: the *Hyp-nut-tist* (1935), which had Bluto making magic the power of his mind before Popeye made mincemeat out of him; *Wotta Nitemare* (1939), where the sailor dreams he, Olive Oyl & Bluto are in heaven; *Popeye Meets William Tell* (1940), *Popeye Meets Rip Van Winkle* (1941); and the spectaculor trio of "two-reelers" (20 minute cartoons) *Popeye Meets Ali Baba & the Forty Thieves*, (1937), *Popeye Meets Aladdin* (1939), and the best of the lot, *Popeye the Sailor Meets Sinbad the Sailor* (1936).

Fantasy reared its wonderful head in several other instances as well. *Popeye in Goonland* (1938) has the sailor and his father battle the big-nosed, giant monsters so ferociously that the film breaks. A live-action hand enters the picture and splices the film back together. In the predominantly live-action *Adventures of Popeye* (1935), a real boy gets pushed around by a bully until Popeye comes out of a book and advises the kid to eat spinach. The same idea is used in *What—No Spinach?* (1936), where a little live-action boy in a theater comes to Popeye's onscreen rescue just in the nick of time.

The Fleischer downfall came about mostly because he did not own his own characters. He made no money from their merchandising and most of his creations were wormed away from him. Before that sad event occured, however, the Fleischer studios made two full-length films—*Gulliver's Travels* (1939) and *Mr. Bug Goes to Town* (1941)—and an expensive series of Superman cartoons from 1941-1944. Although unsuccessful, the cartoons were beautiful and it was a fitting project to "go out" on. The art work was better than any like superhero adventures being drawn and the Superman character was vulnerably human. *Superman in the Mechanical Monsters* (1941), *Superman in the Electric Earthquake* (1942), *Superman in Destruction, Inc.* (1942), and *Superman in Showdown* (1943) are just some of the highlights.

Elsewhere, others were not idle. By 1934, Disney was making money hand over foot and other companies wanted a bit of that action. Already Screen Gems, under the direction of Mintz, was making "Krazy Kat" and "Scrappy the Dog" while Universal Studios had Walter Lantz, who, along with Friz Freleng, Rudolph Ising, and Hugh Harmon were recreating "Oswald." Lantz also became famous for his "Andy Panda" series in 1939, and "Woody Woodpecker" in 1940. Other studios and independent producers figured the best way to hop on the bandwagon was to lure away established directors and

Three original visualizations from the "Night on Bald Mountain" sequence from *Fantasia*. The final animation of the Devil character was by the late Vladimir Tytla, who has been hailed as "the Michelangelo of animators."

animators from the Disney fold. Pat Powers convinced Ub Iwerks to create his own company, the Animated Pictures Corp. a move which would haunt the talented artist the rest of his life. His new 1930 series, "Flip the Frog," was not a long-term success, and, although he returned to Disney Studios in 1935, he had lost Walt's trust.

By that time, Ising & Harmon had created Harmon-Ising Productions, a punny title which led to a very successful tuneful triple whammy. Taking a cue from Disney's "Silly Symphonies," they brought about "Looney Tunes" (1930), "Merrie Melodies" (1931) and "Happy Harmonies" (1934) in one fell swoop. Loony & Merrie became part of Warner Brothers Studio in 1934 with Leon Schlessinger, then Edward Selzer, as producer. Up until then, they had been featuring a slightly negroid character named "Bosko the Talkink Kid," but with the coming of Bob McKimson, Tex Avery, Friz Freleng, Frank Tashlin, Bob Clampett, and Chuck Jones, the studio took on new directions and characters. Among the less-notable creations like "Gabby the Goat" and "Buddy" came such diamonds in the rough as "Porky Pig" (a product of the Tex Avery unit) and what is termed by Chuck Jones as "a wildly insane 'Daffy Duck.' "

The big hits of the newborn Warners crew were two teams, the major being Porky Pig and "Beans the Cat," commonly known as "Porky & Beans." The other duo was two twin dogs called "Ham & Ex." Although most of these cartoons were good, and some were wonderful—like *The Artist's Nightmare*, where a cartoonist falls asleep at his easel and dreams he is taken prisoner by his creations—it is severely doubtful that those early gems will ever be seen, since, for some reason, the networks refuse to show the Warners black and whites.

The only ones they do show are the horribly bastardized recolored versions which are always preceded by a growing asterisk which introduces them as Warner Brothers-Seven Arts cartoons. The story is that these black and white originals were sent to the Orient to be colored by a lazy animation company who did only the number of originals they wanted to. Instead of redoing, let's say, the twelve drawings needed for an onscreen movement, they would do six, maybe eight, and sometimes four or five. Needless to say, they were returned pale shadows of their former selves.

Back in America, the Warner Brothers boys were mounting films of which their main characteristic was insanity. Porky had become a star in his own right, thanks to the great voice characterizations of Mel Blanc, who went on to do almost all of the famous creations, and the maniacal Daffy was premiered in *Porky's Duck Hunt* (1937), a Daffy who looked different than his subsequent self, but was as nutso as the day was long. "Egghead" was turned slowly into "Elmer Fudd" at the same time Porky was finalizing his characterization as a versatile supporting player and "Bugs Bunny" was developed.

Meanwhile, each of the different directors began to cement their own individual styles. Frank Tashlin was a master of sharp-edged schizophrenic insanity, pulling reactions and physical action into the ultimate of exaggeration, a technique both Tex Avery and Bob

The cartoon cast of Disney's *Sleeping Beauty*.

The eternal conflict between Elmer Fudd and Bugs Bunny from their golden age of the forties.

Clampett shared. Avery was a master of motion and expression as well, while Clampett's efforts were like fever dreams, pulpy waves rolling over the viewer. Nineteen forty-one saw the beginnings of Chuck Jones's stark impressionistic style and inventive conceptions. In 1936, Tashlin left the studio to create live-action comedies like *The Paleface* (1948), *Will Success Spoil Rock Hunter?* (1957), and *The Glass Bottom Boat* (1966). In 1942, Avery went over to MGM, and the four leaders left were McKimson, Freleng, Clampett and Jones, each separated into three divisions.

Out of Clampett's came "Tweety-Pie," "Beaky Buzzard" and "Red Hot Ryder," who became "Yosemite Sam." Before he left at the end of the forties to produce "Beany & Cecil," Clampett and his head animator McKimson had developed Bugs into a wise-cracking master of time and space. Out of Jones's department came "Pepe Le Pew," the "Road Runner," and the "Coyote," while, for him, Bugs was forever meeting up with witches, story book characters, and the famous "Martin the Martian."

Daffy turned into everybody's fall guy, appearing in a justly famous cycle of character satires and a classic self-satire of cartoons called "Duck Amuck," where the poor fellow is belittled by every technical problem imaginable: from having the sound go out on him to getting turned into other creatures, to the frame walls sagging, to the film getting caught until Daffy confronts the unseen animator and the camera pulls back to reveal Bugs Bunny at the drawing board. His comment: "Ain't I a stinker?"

The Jones genre satires put Daffy & Porky through *The Scarlet Pumpernickel* (1950), putting on swashbucklers; *Drip Along Daffy* (1951) with westerns as the target; *Duck Dodgers in the 24½ Century* (1953), sending up science fiction, *Deduce You Say!* (1957), Sherlock Somes & Watkins; and *Robin Hood Daffy* (1958). Bugs also hit the satire trail, though his were a bit more esoteric, often using a musical there, like *Long Haired Hare* (1948), *The Rabbit of Seville* (1950), and the crowning achievement, *What's Opera, Doc?* (1957), where Elmer Fudd and Bugs reenact their classic conflict in the form of a Wagnerian Opera.

The Warner Brothers Studio Animation Department went with the wind in 1962, thanks to the money-saving techniques and flawed thinking of the executives, as well as the diminishing market for animation shorts. The other major short subject maker at the time was MGM, who united under producer Fred Quimby in 1937 to produce "The Captain & the Kids," under the direction of William Hanna, and "Barney Bear" under Rudolph

A little older, a little wiser, but still in there plugging. Bugs and Daffy Duck from the recent Chuck Jones CBS special, *A Connecticut Rabbit in King Arthur's Court*.

Ising. Nineteen forty-one was the year they really hit the artistic and monetary big time, with the arrival of Tex Avery and the creation of "Tom & Jerry" cartoons by Will Hanna and Joseph Barbera.

Avery's series of shorts held some undeniable fantasy classics as well as the lovable cycle of "Droopy the Dog" films. One of his first and most famous in both categories is 1943's *Dumb-Hounded*, where Droopy captures an escaped convict, and *Red Hot Riding Hood*, where the characters of the fairy tale revolt against the saccharin aspects of their tale and go through an "R" rated version. Both cartoons established Tex's style of nth-degree reactions and quickly delivered death (with equally fast recovery). Characters' eyes grow big as boulders, their teeth like monoliths, their arms emit from their ears, their limbs fly off in surprise, they shatter like glass, drop into jigsaw pieces, and twist into every imaginable shape.

Other greats of imagination from Avery were *Swing Shift Cinderella* (1945), where the wolf from Little Red Riding Hood switches allegiance; *King Sized Canary* (1947) where a substance called Jumbo-Gro causes all sorts of complications; *The Cat that Hated People* (1948), about a feline who rents a rocket to the moon, finds that craziness abounds, then golfs himself back; and *Bad Luck Blackie* (1949) where a black cat, a specialist in bad luck, comes to the rescue of a persecuted kitten. These capsule descriptions do almost nothing to translate the priceless quality of these insane efforts. They are delirious, demented, delicious, and deserving of the cult that has recently grown up around Avery's work.

But "Tom & Jerry" was where MGM would garner most of its cartoon success and reputation. The first of the lot, *Puss Gets the Boot,* (1941) had a cat named Jasper going after an unnamed mouse on the orders of Mammy Two Shoes, but the second, *The Midnight Snack,* (1941) had the two characters named and their eternal conflict set up, a conflict which was to go into five separate changes. The first cycle was the best and had the best individual fantasy episodes. From 1941-1951, Tom chased Jerry all over the place, smashing into walls, trees, ceilings, stairways, closets and everything else, attempting to either rid the house of the pest or eat him. Along the way,

"Butch the Bulldog" was introduced, as well as some great genre pieces like *Dr. Jekyll and Mister Mouse,* which turned out exactly as it sounds; *Designs on Jerry,* where blue-printed-stick figures that Tom has drawn on plans for a better mousetrap come alive; and *Heavenly Puss,* where Tom is killed by a falling piano and must get Jerry to sign a certificate of forgiveness before he can go to Heaven.

Then from 1951-56, Hanna-Barbera began their cost-cutting techniques, curtailing detail and introducing mechanised, categorized movement. Accompaning the style degeneration was a character degeneration until the delightful characters became almost perverse, especially in one cartoon which Jerry narrates (in a deep human voice) and ends with both characters wanting to commit suicide because their girl friends have run out on them.

The third change came when Hanna-Barbera moved to television in 1957 to produce their series of consistently

Tom the cat putting the hammer down, so to speak. His hopeful target is Jerry the mouse. Theirs was a partnership that would last over thirty years.

worsening cartoon shows. MGM hired Chuck Jones to make a new group of Tom & Jerrys, which he did for four years in a style reminiscent of his Road Runner efforts. The two fantasy-related cartoons by Jones were *Haunted Mouse*, with Jerry in a like house; and *The Mouse from H.U.N.G.E.R.*, secret agent Jerry vs. mad scientist/cheese hoarder Tom. The next move came with Chuck's exit and MGM's decision to make a few cheap cartoons in Czechoslavakia with Gene Dietch as director.

These few were truly weird, combining the stark Czech style with violence-prone Tom & Jerry humor. Needless to say, these didn't last long. The final straw came with Hanna Barbera reintroducing their classic duo in 1975 as one half of the *Tom & Jerry/Grape Ape Show*. Even though that kind of pairing was sacrilegious in the first place, both cartoons were awful. The last-known degradation of the characters occured in 1978, when Jerry the Mouse was featured on Gene Kelly's television special, "An American in Pasadena," (Jerry had danced in the film *Anchors Aweigh* (1944). Initially it sounds like a good idea, but the Jerry that emerged from a limo at the beginning of the show looked more like "Yogi Bear" than a mouse and wasn't even the right color! A sad, sad ending for a marvelous cartoon.

But those two are not alone. Animation on the whole had taken a nose dive in the sixties, and even established creators had to resort to the cut-rate brand of animation. Friz Freleng became part of Depatie-Freleng, the producers of the "Pink Panther," "Jabberjaw," and others. Gene Deitch created the "Tom Terrific" episodes for "Captain Kangaroo." Tex Avery went the way of Jay Ward by going into commercials.

Ward was justly famous for using television's cheapness for humor when he created the characters of "Rocket J. Squirrel," "Bullwinkle Moose," "George of the Jungle", "Super Chicken," and many others, with Bill Scott. He is now kept prosperous by the likes of "Captain Crunch" and "Count Chocula," while Avery took out bugs on "Raid" commercials and resurrected Bugs for "Kool-Aid."

Thankfully, several greats ignore television's cheapness and try to produce excellent animation. John Hubley, an ex-Disney animator and creator of "Mr. Magoo," got in one last shot before his death in 1977—"The Doonesbury Special." Chuck Jones has lent his talent and name to "How the Grinch Stole Christman," "The Cat in the Hat," "The Pogo Special Birthday Special," "A Cricket in Times Square," and many others. He is presently doing a daily syndicated comic strip—*Crawford*—and preparing a sequel to a Warner Brothers classic called "Duck Dodgers and the Return of the 24th and a Half Century."

Rankin-Bass Studio's homogenized view of the number-one hobbit Bilbo Baggins. They adulterated Tolkien's view to fit the vocal talents of Orson Bean.

Other companies work specifically for television. Rankin/Bass have put out all sorts of puppet animation (reminescent of George Pal's "Puppettoons", and cartoon animation for television including "Here Comes Peter Cottontail," and "Frosty the Snowman," but their largest endeavor was 1977's "The Hobbitt," based on the epic work of J.R.R. Tolkien. This largely stiff, but watchable, work was actually animated in the Orient and felt the need to use "big name" voices to supplement the characters, thereby hurting empathy and viewer involvement. To top it off, there was precious little magic in this video version. Filmation has been putting out shows like "Archie" and the animated "Star Trek" profitably but is now doing a little blockbusting by preparing an animated "Flash Gordon" movie with large doses of rotoscoping. But probably the best "made for television" animation in years is to be found in an unpublicized, little seen, half-hour holiday fable televised on NBC in 1977.

Nelvana Limited was the name of the company which produced "A Cosmic Christmas." Clive Smith directed, Frank Nissen was the director of animation, Patrick Loubert and Michael Hirsh produced, and Ida Nelson

A scene from the unjustly ignored *A Cosmic Christmas*.

Fruet, Martin Lavut, Laura Paull and Ken Sobol wrote the story about three outer-space aliens who revisit earth to discover the meaning of an exceptionally brilliant star, 1,977 years ago. A small boy named Peter realizes the significance of their search and leads the three, who bear a passing resemblance to ancient kings, through the dirty streets to rediscover the meaning of Christmas. It was an exceptional effort and one that should have brought forth network hosannas rather than indifference.

Other than this title, it had looked as if animation had run to the end of its line. Disney studios had put out a string of well-drawn but inconsequential features like *Robin Hood* (1974), which didn't need the added dimension of animation—for all the magic that ensued, it might as well have been live action. The same, unfortunately, has to be said of *The Rescuers* (1977), the new fully animated movie by the Disney Studios. Although four years in the making, at a cost over $6,000,000, the full effect of the story was undercut by the decision to use famous voices for the characters. One cannot separate the actors from the cartoon creations to the overall detriment of the movie. The story tells of Miss Bianca

(Eva Gabor), a mouse from the International Rescue Aid Society, who teams up with Bernard (Bob Newhart) to save a young orphan, Penny (Michelle Stacy), in the clutches of Madame Medusa (Geraldine Page) and Snoops (Joe Flynn).

Still, care was taken to toughen up the villainess and tighten up the plot line and the animation is still the best to be found around. Slowly but surely, the Disney Studios seem to be moving back to more substantial animated efforts and audacious subject matter. Their next effort was another step in the right direction. *Pete's Dragon* (1977-8) was the outcome of fifteen years' work, since Seton I. Miller and S.S. Field wrote the original story for it almost seventeen years ago. Malcolm Marmorstein was put to work writing the screenplay when Jerome Courtlan, the producer, rediscovered it in the Disney files in 1975.

In conjunction with Ron Miller, they mounted the twelve-million-dollar live-action/animated musical under the direction of Don Chaffey, who also directed most of the "Prisoner" episodes. Here he's helming a story about a turn-of-the-century orphan (Sean Marshall)

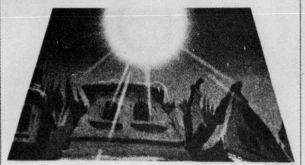

"A COSMIC CHRISTMAS"

WAAA-TV Sunday, 10:00PM

½ Page T.V. Guide

Sunday, Monday, Tuesday, Wednesday,

Thursday, Friday, Saturday,

1 1 2 3 4 5 6 7 8 9 0

:00PM   :00AM

A B C D E F G H I J K L M N O P Q R S T U V W X Y Z

A B C D E F G H I J K L M N O P Q R S T U V W X Y Z

Today   Tonight   Tomorrow

The advertisement for the holiday event.

"A COSMIC CHRISTMAS"

WAAA-TV Sunday, 10:00PM

200 Line Newspaper

What we have come to. A scene from *The Rescuers*, the Disney Studio's latest (© Walt Disney Productions).

who just happens to have a nineteen-foot-long fire-breathing dragon named Elliot as a pet. He escapes from his rotten foster parents (Shelly Winters and Charles Tyner) to settle down in the Maine village of Passamaquoddy with Nora (Helen Reddy) and her dad (Mickey Rooney), who live in a lighthouse. The complications arise when traveling con man Dr. Terminus (Jim Dale) and his sidekick Hoagy (Red Buttons) want the dragon for their own mercenary purposes and Nora's beau (Cal Bartlett) is lost at sea. Since this is a Disney movie, naturally all turns out tunefully well, for both sides. That is, audiences are happy and Disney studios are happy since the movie has made over thirty million dollars while still in limited engagements.

Two different types of Elliotts were created, one full-scale mechanical version built under special effects man Danny Lee, and, of course, the animated version created and implemented by Ken Anderson, an animator with over forty-five years of Disney experience. The talented artist based the dragon on the Chinese visualizations of the creature but drew him, as he put it, "thinking of Wallace Beery". Adding to the overall excellence was Don Bluth as animation director and the vocal abilities of Charlie Callas, who gave versatile voice to the monosyllabic monster. The whole production was created keeping in mind several things audiences take for granted. For example, even Elliott's onscreen skin tone had to alter realistically and his shadow had to fall exactly right.

Presently Disney is preparing their next "four-year special"—for the Disney brand of full animation, it takes at least three years to complete and one to plan—*The Fox and the Hound*. Following that will be one of the most anxiously awaited Disney productions in years—*The Black Cauldron*—a tale of supernatural fantasy and adventure that supposedly rivals *Lord of the Rings*.

And what of *Lord of the Rings?* Originally the rights to Tolkien's epic trilogy—*The Fellowship of the Ring, The*

Sean Marshall, Mickey Rooney, Helen Reddy, and Cal Barlett bid adieu to *Pete's Dragon* (© Walt Disney Productions).

173

Two Towers, and *The Return of the King*—were sold to United Artists in 1971 to be a vehicle for director John Boorman, who, instead went to Warner Brothers to make *Zardoz* and *Deliverance*. After sitting around on the United Artists shelf for awhile, the project went to Ralph Bakshi, who had been dubbed the rightful successor to Disney on the strength of his violent, almost avant-garde cartoons, *Fritz the Cat* (1971), *Heavy Traffic* (1973), *Coonskin* (1975), and *Wizards* (1976). *Wizards* was acknowledged as his "dress rehearsal" for *Lord of the Rings* and smacks of a somewhat-hasty experiment incorporating dozens of other fantasy influences (mostly those of underground cartoonist Vaughn Bode).

Although some proclaim it the first true sword-and-sorcery classic, many find it too derivative and repetitive to herald it as a rebirth of American fantasy animation. Bakshi wrote, produced, and directed the film for 20th Century Fox. It deals with twin brothers, both wizards, who grow apart in temperament and interest in the world of the far, far, far future. Avatar (Bob Holt) is a cheroot-smoking midget in a pointed hat who wants to live in peace while Blackwolf (Steve Gravers), a tall, skeletal sorcerer, wants to take over the world. The evil twin finds a film of Nazi Germany and incites his army of various demons and goblins to march on a valiant race of elves. To prevent devastation, Avatar travels to the dreaded land of Scortch, along with Elinore (Jesse Wells), a voluptuous winged elf; and Weehawk (Richard Ronamus), a hot-tempered elf who knows karate; to confront his evil brother and save his world.

"It is their journey," states the production notes, "pitting their magic against the evil power of technology which provides the basic story line."

Unfortunately, there is precious little magic to be found in the actual film, the most hypocritical moment coming when the twins (who look nothing like each other) face each other and the magical brother shoots his villainous foe in order to win. The high points of the overly padded effort are supplied with some fine background designs by Ian Miller, Johnnie Vita, and Martin Strudler, and nice illustrations by Mike Ploog.

So far, Bakshi has mentioned an unnamed new

Three assassins gather in the dusk of the age of *Wizards*.

The elfin army from *Wizards*.

process in conjunction with *Lord* which is enabling him to produce about 150 minutes of high-class animation in a little over two years. But what is definite at this point is that Saul Zaentz of Fantasy Films is producing, the budget is set at six million dollars, and 150 animators are presently on the job. As of the beginning of 1978, Bakshi had professional pleasure and satisfaction with what had thus far been done. The final product is set to be nationally judged around Thanksgiving 1978.

But if anyone is to be deemed the "official" successor to Disney, it would have to be the man that author John Colhane called "the best guarantee of the future of the animated film"—Richard Williams. This man, who Chuck Jones calls "incredibly talented," started his London-based animation studio in 1955 and made his 1st film, *The Little Island*, which won the British Film Academy Award, among others. Since then, Williams has embarked on a career that is literally stunning in its quality and versatility. His company has done commercials, held seminars, designed advertising campaigns,

created special sequences for live-action films, made short subjects, and aided in one feature while actively preparing another.

Probably Williams is most famous for his feature-film credit sequences. Starting with *Casino Royale* (1967), *What's New Pussycat?* (1968), and *A Funny Thing Happened on the Way to the Forum* (1966), Williams hit a highlight for his sections that acted as bridges for Tony Richardson's *The Charge of the Light Brigade* (1968). The next major breakthrough was his celebrated openings for the *Return of the Pink Panther* (1974) and *The Pink Panther Strikes Again* (1976), which featured the Panther mimicking other movie greats like Buster Keaton, George Raft, Dracula, Gene Kelly and *Jaws*.

Nineteen seventy-six also gave him his first public frustration in the form of the Bobbs-Merrill/ITT produced *Raggedy Ann & Andy*. Although he personally loathed the final product, it just gives one an idea of the quality Williams shoots for, since the film is enjoyable and one of the better efforts in years. One excellent

Williams himself gives a *The Return of the Pink Panther* cell the eye.

The Pink Panther struts his stuff as Dracula during the Richard Williams-animated credit sequence of *The Pink Panther Strikes Again* (directed by Tony White, © DePatie-Freleng).

Scrooge with the Ghost of Christmas Past in a moment from Richard Williams' Oscar-winning short subject *A Christmas Carol*.

Williams influence was listing the animators before the film along with the characters they drew. For the most part, animators have gone through their career uncredited and unacknowledged by feature directors. Williams believes in giving credit where credit is due—therefore hating the interference he was continually having to bear from people who knew nothing about animation. The experience was so distressing to him, that on his large poster-size 1977 Christmas card, incorporating all his studio's characters, Raggedy Ann was being chewed up by a mad dog.

Speaking of Christmas, another highlight of his career was an Oscar for his 1971 version of *A Christmas Carol*, produced by Chuck Jones, narrated by Michael Redgrave, and featuring the voices of Michael Hodern and Alistair Sim. The script was credited to Charles Dickens

and the animation was based on nineteenth-century etchings and illustrations, creating a fascinating, fulfilling, and almost "definitive" work. Throughout his animated life, Williams has stressed versatility, or as he puts it, "enabling the content itself to dictate the style. The animation medium has practically no visual limitations."

He is setting out to prove that once again. For at least the last eight years, the main project of the Williams studio has been a 100-minute animated Panavision film called *The Thief and the Cobbler*. The style is based on the intricate beauty of oriental art and the story has been based on the lyric simplicity of the *Arabian Nights* tales. All proceeds from his commercial work go into this film. One million dollars of his own money have gone into this film. Years of his life and all his talent and experience

Zig-Zag's Alligator Sled races from the land of the One-Eyes. Vincent Price supplied the voice and Richard Williams supplied the artistic genius for the up-coming *The Thief and The Cobbler*.

Richard Williams' preliminary roughs for "Fido," Zig-Zag's pet vulture in *The Thief and the Cobbler*.

178

have gone into this film. This film will feature a hand-drawn cast of thousands and may very well be what Richard Williams hopes it will be: "The greatest animated film ever made." With such dedication, integrity and out-and-out love of his art form, Williams doesn't deserve to be hailed as a new Disney. Disney should be described as "cut from the Williams mold".

Suddenly, the future of the animated film does not look so bleak. With a clear mind one can see general evidence of its resurgence. "There's a whole new world of animation out there that the general public is unaware of," said Christopher Padilla, concept director for Voyage Productions, "unlike the world of Saturday-morning television or those classics from the Walt Disney Studio." He, and others like him, have taken steps to make audiences aware of the bold animation shorts that have already passed them by.

Teamed with Dean Berko, they spent two-and-a-half years collecting, at their own expense, twenty-eight short, excellent animated subjects and then spent 35,000 dollars promoting them locally. After totally selling out its initial run, they convinced Cinema Shares to distribute a 107-minute version, picking out sixteen from the original number, and, in the fall of 1977, *The Fantastic Animation Festival* was unleashed on the nation. Incorporating bold visual advertising, the movie was a celebration of style and enjoyment.

Almost every animation technique was used to great advantage: rotoscoping in *French Windows* and a Levis commercial; model animation in *Icarus, Mountain Music* and the Academy Award-winning *Closed Mondays*; direct drawing on the film as in *Kick Me*; plain, old-fashioned cartoons like *Superman In The Mechanical Monsters*, impressionistic limited animation as in *Nightbird*; satiric and symbolic characterization like *Room & Board* and *Cat's Cradle*; music interpretations like *Moonshadow*; and colorful craziness like *The Last Cartoon Man* and *Bambi Meets Godzilla*. Rounding out the program was *Cosmic Cartoon, Light, Mirror People*, and a 7-UP commercial.

For those who loved *Festival* and for those who should have seen it, another compilation of tremendous cartoons is being readied by the 23-year-old duo that promises to be more ambitious but just as rewarding. The team is not alone in capturing the greats of the past. A compilation of great Bugs Bunny cartoons was put together under the title of *Bugs Bunny, Superstar* by a Cambridge, Mass. group called, suitably, Hare Raising Films. It took them three years of "coaxing, testing, and cajoling" to even get the films out of the storage vaults. Finally, the company, formed under the auspices of the Orson Welles Theatre complex near Harvard, found a wealth of Warner Brothers cartoons in the possession of United Artists and made a deal that finally saw fruition in 1975. With some live-action material of the directors and animators at work sandwiched between nine cartoons made from 1940-1948, the public got their second theatrical crack at Bugs and the gang.

The best of the group, strangely enough, were the three most fantasy oriented. *The Corny Concerto* was a Bob Clampett two-part satire of *Fantasia* featuring Elmer Fudd as a poverty-row Stokowski. He introduces Porky hunting Bugs in the Vienna Woods for the first half and a pubescent Daffy on the Blue Danube for the second. *Hair Raising Hare* is just one of the Chuck Jones fright fests with Bugs going up against a hairy monster with sneakers in a wildly shaped mad scientist's castle. Finally, Clampett's *Old Grey Hare*, which should have been called *2001: A Bugs Oddity*, since it concerns the eternal adversaries, Elmer and Bugs, at the turn of the twenty-first century, really battling it out and featuring some graveyard humor as well as a special guest appearance by God. The entire feature also imparted some interesting technical information—such as the cost of one Warner Brothers cartoon averaged $30,000 and that the voice of Elmer Fudd was actually Arthur Q. Bryan and not Mel Blanc as everyone has supposed.

But that's not all folks, to paraphrase a certain cartoon pig. Animators from all over the globe are seeing to it that quality and imagination do not die. From Italy came Bruno Bozetto, who is one of that country's greats but was not represented here until Specialty Films in Washington saw fit to release his *Allegro non troppo* ("Fast, but not *too* fast") in 1977. This too takes the form of a *Fantasia* satire, but one that is wild, slapdash, and slapstick, as if Fellini had collaborated with Disney.

Between episodes about a fawn too old to make it anymore, a fussy bee whose breakfast is continually interrupted by two humans, and a delirious cat who stumbles about a tenement thinking of it as home, was a live-action story about an imprisoned animator finding love with a washerwoman under the eyes of a flashily dressed producer and obese conductor. The highlights of the proceedings were a manic retelling of the Garden of Eden story, only this time the Serpent eats the apple; and the creation tale, only this time life starts on this planet from a littered soft drink bottle.

Specialty hopes to continue featuring Bozetto's prolific work in the future, work that has garnered him many awards and a great European reputation. Another great reputation is had by the team of Teru Murakami and Fred Wolf, who are represented by the aforementioned *The*

Fantastic Animation Festival

FEATURING: FRENCH WINDOWS / MUSIC BY PINK FLOYD • MOONSHADOW / MUSIC BY CAT STEVENS • ACADEMY AWARD WINNER / CLOSED MONDAYS • AND FOURTEEN MORE AWARD WINNING ANIMATED FILMS • ALL IN ONE SPECIAL FEATURE-LENGTH PRESENTATION

THE GREATEST COLLECTION OF ANIMATED FILMS IN THE WORLD!

© **PG** | PARENTAL GUIDANCE SUGGESTED
SOME MATERIAL MAY NOT BE SUITABLE FOR PRE-TEENAGERS

The Fantastic Animation Festival

The opening of the short *Moonshadow*, based on the song by Cat Stevens and narrated by Spike Milligan. From *The Fantastic Animation Festival*.

A moment from the deterioration of a museum computer in the Oscar-winning clay animated short *Closed Mondays*. From *The Fantastic Animation Festival*.

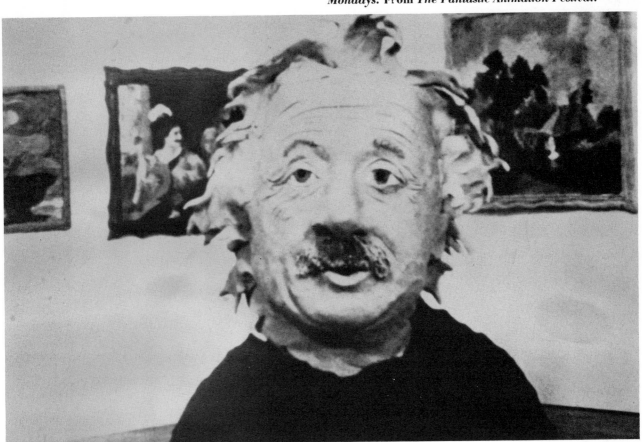

Nine creatures moving slowly toward extinction at the tail end of the "Creation" sequence in *Allegro Non Troppo*.

A rare shot of the storyboards for the Garden of Eden sequence from *Allegro Non Troppo*.

Point and unusual projects like *Dirty Duck* and *The Mouse and his Child*. *Duck* (1977) is an "X" rated satire of a fowl trying to find some sexual happiness in America, nurtured by animator/director/writer/designer Charles Swenson and songwriters/arrangers/conductors/voices Mark Volman and Howard Kaylan, (formerly of *The Turtles* and *The Mothers of Invention*), now known as Flo and Eddie (Murakami and Wolf only produced).

Although quickly played off, the film did garner its share of attention, even in such prestigious circles as the New York *Times*. Their unsigned review called it, "a bit of Walter Mitty and a touch of Woody Allen, with some of the innocence of Walt Disney, the urban smarts of Ralph Bakshi, the mysticism and psychedelic eclecticism of *Yellow Submarine* and the unabashed relish of Robert Crumb." It then added, "For all its lustfulness *Dirty Duck* is concerned with the condition of loneliness," then finished off with, "Beneath the zaniness and constant sexuality lie understanding and affection." Unfortunately they failed to mention that the character and name of Dirty Duck was first created and drawn by Bobby London.

Their more recent title, *The Mouse and his Child* (1978), is a complete change in that it is strictly a Disney-like adaptation of a children's book about two toy mice on a quest to become self-winding. Along the way they fall into the clutches of Manny Rat (Peter Ustinov) and befriend the likes of a Tin Seal (Sally Kellerman) and a stage-struck bird (Cloris Leachman). This lyrical musical fantasy is being distributed by the relatively new company Sanrio, which is also releasing *Five Tales from Ovid's Metamorphoses*, another incredibly ambitious animated undertaking by a Japanese designer/writer/ director named Takashi.

The Ovid cycle of stories were the ancient man's method of rationalizing the workings of his world, and the film is supplemented by the musical contributions of Joan Baez, the Rolling Stones, and the Pointer Sisters. Set for a summer of 1978 release, it promises to be quite an experience. Ambitious seems to be the word to describe all the new animation being planned at the present time on both sides of the Atlantic.

In England, actor Lionel Jeffries is serving as director for the Michael Robson scripted *The Water Babies*, with animation being done at Film Polski in Warsaw. Among the action talent involved in the more than two years of

One of the most prolific and entertaining sources of quality animation is the National Film Board of Canada. This is a moment from one of their most popular cartoons, *Hot Stuff*—a cockeyed history of fire.

Another National Film Board of Canada short displaying a totally different style. This was a realization of the Icarus fable.

production has been James Mason, Billie Whitelaw, Bernard Cribbins, Joan Greenwood, and David Tomlinson. Also being worked on in the Britain by director Martin Rosen and director of animation Tony Guy is *Watership Down,* based on the best-seller by Richard Adams. Some acting greats giving voice to this picture are Sir Ralph Richardson, Denholm Elliott, Roy Kinnear, Michael Hodern, Harry Andrews, and Zero Mostel.

Around these parts, the big news is that Al Brodax, the producer and cowriter of *Yellow Submarine,* is preparing *Devil's Riff,* a story of Heaven, Hell, and love on a musical plane. It opens with Lucifer as part of the heavenly orchestra, but when he hits that first rock note—supplied on the soundtrack by the Electric Light Orchestra—the skies rip asunder and he plunges down to his new, fiery home. Then the contest begins. If the newly crowned devil can corrupt man, he can continue as Satan, but, if not, he should return to Heaven for a second chance.

The bone of contention centers on Manny, a second violinist with the Boston Symphony Orchestra. Because of evil influences, he loses his job and his love disappears. Manny heroically tracks her down to Hell, coming up against Maximus Max, also known as Big Mac, a creature of three heads and many more tongues, who almost devours himself when he speaks; Pin-Pan, a foppish demon whose shirt front opens to eternity and who exists in a mirrored environment—to the point he is multiplied unendingly—and the less esoteric demons of Sloth, Lust, Anger, Jealousy, and Envy, who, according to the credits, "play themselves."

The assorted and sundry people collaborating with Brodax on the project are the authors of *Godspell,* John Tebalack and Nino Faso; animation director Steven Lisenberger; live action consultant David Golden; and the Boston Symphony Orchestra with conductor Seiji Ozawa. Since successful animation is time-consuming, at least we, the audience, are guaranteed of some high-flying visual experiences for the next few years.

INDEX

185